THE GREEKS OF IONIA (Asia Minor)

Sea

D0044760

U.S.S.R.

Sinop

Samsun

Pontic

Fatsa

Amasya

Mountains

Ordu

Aybasti

Trabzon

Niksar

Ayios Antonios
(Iondone)

P O N T I A N S

K E Y

A D O C I A N S

IRAN

Diyarbakir

Karabahçe

Mardin

Aleppo

S Y R I A

I R A Q

Ionians, c. 1200 B.C.–1923

Pontians, c. 800 B.C.–1923

Cappadocians, c. 322 B.C.–1923

Presumed route to exile in 1920

© 2000 Jeffrey L. Ward

NOT EVEN MY NAME

NOT EVEN MY NAME:

From a Death March in Turkey
to a New Home in America, a Young Girl's
True Story of Genocide and Survival

THEA HALO

Picador USA
New York

Library of Congress Cataloging-in-Publication Data
Halo, Thea.
Not even my name : from a death march in Turkey to a new home in America, a young girl's true story of genocide and survival / Thea Halo—1st Picador USA ed.
p. cm.
ISBN 0-312-26211-6
1. Halo, Sano Themia. 2. Greek American women—Biography. 3. Greek Americans—Biography. 4. Greeks—Turkey—Biography. 5. Greeks—Turkey—Social conditions—20th century. 6. Genocide—Turkey—History—20th century. 7. Pontic Mountains (Turkey)—Biography. 8. New York (N.Y.)—Biography. I. Title.

E184.G7 H33 2000
973'.04893'0092—dc21
[B]
                                                           00-023536

First Picador USA Edition: May 2000

10 9 8 7 6 5 4 3 2 1

To my mother and our Pontic family, and to all the Greeks, Assyrians, and Armenians of Turkey who lost their lives, their homes, and their country. May they live forever in our hearts and minds.

IN MEMORY OF:

My father, Abraham and brother, Amos

CONTENTS

BOOK FOUR: AMERICA, AMERICA

BOOK FIVE: JOURNEY'S END

ACKNOWLEDGMENTS

My thanks first and foremost to my mother who has always been my inspiration and who tirelessly dug into her often painful memories to make this book possible. Thanks also to my father whose love of storytelling filled my life with exotic things; to my family who were my cheering committee; to Harry Seiss, without whom we may not have found my mother's land; to Erica Obey for her insight and honesty; Dr. Harry Psomiades, Director of the Center for Byzantine and Modern Greek Studies at Queens College, and Dr. Constantine Hatzidimitriou, Director of the AHIF Center for the study of Human Rights and Hellenism, for their guidance on the historical sections of the book; to the late painter Allen D'Arcangelo for his many tireless readings, dinners, and late-night movies; Arnoud Hekkens for his everlasting friendship and support; Kari Walden, who made the first professional contact for me because of his belief in this book; to the many Pontians and Assyrians whose Web sites helped with my historical research; and of course to my editor, Diane Higgins, at Picador, St. Martin's Press, for her belief in this book, her invaluable insights, and her unflinching courage in calling genocide by its proper name.

DISCLAIMER

Except for the names of my mother's family, the names of the villagers of Iondone are fictitious. They were given names for ease in telling the story. However, the stories about them are real nevertheless. Ruth's real name was either Ann or Ruth. Zohra and Hagop's names are correct, as are those of their children. In addition, Iondone is spelled phonetically the way my mother pronounces it. The Turkish songs were written phonetically as best as I could manage from the way my mother sang them to me. The hamlet of Tlaraz is also spelled phonetically since it is too small to be found on any map and may no longer exist, though there are hamlets like it in southern Turkey.

PRONUNCIATION OF NAMES

Themia is accented on the second syllable, the "i" (which is pronounced "ee"). We are told by Greeks that Efthemia is the correct name, but my mother was never called that. Cristodula is accented on the third syllable, "u"; Nastasia on the third syllable, "i"; Barthena on the second syllable, "e." Varidimei is accented on the second syllable, "i," and the last syllable is pronounced "may." Zohra, Hagop, and Sonya are all accented on the first syllable; Arexine on the last syllable. The "ç," as in *dolmuç* and the town of Karabahçe, is pronounced "sh." Küzel is pronounced like "gazelle." The "I" in Iondone is pronounced like "eye," and the name is accented on the last syllable, "o."

Book One

THE LONG JOURNEY HOME

All I know
is that I know nothing
for certain
But that's the thing
I most often forget

THE RIVER OF DREAMS

NEW YORK CITY—AUGUST 1997
Tourists line the railing of the ferry. I take my place among them and
watch the river dance toward the ocean in shimmering, jagged peaks the
color of steel. Above Ellis Island a single white cloud hangs in a clear
blue sky. August is warm on my shoulders. The ferry rumbles, then cuts
a slow arc around the great green lady holding her torch high above her
head. Does she have a bad side? None I can detect from here.

The great hall of Ellis Island is grand as I enter, but too pristine. I
know it was not so when my parents passed through seventy-two years before. The rows of benches are gone now, but I imagine the clamor of thousands of voices and babies crying as they wait for word. So this was the
last leg of my mother's journey, where doctors felt for telltale lumps and
searched for sickly eyes, weary from the long ocean crossing. I could almost hear the doctor's voice and see his fingers gently touch the scars on
my mother's leg as she raised her skirt for the examination.

"What's this?" the doctor asks my mother of the two small scars.

"All that's left," my mother answers.

*"Hurry!" my father says, grabbing her hand, "before they change
their minds."*

In the photo gallery the faces of hundreds of immigrants stare at me
from the walls, bearing the same expression my mother wears in the photo
of her at fifteen on the day of her wedding. There is no grimace of pain, no
knitted brows; only an unmistakable sorrow that seems to say, *my flame is
almost out.*

"You've got dimples on your leg, Mommy," I once said when my

mother's scars first caught my eye as a child. I pulled down my trousers and looked for dimples on my own leg.

"They're not dimples," my mother said. "You won't find them on your leg, sweetheart."

"Then what are they?" I said.

And for just one moment I saw that look in my mother's eyes as she drifted away from me. "All that's left," she said and closed her eyes. "All that's left."

In the courtyard of Ellis Island, row upon row of silver placards testify to those admitted. I find my parents' names and kneel before them. Sano Themía Halo. Abraham A. Halo. My sister Harty had included my mother's real name on the entry.

"Were you excited when your ship pulled into port and you saw Manhattan across the river sparkling in the August sun?" I once asked my mother.

"Not at first," she said. "I had already learned not to wish for things I couldn't have and along with that went my expectations."

I glide my fingertips over the grooves that spell out their names on the placards and feel the great emotion denied my mother on that day welling up in me.

⁊   ⁊   ⁊

There had always been only us: my mother, my father, my five sisters and four brothers, one uncle, an Armenian aunt—probably with her own sad story to tell—and their daughter who married and moved away too soon. Then a void.

We lived on West One hundred second Street in New York City, but it was very different from the way it is now. In the '40s and '50s it was like a page out of *West Side Story*. We lived in a five-room railroad flat; each room led into the other like boxcars. It was a five-flight walk-up above a half-flight brownstone stoop. For the twenty years that my family lived there, my mother carried bikes and babies, sometimes one on each hip, and groceries and toys, and all the other things one carries up and down, up and down those five flights of stairs.

We grew up among the Irish mostly, although there were other races and nationalities in the surrounding neighborhoods and in our schools. But our heritage had been a mystery to us as children. We came from two lost civilizations. Both my parents came from Turkey, and their people had been there for thousands of years, but they were not Turks. No one had ever heard of my mother's people—the Pontic Greeks of Asia Minor (Turkey)—and my father's people, the Assyrians, were believed to have lived only in ancient times but were no more. As a child I never mentioned my mother's heritage, and the few times I responded to questions of my father's heritage I was corrected with great authority.

"No, dear. You mean you're Syrian. The Assyrians are an ancient people. They don't exist anymore." Even my teachers told me that.

How could I be something that doesn't exist?

"They called us Rüm," my mother would say about her own people, pronouncing the word "room." And that was even more confusing. What was Rüm? Even my mother's language was lost to her because she had no one with whom she could speak her ancient Greek. Without even the sound of her Greek language to help me identify with her culture as a child, I was left with nothing but her few stories.

But Rüm or Pontic Greek, as a child of the '40s and '50s, I had just assumed that all mothers were more or less like mine. Or rather, I would have assumed it had I given it any thought. She had the kind of figure you might expect on a mother in 1950s America; kind of plump but not fat; perfect for those short-sleeved housedresses that buttoned down the front. They were usually full of flowers. She had a sweet, wistful smile and those innocent black eyes—with just a trace of sadness about the brow— that smiled out at you from beneath the rolled wreath of black hair that framed her lovely face.

As to her birthday, my mother had never known the real date of her birth, so someone somewhere along the line had chosen May 10. It usually coincided with Mother's Day appropriately enough. With ten kids— I was the eighth—I don't remember her ever just sitting without doing something. There was always so much that had to be done. She was always cooking or cleaning, baking, making clothes, crocheting. And she was always singing. I could recite her favorite songs: "Blue Skies," "Little Man You're Crying," "Oh, Johnny," "Paper Moon," and a hundred more like those, all as American as the proverbial apple pie, which she also baked to perfection.

Her musical ear gave her an easy grasp of languages so I never really noticed an accent. But there were a few words that made us all laugh, like the way she pronounced "wheat" with a heavy emphasis on the H. Haweet. And her attempts at the American slang of the '50s could have you rolling in the aisles. Each time we laughed at her, all she could do was cover her face with her hands and laugh with embarrassment.

"Oooooooh sugar!" she'd say.

Since my mother rarely talked about her childhood there wasn't too much to remind us that she wasn't born in America. Considering her circumstances when my father happened upon her, some might say he rescued her from oblivion, but sometimes I wonder who rescued whom.

She cooked all of America's traditional fare, and for Christmas there was turkey with rice and chestnut stuffing; sweet potatoes, topped with pineapple and marshmallows; fresh cranberry and walnut sauce; mashed potatoes and gravy; apple and pumpkin pies. But there was also the stuffed grape leaves on holidays, and the meat pies my mother called *chamborak,* which she fried in a pan, and her special rolls with black seeds. All those exotic scents would mingle to fill the air. My father bought sweets from the Middle Eastern markets: Turkish delight; the pressed sheets of apricot we called *garmardine;* a sweet made of strung walnuts or pistachios surrounded by a thick grape coating and sprinkled with powdered sugar; and the tins of halvah, and baklava that he'd spread out on the table.

It was those little things like the words mispronounced, a foreign word thrown in, the stories and songs, and the Turkish delight and stuffed grape leaves that reminded us our parents came from someplace else; that there was something unknown about them; that they were separate from us in some unfathomable way.

2

THE LONG JOURNEY HOME

As a child I couldn't imagine my mother being able to protect herself in the outside world even though she took care of us to perfection. The image of her as an innocent, as a pure being unable to cope with the complexities and cunning in the world persisted in my mind. She was without guile; so full of love and song when I was a child that somewhere along the way I appointed myself her protector. It wasn't a conscious decision. In fact, only later, when I began to reflect on my childhood, did I realize the decision had been made. And only then did I realize that some of my siblings had also appointed themselves her protector. Perhaps there were other reasons for our protectiveness besides her artlessness and seeming innocence, but I had never defined those reasons as a child. I hadn't completely understood what had happened to her except that her family had been driven from their homes at gunpoint by the Turks. She made only passing reference to the loss of her family, never dwelling on it for too long. But when we didn't behave, on rare occasions she'd say, "Don't wait until I'm gone before you realize how much you love me." On rarer occasions she'd say, "I loved my mother more than life." Then she'd close her eyes to hold back the tears.

It was on one of those occasions, when I was still quite young, that I promised to take her back to Turkey one day to search for her home. I promised her a lot of things when I was a child. I promised she would live forever, and that I would buy her a big, beautiful house one day too, because even then I wanted to pay her back for my childhood. But taking my mother to Turkey to find her home was one of those magnanimous, well-intentioned promises kids make that somehow sit in the same slot in the distant future no matter how many years pass. Many years did pass before I realized it was one promise I wanted to keep.

But by the summer of 1989, we had still not found her village on a map. Over the years, even before I was old enough to help with the search, the efforts of my older sisters had ended in failure, as if my mother's memories had been a dream. My own trips to the New York Public Library to look at maps of Turkey revealed nothing, even when they were pre-World War I maps from countries such as France and Britain. On each map I carefully searched the Pontic mountain range below the Black Sea where my mother's villages had been, but still found no mention of my mother's villages: the three Greek villages called Iondone.

We knew some of the Greek names for towns and villages had been changed after the end of World War I, when General Mustafa Kemal— later known as Atatürk, literally, "father of the Turks"—successfully defeated his rivals to rule Turkey. In his effort to nationalize and modernize Turkey, Atatürk set various programs in place. He changed the name of the famous city of Constantinople—previously known as Byzantium—to Istanbul, and many other Greek names took on a Turkish form. The black veils covering the faces of Muslim women were banned, along with the Arabic script the Turks once used for their writing. In its place Roman letters were used to simplify the Turkish language and make it more accessible to other nations. Educational programs were also initiated to raise the literacy rate, and monogamous marriages replaced the earlier acceptance of multiple wives—all in an effort to realign Turkey with the West.

But the most dramatic change in Turkey was the slaughter of 1.5 million Armenians, 750,000 Assyrians, and 353,000 Pontic Greeks, and the cruel death marches to exile of 1.5 million more Greeks of Turkey; death marches on which countless other Pontians lost their lives, all between 1915 and 1923. This genocide, euphemistically termed "ethnic cleansing," and "relocation," eliminated most, if not all, of the Christian minorities in Turkey, and brought to a tragic end the 3,000 year history of the Pontic Greeks in Asia Minor.

So much had changed, both in Turkey and in my mother's life since 1920, when, at age ten, my mother and all the people of her villages were sent on their own devastating death march to exile. It was certainly possible she wasn't remembering the name of her village clearly—seventy years had come and gone—but I never doubted her memory for a moment. On one of my visits to her in the summer of 1989, when she was seventy-nine years old, I suggested we start on her quest to find her home as soon as possible, still not knowing where our search would lead, or what we would find if, by chance, we arrived at our desired destination. We had heard all the usual horror stories about Turkey, and my mother knew firsthand of Turkey's capacity for brutality.

After an almost imperceptible hesitation, my mother smiled. "I've waited a lifetime," she said. "My bags are packed."

3.

RECROSSING

ANKARA, TURKEY—AUGUST 1989

After a brief stop in London, our plane landed in Ankara—Turkey's capital city—on the afternoon of the second day. We had chosen Ankara instead of the famed Istanbul because Ankara was in the center of the country, much closer to the area my mother once called home.

At the hotel, the room we were shown, though somewhat drab with its brown bedspreads and beige walls, was clean and comfortable. It was early evening by the time we got settled in the hotel. We took a short walk, but it didn't take long before we were ready for that horizontal position we had been deprived of during the last two days of travel. I bought some Turkish sandwiches, which we ate in our room. Then we showered and got ready for bed.

The traffic in the street roared, sending plumes of exhaust up the six stories to waft through the door to the balcony.

"Maybe we should close the door," I said.

My mother nodded and climbed under the covers of her bed.

"Do you want the lights out?"

"That's a good idea," she said. "Good night, sweetheart."

"Good night, honey," I said, using a term that had become comfortable for me. I don't know when I stopped using the word mom, or mother, or other terms that connote motherhood, but at some point in time those words simply fell away.

I pulled the balcony door shut and climbed into my bed. I could still hear the trucks below rumbling down the street. I turned out the lights and lay there staring at the ceiling. Would we really come to a village that had once been my mother's and stand on the threshold of her home? The thought of it was rather eerie. There was a whole lifetime of references to a family I would never know. Her world had always sounded so ancient, more like stories from the Bible than a time in which my mother could have lived. I tried to imagine my mother with her family as a child, to imagine her villages and her people tucked away in those mountains for hundreds, maybe thousands of years without major contact with the outside world, but I drifted off to sleep instead.

We rose early the next morning, anxious to get started with our search for my mother's home, but we thought it best to stay over for a day in Ankara to give my mother a rest before starting on our journey. After the traditional Turkish breakfast of tomatoes, feta cheese, bread, olives, and tea, we ventured out.

We visited an old stone ruin of ancient Roman baths, then walked up a narrow stone street. Two women sat on the ground sorting wool of various colors while a third woman worked at a small loom weaving a brightly colored rug. We walked past them and up the hill until we came upon the low, broad structure of the archeological museum squatting on a long row of steps.

The museum was too hot inside for my mother, so I brought her outside to sit on a bench in its garden under an umbrella of trees. Two young Turks immediately made room for her and invited her to join them. Both spoke English well. One was just a boy of fourteen. The other was somewhat older, but still quite young. He was an architecture student, twenty-one years old, he later told us. Both were well dressed and obviously educated.

After determining my mother was safe with them, I left her in the garden and went back into the sweltering museum to look at some of Turkey's treasures. Remnants of my mother's people stared at me, scattered among the remains of other inhabitants of that strange and beautiful land.

When I came out again, I found my mother talking with the two young men. She rose to leave and they asked if they could show us some points of interest. The fourteen-year-old walked with me while the architecture student walked behind us with my mother.

"What are you studying in school?" I asked the boy as we worked our way along a wide avenue.

"I want to be in the International Secret Service," he said.

I couldn't help smiling to myself. "What does the International Secret Service do?" I said.

"They catch smugglers and spies."

"Like James Bond?" I said. But I thought of the horrific film *Midnight Express*, about a young American man who got caught smuggling marijuana into Turkey. He was jailed in a filthy prison under horrendous conditions and fought for years to be released.

The boy laughed shyly as if caught in a secret.

"It would be interesting," he said, "and I'd get to travel."

I glanced back to see if my mother and the architect were still behind us. They were deep in conversation.

"What do you think of the Bulgarian government expelling all the Turkish Nationals?" the boy said. "Don't you think it's terrible?"

His question took me by surprise. I hadn't intended to get into political discussions while in Turkey. But I said, "What do you think of what the Turkish government did to the Greek and Armenian Nationals in the past?" And when I said it, I found I did so without emotion—more with the objectivity of a journalist than with the outrage of a daughter of one of those decimated peoples. But the realization registered only slightly, and I pushed the thought aside as I turned to listen to his answer.

"But this is different," he said.

"How is it different?"

"The Turks live in Bulgaria. Some were born there. That's their home." His young face was earnest.

"Yes," I said. "You're right. This is different. Very different. In Bulgaria, they only expelled the Turks and let them leave with their lives and their belongings. In Turkey, they murdered hundreds of thousands of Greek, Armenian, and Assyrian Nationals, and drove the rest out on long, devastating death marches."

The image described by Ernest Hemingway when he was a war correspondent stationed in Turkey during World War I, flashed through my mind. It was an image of a file of Greek exiles near Smyrna that was twenty miles long. How many people, two to four abreast, fit into a file twenty miles long? The sight had distressed Hemingway deeply. I thought of the waste of human life, but even then there was that strange detachment without the full emotional impact that so moved Hemingway as an eyewitness to the devastation. It had so moved him that he included the scene in one of his short stories, "On the Quay at Smyrna."

The boy's mouth fell open in disbelief. "But that never happened," he said. "That couldn't have happened!"

I could see he was sincere and I could feel myself becoming annoyed. Not at him. That part of Turkey's past had evidently been kept from him for obvious reasons. Not only were the young Turks unaware of their past, but the Turkish Government was "buying history" at American universities by giving them large endowments to keep its barbaric past from the American university agenda—a past filled with such atrocities that it had inspired Hitler. "Who remembers the Armenians?" Hitler had asked to justify his slaughter of the Jews and other designated enemies of the state. Indeed. And who even knew the Pontic Greeks ever existed?

I again looked back to check on my mother. She and the architect walked along behind us as before.

"It did happen," I said, turning again to the young boy. "They just didn't teach you about it in school. But it's important that you know your country's history."

To his credit, he didn't run off angrily. We walked in silence until we came to an ancient stone wall. The young men helped my mother climb the high, broken stone steps that led to a place on top where we could look out over Ankara.

"It's beautiful from up here, isn't it?" the boy said.

Ankara spread out before us as far as the eye could see, dotting the distant hills with small houses. No hint of Turkey's genocide sprang from the scene, and the gentle people we had met thus far gave no hint of the extraordinary capacity for brutality that was their country's past.

"Yes," I said to the boy. "From up here, it's beautiful."

4

IN THE BLINK OF AN EYE

Our preliminary destination was to be Fatsa, a town on the Black Sea my mother had heard her father and grandfather speak of when she was a child. We thought it a good place to begin our search for her home since we had still not found her villages on a map. But the trip to Fatsa would take twelve hours, and I thought it too long for my mother to be cooped up in a hot bus. We decided instead to make our first stop a town called Amasya, because it was halfway between Ankara and Fatsa. That decision could not have been more fortuitous.

We boarded our bus in the late morning in the full heat of the August sun and settled into our seats. Just before the bus left the station the driver entered. He turned on the air conditioner to show the passengers the bus had one, and that it worked. The bus company had charged extra for it after all. Then he turned around to face the passengers with a big mustachioed smile, and promptly turned the air conditioner off again. He tucked his six-foot frame behind the steering wheel, started the engine, adjusted his mirror, and we started down the road.

A tall, wiry attendant, with a friendly, weather-beaten face, was next to make an appearance. Working his way down the aisle with a bottle of eau du toilet, he stopped at each row of seats to offer each passenger a sprinkling.

"Hold out your hands, honey," I said to my mother as the attendant approached.

"What's that?" my mother said.

"Toilet water."

She held her palms over the aisle while the attendant sprinkled them with the lemon scent. I also held out my hands, then spread the scent over my bare arms and neck. My mother did the same. A cool, tingling sensation followed my dampened hand as it traveled over my bare flesh, then dissipated in the heat of the bus.

"Do you want to know what they say about the Black Sea?" I asked my mother.

"That would be nice," she said.

I pulled my friend's guidebook from my bag and looked for a section that covered the Black Sea, but found nothing, so I browsed through the book looking for something that might be of particular interest—something relevant to our trip. I turned back to the beginning of the book where they gave a brief history of Asia Minor (Turkey) before Ottoman rule, and read aloud the brief account back through 9,000 years. But only the Hittites and a reference to some sea people were mentioned other than the Turks. The Hellenic, Byzantine, Assyrian, Armenian, and Roman civilizations, and all the other peoples embedded in Asia Minor's past were absent.

I turned to the insert about Amasya, our interim destination, and read aloud a passage about the tombs of the Greek kings. Then I closed the book and lay back in the cushioned seat and closed my eyes.

I had been hoping to find the history of the Pontians, my mother's people, but there were only small references related to archeological sites as far as I could tell. There were still many ancient Greek ruins in Turkey left over from the Hellenic periods. Perhaps the most famous city, besides the former Constantinople, was the city of Troy. Just the mention of Troy conjured up for me all of Homer's tales of Greek gods and goddesses, of warriors like Odysseus and Achilles, of Trojan horses, and Greeks bearing gifts.

I was fourteen years old when I discovered Homer in my neighborhood bookstore. I don't know why, out of all the choices, Homer's books found their way into my hands, but once I picked up *The Iliad* and then *The Odyssey*, and read their covers, I was fascinated. Homer's epic poems of the Bronze Age, among the earliest written literature, brought Achaean heroes like Odysseus, and the other early people of Greece, back to life. I devoured both of those great works one after the other, never dreaming he spoke of people even remotely related to my mother's people, and never knowing that Homer, a blind poet, was himself an Achaean from Asia Minor.

I then read every book on Greek mythology I could find, yet I never once thought of myself as a Greek. I hadn't thought of myself as an Assyrian either. After all, my father's people no longer existed. It was only as an adult that I occasionally mentioned my mother's heritage, but it usually brought an embarrassed stare and that inevitable response: Pontic Greek? I've never heard of them.

As an artist, a painter, I had moved in intellectual circles from the age of seventeen. I had lived in Spain, Morocco, and Italy, and had traveled extensively, beginning at an early age, throughout the U.S., Mexico, Canada, western Europe, Greece, Egypt, and even China. Except in Greece, I had never met anyone who had ever heard of the Pontic Greeks, so completely had the memory of their existence been obliterated for most of the world. For most of my life therefore, such was my isolation from, and ignorance of, my heritage. It would be years later that I would discover there was a whole community of Pontians living in Queens, New York, and there were Pontic Greek societies and communities throughout the U.S. and Canada. There was even a large community of Pontians living in Australia. But in 1989, at the time of our trip, I had still neither met, nor heard of, a Pontic Greek other than my mother. No one else I knew had heard of them either. It was as if my mother was the only Pontic Greek in the world.

Nor had I ever met or heard of an Assyrian other than my father. It would also be years later that I would hear of a large community of Assyrians living in Chicago.

My older sisters became Egyptians when, as teenagers, they grew old enough to need an identity larger than themselves. They weren't modern-day Egyptians. We didn't know what modern-day Egyptians were. As a child I had been told on more than one occasion, again with great authority by my friends, that Egyptians were also all dead and mummified thousands of years ago. But that didn't stop me. I too became an Egyptian when I found a need for an identity larger than myself. We were ancient; mythical; kin to Nefertiti. We were citizens of the world.

My brothers, oddly enough, became Turks. Not the Turks who had slaughtered my mother's people and driven them from their lands. Nor the Turks who had slaughtered my father's people, kidnapped his sister, confiscated his land, and exiled his family. My brothers became mythical Turks.

Neither my father's stories, nor my mother's had ever sounded hostile toward the Turks when I was a child, so we grew up thinking of the Turks as big, strong men who never drew their swords without drawing blood, even if it had to be their own. It was a romantic image without the horror it implied.

"Make sure you tell people you're an Egyptian," my older sisters would warn my mother when they introduced her to a new friend.

"What do I know about being an Egyptian?" my mother would say. But to questions of her origin she'd say, "Cairo," for their sake, sensing how important it was to them. Then she'd quickly change the subject. It had never occurred to any of us, that in our struggle to have an identity of our own, we had negated hers.

𝔶　𝔶　𝔶

The bus rumbled down a steep incline gouged out of the cliffs, then slowed, as its gears began to grind hoarsely.

"What time are we supposed to arrive in Amasya?" my mother said.

"I thought you were sleeping."

"It's too hot to sleep," she said.

The bus was sweltering, and each time someone opened the roof hatch to let in a little air, it was slammed shut again soon after. The sound of the roof hatch slamming shut would become a familiar one on our six-hour journey.

"Do you think they have water?" my mother said.

I took out my Turkish-English dictionary and looked up the word for "water." Then I turned around and got the attention of the attendant who sat at the rear of the bus.

"Water, please," I said in Turkish when he approached.

He went to the back of the bus and returned with two small bottles of cold water he had taken from a cooler.

"And the window. Could you open the window?"

The attendant looked at me blankly.

"Wait," I said, holding up my hand like a traffic cop. I rummaged through the dictionary again.

"Air," I said in Turkish and pointed to the roof hatch.

He smiled and nodded, then reached up and opened the roof hatch.

I looked around the bus to see if anyone looked uncomfortable with the open roof hatch. A few children slept on little rugs on the floor of the bus at their parents' feet. No one seemed to grimace or complain. I felt as I usually felt in settings like this, where I am a willing captive for a short time surrounded by the people of a foreign land: a strange, anonymous closeness, almost familial. I don't know why I have that feeling, but somehow I suspect it's tied to my parents' stories as a child.

"How's that?" I said to my mother when a cool breeze that smelled of summer sailed toward us.

"That feels good," my mother said. "Being in this country, it's almost possible to forget how much time has passed and how much the world has changed."

"What do you mean?" I said.

"Oh, I just mean it's nice to have someone bring water on a bus when you need it. Things are slower here. It almost feels like America forty or fifty years ago."

She shook her head and looked out the window. "Everything changes so quickly," she said. "It's hard to believe men are traveling through space and walking on the moon. I would have liked to go to the moon and walk through space. Something different. I like that. Imagine. No one really knows what's up there. I would have liked to find out."

I tried to picture my mother in a space suit walking a weightless, slow-motion walk through the universe surrounded by a billion stars.

The gears on the bus ground again and then, with a long whush and sigh, the bus pulled off the road beside a small store and came to a halt. The attendant came down the aisle and reached up to slam the roof hatch shut as the door of the bus opened with another sigh, and the passengers began to stretch and rouse themselves.

"Are we in Amasya already?" my mother said.

"I don't think so. I think we have a few hours yet. Amasya?" I asked the Turkish woman across the aisle.

She made a clucking noise with her tongue against the roof of her mouth and waved her finger at me to indicate a no.

"I guess we're just stopping to stretch our legs," I said.

The roadside store was a simple, one-story building. Rows of huge burlap sacks sat like fat Buddhas outside the store and inside on the floor. Their tops were opened wide to display their contents. Gold-, olive-, and cinnamon-colored herbs and spices, dried fruits, legumes, grains, and other richly colored foodstuff filled each sack to its brim. The shelved wall held big glass jars full of other grains and comestibles. Everything had that turn-of-the-century, matter-of-factness about it, devoid of designer debris.

On the counter I spied flat sheets of *garmardine*, the kind of apricot paste my father used to buy. I bought a few pounds of the preserved fruit and roamed around the store inhaling the exotic scents. I could almost feel my father's strong hand on mine.

🕊   🕊   🕊

Back on the bus, my mother and I once again settled ourselves in our seats as the bus pulled away and started down the road. The craggy, sun-drenched scene outside the bus window was beginning to show more signs of greenery as we slowly slanted toward the north. Again the heat began to build inside the bus and again I turned around to search for the attendant. I caught his eye and signaled for him.

"Air," I said in English this time. I pointed to the roof hatch and he knew what I meant. He reached up and opened it and again the scent of summer sailed toward us.

It never occurred to me that we might not find my mother's home. The bus was speeding down the highway at 70 miles an hour toward Amasya, but I still hadn't devised a plan to find her villages. I had always just relied on my own ingenuity to do what was needed when I traveled. This time was no different. In fact, I had never even traveled with a guidebook before; a dictionary always, but never a guidebook. I had preferred to just arrive in a foreign place and take it from there, feeling my way as I went along. It made me a haphazard tourist at best, but I liked strolling down a street and coming upon some extraordinary thing waiting in my path, like the ethereal spires of a cathedral rising from the ground and reaching for the sky. Or a marble mosque, with its arched portico forming an arcade of rapid-fire columns and curves. Or something as simple as a stone arch around the doorway of an ordinary house in a style I had never seen before. I had always been afraid that a specific destination each time I left the hotel would cause me to miss all those treasures not listed in the guidebooks. Or maybe it was just that I had never liked being a "tourist."

But this trip was different. This time we had a very specific destination in mind with a very specific goal. The problem of researching the location of my mother's villages had been a difficult one. Before I left New York, I had done all I had known to do at the time. I had even looked up old newspaper articles in the *New York Times* archives, dating back to the early 1920s. I found only one, two-inch item mentioning some Greek exiles of Turkey.

I pulled the *garmardine* from my bag and offered some to my mother.

"I used to love it when Pop brought this home," I said.

"Someone finally got the idea to make a popular version of it in different flavors," my mother said.

"I know," I said. "They call them fruit-rolls, or roll-ups, or some such thing."

The Turkish woman in the seat across the aisle looked over at us and smiled when I looked back. Her child, who had been sleeping at her feet on the floor of the bus, was now awake and sitting on her lap.

"Offer her some *garmardine*," my mother said.

I reached across the aisle and held out the package of apricot sheets as an offering. The woman smiled again but refused shyly.

"It's okay," I said in English, hoping my smile would encourage her.

Again I made a gesture of offering, this time indicating her child. The woman reached across the aisle and tore off a small piece and thanked me.

"Can you believe you were ever that young?" my mother said. She took a long drink of water, recapped the bottle, and leaned her head back against the cushion. "Sometimes I look in the mirror and it's hard to believe the person looking back is really me. There are times when only the mirror knows my age." My mother smiled. "And sometimes my aching bones."

I closed my eyes and tried again to imagine my mother as a child, but I could only remember my own childhood and the young mother who cared for us so tenderly.

I could see her sitting in our old dining room by the potbellied stove. She's crocheting a little dress with pale yellow thread. Tiny pink crocheted roses adorn the bodice. She's singing "My Bonnie Lies Over the Ocean" as I stand before her, no more than four years old. I spread my arms out so wide my little hands touch behind my back, and I tilt my head to gaze into her dark, smiling eyes.

"I love you this much," I say. "I love you from the top of the sky to the bottom of the ocean."

My mother stops singing, rests her crocheting in her lap and smiles. "I love you from the top of the sky to the bottom of the ocean too," she says.

Ah. There I am at seven. My brother Tim, three years older than I, is practicing his jujitsu on me. He flips me over his shoulder, then gives me a full nelson. Then I do it to him and taunt him by singing a song my mother often sings. But I change the words to fit the occasion, and when Tim chases me, I run to hide behind my mother as she irons my blouse.

"Ma, he's making eyes at me. Ma, he's making eyes at me."

"It's getting late," my mother says.

"Ma, I flipped him over my head. Then I threw him down on the bed. Ma, he's chasing me."

"Come and eat," my mother says and laughs. "You don't want to be late for Sunday School."

"There go the Halos," the neighbors say as we trooped down the street bright and early every Sunday morning, our clothes starched and pressed to perfection, and the taps on my black patent leather shoes clicking with each step. I put my hand in my pocket and finger my Sunday School offering sealed in its tiny envelope.

There she is with her arm around my shoulder. I must be seven, or maybe eight. She's leading me out the door.

"Where are you going?" my father asks.

"We're going to church," my mother says.

It's not such a farfetched lie. With all the other things my mother had to do, she still found time to help out at church, cleaning silverware, setting up bazaars, filling baskets for the needy. But every so often after telling my father we were going to church, we'd head to a movie theater and for the rest of the afternoon we'd be lost in the magic of cinema. That was probably the only thing my mother did purely for herself, and I was grateful she always took me with her.

"What he doesn't know won't hurt him," my mother says, knowing my father didn't approve of movies. But it was not in her nature to deceive, so eventually she told him the truth.

There I am at nine. I just had a fight with a girl twice my size. I did my best to ward her off, but she towered over me. I feel humiliated, hurt.

I never tell my mother such things. I don't want to burden her. All I need is to be near her, to listen to the sound of her sweet voice and feel her warmth.

She's standing at the table kneading dough for her special rolls with black seeds. Soon the house will be filled with their steamy, exotic scent to mingle with the aroma of roast with carrots and onions, baking in the oven.

She's wearing her dress full of flowers and singing "Paper Moon." Her black hair, as usual, is rolled in a wreath around her head. I kneel beside her on a chair to watch her strong fists sink into the supple dough in a rhythmic, almost slow motion, punching and rolling. Then she folds the dough in two and starts again. She's already let it rise under a clean cloth until it doubled in size. She tears off piece by piece and rolls each one into a small log, then curls it into a bun. She lays them on a baking tray, brushes the tops with beaten egg, and slips them into the oven.

"It's a Barnum and Bailey world, just as phony as it can be. But it wouldn't be make believe if you believed in me."

Why did I always think she was singing those words to me . . . to us? I do believe in her. I'm already healed.

I opened my eyes, and the flood of childhood memories dissolved in the dazzling sunlight that filled the bus. My mother was staring out of the window. Her head, with its shock of cropped white hair, rested against the cushion of the seat. I looked at its whiteness as if for the first time. The contrast with my memory was so striking that for a moment I found it difficult to reconcile how many years had passed since I was a child. My life was so busy. I was always working, always striving, and the years that had turned each strand of my mother's hair from black to white had marched by without waiting for me to fully register the change. My own hair had strands of white tucked between the brown. They had also worked themselves in without trumpets or fanfare to announce their arrival.

"Have you ever set a timer for three minutes to boil an egg?" I said to my mother.

My mother smiled. "Yes. Why?"

"Did you ever notice how long three minutes is? You can wash the dishes, dry your hands, and do a number of other things before that timer goes off. Three minutes, or even one minute for that matter, seems like such a long time when you're waiting for it to pass."

My mother again looked at the child across the aisle who was sucking on the small strip of apricot. "Yes," my mother said. And as if reading my mind, "three minutes seems like such a long time when you're waiting for it to pass, but your life rushes by in the blink of an eye."

The roof hatch of the bus slammed shut again, and my mother and I looked up in time to see the attendant turning the handle to secure it tightly. My mother looked at me and smiled, and I wanted to put my arms around her and hold her as she had held me so many times as a child, but I leaned my head on hers and closed my eyes.

5.

STEP BY STEP

We arrived in Amasya in the evening. The sun had already slipped behind the mountain, but the light lingered for a few more hours. My friend's old guidebook listed only one hotel for Amasya. We walked the quarter mile from the bus stop to the hotel across a small bridge and checked in.

The next morning my mother dressed for walking in a pair of slacks and a loose-fitting blouse. The purse I bought her in New York that one wore around one's waist like a belt to free the hands, was securely in place around hers.

We had decided to spend at least a day in Amasya before heading on to Fatsa to begin our search. Again we walked across the small bridge. In the brilliant light of morning one could see why the Green River was called by that name. It ran like an emerald ribbon thrown to the ground, cutting that portion of the town in two as it wriggled toward the hills. High up, on the hotel side of the river, the mountain came right down to the river's edge. Eerie window and door openings of long defunct Hellenic tombs stared down at us from the face of the mountain like colossal, haunted eyes.

"Those are old Greek tombs. They were built for the kings," a young man's voice said from behind us.

We turned to find two young men who looked to be about eighteen or nineteen standing there. Both were about five foot six or seven, approximately my size.

"How did you know we speak English?" I said.

Mustafa, the dark one, laughed and repeated in Turkish what I said to his fair-haired friend.

"I don't know," Mustafa said, turning back to me. "I just guessed. Anyway, you're not German, and I only speak English and German . . . and Turkish. Where are you staying?"

"In the hotel across the bridge there," I said. "The guidebook says there's only one hotel in Amasya."

"There used to be only one, but now there's a *pansiyon*. It just opened fifteen days ago. It was an old Armenian mansion years ago. An architect restored it and opened a *pansiyon*. Do you want to see it? It's not far."

I looked at my mother. She nodded a yes.

"Sure," I said. "How is it you speak such good English?"

"I live in Germany with my family. I grew up there and learned English there. But I was born in Amasya so I come here with my mother every summer."

"And your friend?"

His blond young friend stood patiently wearing a sweet smile on his handsome face.

"Oh. He lives here always. He doesn't speak English."

They led us the half block to the *pansiyon* down a narrow stone street where a few stone earthquake arches connected one stone building to another high up on their facades. It created a tunnel-like effect and a feeling of great age.

Surrounding the *Ilk Pansiyon*, as it was called, was a high wall that hid it and its inner courtyard from the street.

"This is Ali," Mustafa said when the *pansiyon's* architect opened the door to our knocking. Then turning to Mustafa, "They want to see the *pansiyon*. I can show them around."

Ali, a man in his thirties, stepped back cordially. The rim of his glasses formed a thick black line around his black eyes, and the heavy black stubble of his cleanly shaven face was still prominent.

"Welcome," Ali said.

We stepped over the low partition in the doorway and entered the courtyard. Flowering plants stood in clay pots on the ground, and four or five round tables with chairs waited for guests. The *pansiyon* was quite simple and very beautiful. Honey-colored wooden doors and window frames trimmed the beige, mortar-covered stone walls, and hugging the front of the building was a stairway, which led up to the main entrance.

Mustafa showed us the rooms on the first floor of the living area, then led us up another flight of stairs directly in front of the entrance, and walked us through the two large but simple rooms on the second floor. There too, the wooden doors, trim, and wardrobe, made of the same warm, honey-colored wood, created an elegant, rustic finish to the rooms. Under a wall of windows that opened out over the courtyard, a wooden window seat, covered with cushions and multicolored kilim rugs, ran the full length of the wall.

"What do you say, honey?"

"It's beautiful," my mother said.

"We should stay here," I said. "I have a feeling we won't ever find another place like it."

Mustafa smiled. "I knew you'd like it. It's decorated like in the nineteenth century."

We went back downstairs and I left my mother sitting in the courtyard with the other young Turk, whose name she couldn't pronounce, while Mustafa and I went to fetch our bags from the other hotel. When we returned, an American man with a game leg was moving into the *pansiyon* right before us. We stepped aside to let him enter. He had also stayed one night at the other hotel and had found the *pansiyon* as we had. His name was Harry Seiss. He was about sixty-five years of age, a retired jeweler from Pennsylvania he later told us. He also told us he had been on the same bus that had brought my mother and me to Amasya from Ankara.

Mustafa and I brought our bags up to the room my mother and I had chosen for our own. Then I went to ask Ali, who spoke English fairly well, if he could help us locate my mother's villages. Ali questioned one of his workers who came from Fatsa to no avail, and in that moment I realized how hard it was going to be to find three small villages in some remote mountain area with only a vague notion of where they lay. When I returned to my mother sitting in the courtyard, I found she had already been joined by Harry at one of the small round tables.

"Your story is my story, Sano," Harry was saying to my mother as I sat down. "My parents were also Pontians and they were also exiled in the early 1920s. They came from a coastal town of the Black Sea not far from

Fatsa. I'm here to visit their home. Let's see. You say your village was called Iondone and it was just below Fatsa and Ordu."

Harry pulled a large map from the leather bag that still hung from his shoulder. It was a Greek map. He opened it wide and spread it out on the table to give us all a better chance to look. Then he leaned over it and adjusted his eyeglasses.

"Here's Fatsa," Harry said and fingered a spot on the coast of the Black Sea. He trailed his finger downward. "Go south and look! Here are three crosses. That means they were Greek villages. And one of them is called Ayios Antonis. Saint Anthony. That's the real name of what you call Iondone."

I looked at my mother who was staring at him in wonder.

"Could it really be true?" she said.

"Here it is, right here," Harry said, tapping the little crosses with his finger.

What we hadn't been able to find in decades of searching, Harry had found in the blink of an eye. And it was no wonder we had never found it. We had only known the name in dialect. Or maybe Iondone was just the way it was said in the villages when one pronounced it quickly, the only way my mother had ever known it.

I couldn't tell what my mother was feeling. I only knew that I felt as if I had found some precious, mysterious thing I could never name, but that I had searched for my entire life, and now it was finally within reach. I ran to Ali to tell him the new arrival had found my mother's villages on his map. Ali seemed almost as excited as I. He followed me back to the table and sat down.

"Will you do me a favor?" he said to my mother.

"What is it?" my mother said.

"Will you wait here for one extra day until I can take care of business? Then allow me to take you to find your home. I want to see your face when we find it."

My mother lowered her head and her eyes filled with tears. "Thank you," she said.

☙ ☙ ☙

For the rest of that day and the next, my mother and I roamed around Amasya and neighboring towns with our two young Turkish friends. Now that we had been assured we were close to our goal, at least by knowing where the villages lay, we decided to enjoy the few days' wait for Ali.

That night my mother and I lay in our low beds in the *Ilk Pansiyon* as the dim light from the courtyard came through the open windows. I tried to sleep but the disparity between Turkey's past and the people we had met thus far, kept clamoring for my attention. Everyone, from the man who practically took me by the hand and brought me to my destination at the bus depot in Ankara, to the hotel clerk, and now Ali and the young boys, were as courteous and generous as one could hope. It was a strange dichotomy knowing of Turkey's atrocious history, and its intermittent rampages against the Kurds, and then visiting the land and finding a warm, receptive people. Where did that barbarism come from? How was it born? All the typical answers came to me of greed, territory and conquest, of fear and jealousy, but they were just words. As usual, it was difficult to reconcile the incredible brutality of a country's history with the seeming gentleness one finds in its people.

I had that bizarre feeling one gets when looking at the face of a perfectly made-up drag queen at a burlesque show. You can stare at that face for as long as you will, knowing it's not the face of a woman, but that of a man, yet it's difficult to reconcile it emotionally. A kind of fascination sets in; a lack of desire to let go of the illusion. Which image of Turkey was the real one? Or were both images equally real?

"Are you awake?" I said to my mother.

"Yes," she said.

"The people here remind me of Spain years ago," I said. "I don't know what it's like now, but when I lived there, if you asked someone directions, they took you by the hand and walked you to your destination, even if they had been heading in the opposite direction. The Turks do the same thing. You think of the history of Turkey, the conquests, the slaughters, the pillaging, and you half expect to find barbarians grunting along, out to steal even the dust from your boots."

"It was never the people," my mother said. "At least not where we came from. It was the government. Mustafa Kemal. Atatürk. He was the one. Not the only one, but he was the one."

"But they obeyed him," I said.

"What else could they do? They were soldiers. But it's true," she added after some reflection. "Some of them were cruel."

"You never seem to hate them," I said, "even after all you've suffered."

"Let's just say I wouldn't want my daughter to marry a Turk. It would be too much of a reminder. But no. I don't hate them. How could I hate them? All the surrounding villages and towns were Turkish. We lived peacefully side by side with the Turks, probably for centuries, sharing our workloads by bartering. There were no problems, except perhaps those of the heart."

And what of my mother's heart? I wondered if she had ever been courted, had ever felt the thrill of young love. I was tempted to ask, but decided to leave it for another day.

꙳ ꙳ ꙳

Early the next morning, Harry, Ali, my mother, and I set out on our search for Iondone. The sun was shining brightly but in the distance, rain clouds peaked over the mountains. The car worked its way out of the hills of Amasya and onto the plains. In the front seat Harry and Ali conversed softly as my mother and I watched the scenery change from the backseat.

"Look!" Harry said. "There's a rainbow. It must be a good sign."

Directly in front of us, an enormous colored arc stretched from one end of the flat plain to the other, right up to the edge of the horizon. Through the middle of the arc, a purple mountain with a flat summit rose in the distance like a scene from *The Wizard of Oz*.

"Do you think that means we'll find our prize at the end of our journey?" I said.

"I hope so," Ali said.

At Niksar, Ali suggested we stop for lunch. It was a fairly big town where the ancient city of Cabeira, a great stronghold of the Pontic Greek kings, once stood. We parked near a large marketplace where merchants displayed their rugs, produce, and handmade brooms. The town was unlike the others we had seen so far. This one had such broad streets with low buildings. There was such an empty—or perhaps a better word would be quiet—feeling about it. Only the marketplace and the streets surrounding it bustled with life and color.

"Something seems so familiar about this town," my mother said.

"We're still so far from where your village is," Ali said.

"But I feel like I've been here before."

It was the first time since arriving in Turkey that my mother had such a sensation. We walked up the road to a two-story building, then up a flight of stairs to a restaurant. The maitre d' showed us to a table near a large window that overlooked the wide, empty crossroads. We took our seats and were given menus. My mother looked out the window.

"When my grandfather threw us out of the house, we settled in a large town like this for a while. Or maybe this was where my grandfather had his shop."

"Your grandfather threw you out?" Harry said. "Why would he do that?"

My mother looked at Harry with surprise, then turned to me and Ali, but each of us looked back at her, curious to know what she'd answer.

"Oh," she said. "A misunderstanding. Just a misunderstanding."

We waited expectantly, but she again turned toward the window.

"Anyway," she said, "this town reminds me of the town we came to. And that corner reminds me of where my father had his shop."

"Could be," Ali said. "Could be."

By late afternoon we arrived in a small mountain town called Aybasti. Ali had determined Aybasti to be the town at the foot of the mountain where my mother's villages lay. There was nothing distinguishing about the town, except perhaps the fact that there were four-story buildings in such a tiny place. It had a kind of close feeling about it, as if it were squeezed between two mountain peaks, the exact opposite feeling of Niksar. The main street, or rather a small square, sat in the middle of the village around which the buildings seemed to radiate helter-skelter. There was a smoky quality to the air when we arrived, and a cool dampness made it seem like early fall rather than midsummer.

"Now what?" I asked.

"You find the richest man in town," Ali said, "and you ask him what you want to know. They know everything, or at least can find out."

He parked his car in the small square in front of the Perelli Tire store. Except for Perelli's, I saw nothing resembling city life or city business.

"This looks like it," Ali said. We got out and went inside. Ali asked for the owner and was shown into a room behind the small showroom. My mother, Harry, and I waited patiently.

"Well?" I said when Ali returned.

"He knows of Iondone. He said the road is rough. We will stay here tonight and go up the mountain in the morning. We can hire a dolmuç to take us. That's a kind of minibus taxi."

By then it was late. We walked up the steep flight of stairs to the second-floor office of one of the only two hotels in the village. It was crude. We checked in and were given keys to two rooms on the fourth floor. Harry and Ali joined us in our room for a short time and then said good night.

My mother and I looked at each other. So close. So close.

6.

ON THE ROAD TO IONDONE

In our small hotel room at the foot of the mountains my mother once called home, I climbed into the bed near hers and turned out the lights. For the first time in my life I realized I didn't know her. It was so easy to think one's parents had just sprung up full grown in the role of parent, and my mother had played the role of mother so well. I looked over to where she lay in her little Turkish bed. Her white hair caught the faint light of the room.

"You know," I said. "There are so many things you never told me."

"About what, sweetheart?" my mother said.

"About how you grew up and what it was like. You've told us stories over the years, but I know there's more than those few stories. We came all this way to find your past, your home, and I realize I don't know those people you call family. I never felt they were mine, that they belonged to me too. What I remember most is that you named me after your calf."

My mother smiled. "Not really," she said. "But I did name my calf Mata. That was short for Mathea."

In fact, as a child, I remembered my mother's story of her calf most of all. The thought of owning such a large, docile animal had filled me with awe. I could recite the names of her family, but they had remained just names. Her mother's name was Barthena. Her father's name was Haralumbos, or Lumbo as they called him. They lived with her grandfather, Varidimei, and step-grandmother. Her uncle Constantine and his wife and little girl also lived with them, all together in a log cabin. She had a second uncle, Nikolas, who lived with her grandfather's brother. The men of the family were blacksmiths, but her father also made and played the viol. Her grandfather played the flute. She had a sister named Cristodula who was a few years older, and only one brother who was a year younger. Yanni was his name. Then there was little Nastasía who was five years younger than Yanni. And later there were the twins: Mathea, the one my mother named me after, and Maria, the one after whom my eldest sister Mariam was named.

My mother's few stories of life in her ancient village had also stayed with me: how the women bleached the newly woven cloth by laying it on the ground and covering it with cow manure because there was something in the manure that bleached the cloth. Then they washed it again and again and it became pure white. She told how her mother made butter from the milk she collected each day from their ten cows. First she boiled it so it wouldn't spoil. Then, when she had enough milk, she made yogurt, and from that, she separated the butter by putting the yogurt in a barrel that hung from ropes under the porch, and she shook the barrel until the butter formed on top. And she told how her father went into the woods in autumn and collected huge snails and carried them home in a big basket for the family to eat like escargot.

Of course, I knew the Turks had driven them from their homes, but my knowledge of that was also limited.

"Tell me what you want to know and I'll tell you," my mother said.

"The little things of your daily life," I said. "And the big things. You never told us the details."

"The details," my mother said. "Yes. What are the details? I suppose a detail is the way the light shone on my mother's face from the glow of the fire. Or my father sitting on his stool with his viol on his knee, playing and singing after the evening meal. Or the sound of my family talking as I lay in my bed in the dark. A sunrise. A sunset. And then the dying. Always the dying. Those things are hardest to remember because then I'm reminded of what I lost. Being here in this country after so many years brings back so many memories. Where should I begin? Where should I begin?"

I closed my own eyes then and listened to the sound of my own mother's voice in the dark, and again, a flood of my own childhood memories swept over me.

"Did I tell you we lived in log cabins in our villages?" my mother said. "The whole village used to get together to help build a house for a couple when they were first married if they had no family to live with. The sons usually lived in their father's house when they married. The daughters went to their in-laws. I don't think the Turks built log cabins. At least I never saw any when they drove us from our homes. I saw a few homes in the north that were built with wooden slabs, and in the south they used mud bricks, but never logs. Even the Turks who lived in villages near ours didn't build log cabins. I wonder why."

"Why didn't you ever tell us what really happened?" I said.

"When I first went to America, I tried a few times to tell your uncle Elias, but he got angry with me. He said, 'Come on, sister! Forget it.' It made me feel so . . . I can't think of a word to describe it. Maybe ashamed. His wife, Agnes, was Armenian, but they lived in the Bronx and I rarely saw her. I had no one of my own people to talk with. I couldn't burden my young children with what happened to us. It was too horrible to tell. Finally I stopped trying to talk about it. But I never stopped thinking of my family. I never stopped thinking of our home and land and the way we lived there. I pictured every detail in my mind over and over all these years so I wouldn't forget; so I could keep them alive in my heart. I can close my eyes now and see our beautiful landscape. I can close my eyes and see my family too."

My mother stopped speaking then and I could feel the silence fill the room.

"Are you all right?" I said.

"Let's sleep now," my mother said. "We have so much to see in the morning."

"Can I get you something?"

"No, sweetheart. Just sleep."

I suppose the past had always been a kind of poetry for me. All the insignificant moments of one's life fall away and only the most essential memories remain. Even bad memories have their poetry. Even they have the power to fill one's heart and mind with a life lived.

Now in Aybasti at the foot of Iondone, as Harry and Ali slept in a room down the hall and my mother and I lay in our beds, I couldn't help wondering what we would find. I knew the impossibility of finding my mother's family there, but I couldn't shake the few pictures I had of them in my mind.

I could see her little calf standing there tied to the old apple tree and her mother and father sitting by the fire. I imagine a glint from the glow of the fire catching a tear in my grandmother's eye as she looks up in surprise and realizes who we are. My grandfather has his viol perched on his knee. His right hand holds its bow suspended, waiting to once again slide it across its strings, while my great-grandfather sits with his flute raised to his lips. My mother's brother and sisters are also there, Cristodula, Yanni and Nastasía—my aunts and uncle—as young as when my mother last saw them seventy years before. They run to us, curious to know us and touch us, to see if we are real. They embrace us, then speak while I stand there with that frozen grin that says, "I can't understand a word you're saying, but I'm so grateful to hear you say it all the same."

"Oh, God," I thought. "If only one could make time stand still; if one could erase all the horror and inhumanity in the world."

My mother finally told me her story. I've written it down in an effort to share her life and her people. And although I can't alter the horror, I wrote it in an effort to make time stand still. I had taken my mother on her quest to find her home. She had waited a lifetime. But that night, lying in the hotel room in the dark, I realized the quest was also mine; that I had also waited a lifetime to know her, and to make her people mine.

Book Two

NOT EVEN MY NAME

The tears are deep inside me
Even I am not always aware
that I weep
Perhaps I should go in there
where the crying is

The earliest record of my mother's people is intertwined with the Greeks of mainland Greece and Crete. In the Middle Paleolithic, or Stone Age (c. 55,000–30,000 B.C.) the humans who occupied Greece made finely crafted tools of wood, stone, and bone and survived as hunter/gatherers. With the recession of the glaciers of the Ice Age, sea-fishing in small boats they crafted from reeds and skins was added to their activities around 12,000 B.C. Between 6,500–3,000 B.C. the inhabitants began to cultivate the fields and domesticate animals, a practice begun 2,000 years earlier in Asia Minor, the land across the Aegean Sea that the early Greeks called Ionia.

The development of bronze in the Near East in the fourth millennium B.C. reached Greece around 3000 B.C., marking the beginning of the Bronze Age. As other metals, such as lead, silver, and gold were also developed and became widely used in Greece, and economic and cultural trade was extended outside its own borders, Greece began to flourish. Between 2100–1900 B.C., people who spoke an Indo-European language common to a wide range of peoples, which developed into an early form of Greek in the Greek territories, came down from the mountains in the north and east bringing with them both their gods and destruction to many of the Greek settlements. On their arrival, these invaders adopted some of the arts and customs of the Greeks whose strongholds they had conquered and introduced their own. A 500-year period of cultural stagnation followed, after which a regeneration took place in the late Bronze Age 1600–1150 B.C.

Through association with Crete, Phoenicia, and Egypt, Greece continued to develop culturally. Cretan tablets dating back as early as 1800 B.C. show an early form of writing. With the takeover of Crete around 1450 B.C. by Mycenae, a leading Greek city in the Aegean civilization, the late Bronze Age reached its height of prosperity and glory. The last 300 years of the Bronze Age became known as the Mycenaean Period, named after "golden" Mycenae, where some of the finest examples of crafts of the Bronze Age, especially jewelry and various articles in solid gold, were found. It was from this great city that King Agamemnon set out with his legendary army around 1250–1225 B.C. for Troy—a city on the western banks of Ionia—to retrieve his beautiful queen, Helen.

Around 1200 B.C., invaders again came from the north like those before them, and with that, the Dark Age began. The destruction the invaders wrought was so great even the art of writing was lost. A massive redistribution of peoples took place around 1200 B.C. when Greeks moved across the

Aegean Sea to the islands and shores of Ionia. For 300 years the memory of the Bronze Age remained only through oral poetry.

In 1000 B.C. the Dorians, Greek-speaking people from the Pindus Mountains, settled in Greece. In 800 B.C. the Greeks once again developed an alphabet and began to construct temples. In 776 B.C. the first Olympian games were started. The renewal of Greece had obviously reached Ionia, since it was during this period of renewal that the blind poet Homer, an Achaean Greek from Ionia, wrote down the history of the Trojan War around 750 B.C., 500 years after the actual events. Homer's epic poems of the Bronze Age, The Iliad *and* The Odyssey, *brought the Trojan War and its players, King Agamemnon and the ancient Achaean heroes of Greece, such as Odysseus and Achilles, back to life, and immortalized the daughter of Zeus and Leda, the beautiful queen, Helen, whose "face had launched a thousand ships" when she was kidnapped from golden Mycenae by Paris and brought to his palace in Troy.*

Around the time of Homer's epic poems, city–states emerged in Greece (750–700 B.C.), and colonization again took place. In Ionia, colonists migrated north and east settling throughout the Pontic Mountains and the southern shores of the Black Sea. Sinope was the first Ionian city to be founded there by colonists from Miletus in 785 B.C. From Sinope other cities were founded including Amisus (Samsun), and Kotyora (Ordu) and in 756 B.C., the famed city of Trapezus (Trapezunta/Trebizond/Trabzon).

Pontus is an ancient Greek word that means "Sea." Pontios means "a person of the sea." It is from these ancient Greek words that both the mountain range and the Greek people who inhabited them, the Pontians, or Pontic Greeks, derived their name. It was here that Xenophon and his 10,000 soldiers found safe haven after their retreat from Mesopotamia in 400 B.C. The legend of Jason and the Argonauts quest for the Golden Fleece is associated with the Pontians, as is the legend of Heracles obtaining the Amazon Queen's girdle. The philosopher, Diogenes, (c. 412–323 B.C.), who was said to have gone about with a lantern in search of an honest man, and the great historian and geographer, Strabo, (c. 63 B.C.–c. A.D. 23) were both Pontians.

These Pontic Greeks were my mother's people, and this is her story.

7.

NOT EVEN MY NAME

THERE I WAS in Aleppo, Syria, a thousand miles from home. I was just fifteen years old, and getting married to a man I didn't know who was three times my age. At least I think I was fifteen, but for all I know I could have been younger. I still had no breasts, and I still didn't menstruate. In fact, I still didn't know what that was, or that it existed at all. I didn't have any friends I could talk to about those things, and I had lost my mother too soon, so my knowledge of what it meant to be a woman came only from the people I lived with. They told me nothing.

Their names were Hagop and Zohra. They were an Armenian couple from Diyarbakir, Turkey. That's where I had met them. They lived with Zohra's mother. Or rather, Zohra's mother lived with them. Nana, as they called her. I never called her anything.

Zohra was a patient woman who tended to her chores in silence. Hagop was a carpenter. He made musical instruments and wooden utensils used in the kitchen. He also made cob-cobs, a kind of wooden sandal, similar to the Japanese style that elevates the wearer four or more inches off the ground. He was a kind man. Not prone to too much talking.

Nana was something else entirely. She was quite old and bent over like a broken twig. She couldn't stand upright at all. She had to hold on to her own knee to keep her balance as she walked so she wouldn't just topple over. But she never rested for a minute. She was just as active as a young woman, only twice as bossy. Her hands were always busy taking in wash to make extra money, or crocheting the edges around handkerchiefs, which she sold. She had the will and determination of a bull, and the eye of an eagle.

I was only ten years old when I lost my mother. She left me with a woman in a little mud village in the south of Turkey. But the woman she left me with only wanted a slave. Of course she didn't say that when she asked my mother if she could keep me. When the woman asked for me to stay, at first Mother told her she couldn't leave me because I didn't belong to her. She didn't want to disappoint the woman I guess. Mother said she couldn't bear to let me go. She cried and cried. But then, when she saw how little food we had collected for the family, she changed her mind. I know she did it to save my life. So many of our people had already died and my own family were dying one by one.

After a few years of that woman's abuse, I finally ran away from her, all the way to Diyarbakir. In Diyarbakir I lived with another woman for a few days who didn't want me. That's when Zohra asked me if I wanted to come and live with her and her family. She and Hagop had two small children. That's where I came in. She said I could help take care of them. Actually, at that time, Zohra only had one child. The other was on the way. I don't know what would have happened to me if they hadn't taken me in. That woman I was living with probably would have just locked me out one day to starve in the streets. So when Zohra asked me to live with them, of course I said yes. Where else would I go at twelve years old in a large city without anyone to call my own?

I lived with Zohra and her family in Diyarbakir for a few years. Then we heard Turkish soldiers were coming to expel the rest of the Christians from Turkey, even those in the south. Hagop and his family decided to leave. They owned a nice house in Diyarbakir but they left everything they owned behind. All the other Armenians left too, I think. That is, all the Armenians the Turks hadn't already killed.

They took me with them, and we headed for Aleppo, Syria, where we would be safe at last. They rented a small apartment there. It had just one room on the second floor of a two-story building with a courtyard. Six of us all slept and ate and rested in that one room.

I guess you could say Hagop sold me into marriage, because he asked the man I was going to marry to pay him twenty pieces of gold— $100.00. That was quite a lot in 1925. When Hagop told me I was getting married, each time I'd try to imagine it, I'd think of the old man I was going to marry and all my images would disappear. I needed a father, not a husband. I needed my mother most of all.

I just wanted to go home. But there was no going home, and there never would be again. I had lost them all; everyone and everything I had ever loved. All I had left were my memories and two small scars on my leg. By the time I was ten years old, nothing else was left to me. Not even my name.

🕊 🕊 🕊

My memories of the last summer we spent on our land were probably the most beautiful memories of all. It was the summer my grandfather gave me a calf to call my own, and the last summer I would spend as a carefree child.

My name wasn't Sano then. My name was Themía, and I was nine that summer, I think. Birthdays weren't something we celebrated in those remote mountain villages of north central Turkey. The Turks called us Rüm. I had always thought that meant Greek, but it meant Roman. We were Pontic Greeks, going back in history to when the Roman Empire ruled the land and even before, all the way back to the eighth century B.C.

Our villages sat high in the mountains south of Fatsa and Ordu on the Black Sea. Today they're just a few hours drive by car, but in 1919, travel was more difficult. Donkeys and gamish, a kind of water buffalo, trudged along the dusty paths winding up the mountain, drawing their carts or saddled with bags to carry provisions. Father and Grandfather often talked of those far-off towns, and occasionally they went to them to bring back supplies.

Once, Grandfather brought back a new prize. She was a Protestant woman and she came with her finery and settled in. She brought linens with her, and towels . . . a real luxury in our little village. My real grandmother had died in childbirth a few years before. They had laid her out in the summer room of our home wrapped in white cloth. Her gray face peered out from the halo of white that surrounded it with that serene grace only death can bring with certainty. For many years after, being too young to grasp the details, I thought they had also buried her somewhere in the house. So when my new grandmother came, I often wondered if one day, while cleaning or sorting things out, she would come upon her rival, cold and unmoving, with pebbles on her eyes to keep them shut.

The First World War had only ended the year before. It was a brutal war that lasted four years with a death toll of at least 13 million souls. Turkish soldiers had periodically swept through our villages to snatch our men from the fields and roads. They sent them to labor camps to build highways and dig trenches. Most of them never came back.

But that summer the air smelled of hazelnut fires and freshly baked bread, and the pear trees on the slope of the mountain below our log homes dragged their branches with the weight of their fruit. The hills and valleys spread out in a mass of greenness with rows of corn, the pear trees, and our great garden, which was our survival. And the golden fields of barley and wheat were ever waving in the sunshine.

An occasional muddy path along which the cows tramped from home to field and back again played peekaboo with the sky, while great billowy white clouds often rose above the mountains like majestic castles in a fairy tale.

There were three Greek villages in those mountains. Three sister villages you could call them. I don't remember the name of our village or the other small village, but the largest one, the one where the cathedral stood, was called Iondone. It sat on the other hillside, down the valley from our village and up the other side. There were thirty homes in our village and twenty-eight in the other small village, but more than 250 in Iondone.

We had wonderful forests in the north, but only the Greeks built log cabins. In our house, my grandparents' bedroom was also the kitchen, our dining room, and what one might call our living room. That's where the fireplace was. Then there was a summer room, where Uncle Constantine and his family slept, the utility room or pantry, where we kept the food supplies for the year, and our room, the only other room with a fireplace. The bathroom was a kind of indoor outhouse you might say; a small separate room that jutted out from the outer wall over the ground. One stood straddled over a hole in the floor, Turkish style, to relieve oneself over the cow manure down below. The animals lived under the house. The warmth of their bodies rose to help warm the rooms above.

One of my greatest sources of pleasure was my little calf Mata. I rode her once. It wasn't something I usually did, but one day my older sister Cristodula climbed on her back to ride her home. She bounced up and down to encourage Mata to carry her.

"Let's go," she said. But Mata pulled back her head and planted her tiny hooves in the grass. I tugged on her furry neck to make her run along beside me, but the more I tugged, the more obstinate she became.

"Push her from behind," my brother Yanni said.

He leaned against her rump with both hands and pushed as hard as he could. But Mata would not move.

"You push and I'll pull," I said. I yanked her with all my might while Yanni leaned his back against her rump and pushed, digging his heels into the grass. But Mata still would not move.

"Come up with me Themía," Cristodula said. "Maybe then she'll move."

I picked up a rock and moved it closer to Mata. Then I stood on it to give myself a boost and sprung up onto her rump on my belly before pulling myself up to straddle her behind my sister. I also bounced up and down.

"Let's go," I said bouncing and kicking in unison with Cristodula. "Let's go, you little rascal."

But Mata only mooed the sky.

"I'll go get a twig. That will make her move," said Cristodula.

She swung her leg over Mata's head and slipped off her back. But no sooner had she slipped off and turned away, then Mata decided to run. Surprised and delighted, I grabbed her fur to hang on, my legs flapping.

"Wait!" Cristodula screamed after us, running as fast as she could. Yanni was right behind her. "Wait for me," she cried.

But Mata ran and I laughed all the way down the slope and up toward the path for home, with me hugging her 'round the neck to keep from falling, and planting kisses with each bounce of my head against her fur.

8

A CARAVAN OF COWS

IT WOULD BE easier to explain what happened to the Pontic Greeks if I could simply say the Turks and Greeks hated each other, and that's why the Turks did what they did to us, but it wouldn't be true. At least it wasn't true where we came from. All the surrounding villages were Turkish, and as far back as I could remember we had lived side by side with the Turks without major incidents of any kind, except occasionally those of the heart. But that always seemed so romantic. That last summer, a Greek girl from one of our villages ran off with a Turkish boy to be married. It caused quite a commotion in our villages. She was kidnapped some said, but I don't think anyone really believed that.

On the day we heard about it, I remember lying in my bed that night fighting my drowsiness, staring at the blackness of the beamed ceiling. Little Nastasía slept beside me. Her warm feet were pressed against my thigh. The sound of her breathing rose and fell like the hills and valleys surrounding the orchards of our gentle domain. Cristodula also slept near, and Yanni nestled himself near her to keep warm.

In the next room my parents and grandparents talked about the young people who had run off. I forced my eyes wide open, as though that would help me hear better in the dark. Between my inhales and exhales, I picked out whole words from the low hum of their voices squeezing under the crude wooden door along with the dim light of the fire. Turk . . . child . . . ruined . . . Greek. I wondered what it was like to run off and leave everyone behind, mother, father, everything I held dear.

By morning it was over. I had drifted off to sleep, surprised to find the gray light filling the room in the morning. The sound of the fire crackling and the smell of coffee nudged my senses. I sat up in bed and through the window I could see only the tops of a few pear trees not hidden in the dense fog.

"Cristodula." I whispered. "Are you awake?"

"No," she said, rolling over and nudging me with her behind.

I crawled over Nastasía and slipped my feet onto the cool wooden floor between the mats, still wearing the new cowhide shoes Grandfather had made for me the day before. They were so soft and pretty. I hadn't wanted to take them off.

In Grandfather's room the fire was already licking at the great beam, which was its mantel. They were all assembled at the long wooden table Grandfather had built many years before: Grandfather, my step-grandmother, Mother and Father, Uncle Constantine and his wife. They were drinking coffee and eating bread. Their mats and blankets were already folded neatly and placed on their shelves to clear the floor.

I stole quietly into the room and planted myself on an empty stool beside Grandfather, then leaned my head against him. His strong arm circled my thin shoulder automatically, and he patted my arm.

"The boy was beaten by the men of the village," Father was saying as he settled himself in his seat. The chill of an early-morning excursion still lingered on his clothes and hair. Mother poured a demitasse for him from a small brass pot, then continued pouring melted butter over the flat bread she had baked for breakfast.

"They shouldn't have run off," Grandfather said. "She's a Christian and he's a Muslim. What kind of future could they have together?"

"What happened to the girl?" Mother asked, directing her question to my father. It wasn't proper for a woman to speak directly to her father-in-law.

"The girl was returned to her parents. It's a nasty business," Father said.

Later that day the women of the village gathered to bake their bread in the stone oven Grandfather built near our home.

"I can't believe she would go of her own free will."

"He must have dragged her off."

"You can never tell what's in the heart of a young girl," a third woman said softly. Almost immediately she lowered her eyes and fumbled with her apron as if remembering a sinful kiss.

It was a simple life that we lived, and except for that incident, we had no trouble with the Turks that summer. There was only one incident of violence, but it came from one of our own. That was rare in our villages, but there's good and bad everywhere I suppose. It happened to my mother. Just to think of it makes my heart ache.

We were making our daily round to the garden, just Mother and I, when we came upon two boys near our wheat fields. A gentle breeze, drifting over the mountains from the south, brought a feeling of peace to the village, which brushed away any sense of fear. The dense and varied greens of the mountains had deepened, and rippled over the landscape like richly embroidered cloth. Wildflowers peered from every crevice, and eagles waltzed on the currents high above our heads. On days like that it was difficult to believe there had ever been a war or there was still danger lurking ahead.

The boys were tall, with ruddy faces and thick black hair. One was about seventeen; the other a year or two younger. They had allowed their cows to wander through our wheat fields to graze on our wheat.

"Hey, there!" Mother called to the boys. "Don't you know better than to allow your animals into the wheat fields?"

Mother headed toward the boys and I followed. The sticky sheaths of wheat gently beat against my chest nearly to my chin.

"Mind your own business!" one of the boys shouted at her. "Go on your way if you know what's good for you."

"Well, this is my business," Mother called. "What would your parents say if they knew you were destroying our wheat?"

At that the boys moved menacingly toward us and stood belligerently before her, as close as they could without touching her, one on either side. Mother reached for me to press me behind her out of harm's way. My heart began to race and my breath reached only to my throat and back again. I looked at her for some sign. She stood dark and proud; a kerchief tied around and under her long black hair, framed her beautiful face.

"Who will tell our parents?" the boy said.

"You better not touch my mother!" I shouted, intending my fierceness to drive them away.

But the taller one leaned his downy, smirking face close to my mother's. His rugged build and rosy cheeks were striking against the blackness of his thick hair and mocking, peasant eyes. I struggled to break free of Mother's protective grip, but she held me tight.

"My father will kill you if you touch her," I shouted again.

"So?" he said, jutting out his thick neck to force his face even closer to my mother's than before. "Who will tell our parents?"

Mother began to turn away, but the boy grabbed her by the shoulder and pushed her to the ground.

"Run!" Mother cried. "Run!"

And I did run as the boy lifted his hand to strike her. I heard the blows pound against my ears as if they were falling on my own body. I ran. No. I flew like a butterfly above the ground, rising and falling in flight over rocks and dips in the field, rising even above the wheat, above the clawing sheaths that grabbed at my long, brightly colored dress, above the sting and lashing to my tender flesh. I flew into the clearing and up the hill and around the house to my father's blacksmith shop. There I exploded into the room with my chest heaving and my cheeks stinging and wet with tears.

"My mother! My mother!" I cried.

Father looked up from the flames where he held molten metal with great claws of steel as Grandfather worked the giant bellows.

"The wheat field . . . they're beating her," I said between sobs.

Father dropped his tools and burst out the door. I raced behind him, making it to the edge of the wheat field before my legs would go no more. I stood panting and sobbing as I watched my father race on, bounding through the field toward the boys.

They laughed together as they walked along, until they caught sight of the raging hulk that vaulted toward them. Then they turned to run, hopping and pitching through the wheat like vultures heavy from a recent feeding. I stood long enough to hear my father's voice and see his right fist come down on the tallest boy; long enough to see his left arm swing out and crash against the other's jaw, and long enough to hear their cries as blow after blow crushed their arrogant laughter, and restored my mother's honor. Then I limped to where my mother lay wounded and collapsed in a heap, my head upon her breast.

At breakfast the next morning, a knock came at the door. Mother sat beside me. The bruises were beginning to show through the red swelling near her eye and on her cheek.

"Lumbo!" a voice called through the thick wooden panels.

Father rose and went to the door with nine pairs of eyes silently watching him move across the room. He swung the door wide.

"My sons are missing," the man on the other side said with hat in hand, not raising his eyes from the floor. "They didn't come home last night. Could you help me find them?"

Father looked back at us waiting expectantly. His eyes settled on Mother. She looked at him for a moment, then lowered her eyes and nodded her consent.

The boys had hidden themselves in the mountains, afraid to come home. Father showed the way. There was no mention made of the beatings given or received. That was the way in our Greek villages. There were no police or magistrates. Punishment was swift for a wrong done. No one questioned it. Not even the family of the one punished. It was a question of honor to acknowledge a wrong. That's what kept the peace.

❧ ❧ ❧

It's strange how little snippets of your life can sometimes race through your mind. I always tried to think about my life in our village, but sometimes it would just come back to me without trying. Sometimes just seeing the sun slanting through the window would remind me of home; of the way the early morning sun slipped into Grandfather's room, caught the edge of the table and ran a sliver of gold down the wall, then rested on Father's viol leaning there.

Sometimes Cristodula, Yanni, and I would drag ourselves from our bed, even before the sun rose, and dress in the dark. Mother was already awake, lighting the fire, milking the cows, and preparing our food. We'd eat breakfast by the glow of the fire, then rouse our ten cows, and my little calf Mata, and march them through the village. Cristodula was about twelve then, because she was three years older than I. Yanni was eight, one year younger.

"Children!" a frail voice called out from a window on one of our excursions. "Where are you going so early in the morning? The sky is not yet bright."

"We're going to pasture," Yanni said.

"Would you take my cows to pasture also?" the old woman asked as she tossed a few more grains of corn with her veined, bony hand, to the chickens below her window.

"Sure," I said. "We're going to the mountain on the other side of Iondone."

"Oh, good!" The old woman sounded pleased. "The grass is rich there. But don't let the Turkish ghosts capture your spirit."

"No. We won't," I said quickly, not understanding what she meant.

I trooped into the underbelly of her home where the animals were kept, with Cristodula right behind me. We brought out the old woman's cows, then continued down the road toward Iondone, our caravan of cows growing larger and larger along the way.

As we paraded up the final slope at the edge of the village, an occasional moo mingled with the twitter of birds. A rooster crowed and then another, and another rooster answered their call. A donkey brayed. Another cow mooed the distant hills, and myriad birds chirped and sang and sprang from twig to twig to praise the dawning, until the whole valley and the surrounding hills were alive with the music of donkeys and cows and birds, and red-plumed roosters staking their claims. Like a hunting party thrashing the ridges to scare the sun from its hiding, their riotous voices reached a crescendo worthy of a sunrise.

As if drawn by a gossamer thread, my eyes turned to the east as the sun peeked its brilliant face above the mountain. My sister's hair flamed before me and golden sunlight drenched the hills. My own hand bled a golden light that soaked the fur of the calf it was leading. Even the grass confused its color; first gold then green then gold once more as it flirted with the sun. Then the sun cleared the ridge of the mountain, and gathering its full strength, sucked back its gold and exchanged it for silver.

As we descended the slope toward Iondone, a garden spread out at our side. The pumpkins were already quite large, and the corn stalks stood row upon row, thick and impenetrable; their cobs, like little green canons, had already shot their silken threads. There were fava beans and cabbage and a green we called *lahana* that Mother dried for winter soups. The abundance of that summer was everywhere.

"Potatoes," said Cristodula, pointing to a large patch of low, green leafy plants. "Wouldn't it be nice to roast some potatoes while the cows are grazing?"

"Where?" said Yanni. "I don't see any potatoes."

"They're under the ground" Cristodula said.

"How do you know they're under there?"

"I just know," she said. "Because the leaves grow on top to tell you where they are."

"Well how can we get some?" Yanni said.

"We could dig them up with a stick and our fingers," I said, imagining the hot potatoes melting in my mouth.

"Do you think they'll mind if we take some?" Cristodula said.

"If we take just a few each," I said, "maybe they won't miss them. They have so many."

We set to work then without giving it another thought, except perhaps to crouch down and become really small in case someone was watching. But we knew the owners would only smile. Cristodula and I tucked our potatoes into our skirts. Yanni tucked his in his waistband and we continued on our way.

We washed the potatoes along the way in a stream of water spilling from a crevice of the mountain, then followed the path that wound its way up in twists and turns until it cleared the forbidding facade. On top, a lush plateau opened before us above a protected valley where a small stone house, the only house in the whole landscape, squatted in the sun. We released the cows to graze, then collapsed playfully on the rich, green grass. We picked wildflowers and played games, then went through the nearby forest to gather wood for a fire.

On a flat rocky place we dug a small pit and wrapped our potatoes in large, moist leaves. Then we put them in the pit and set a fire above it. Our matches were made of tree mushrooms that had been pounded and pounded until they were flat, then dried and cut into tiny strips. I held one in my hand against a small white stone, then struck it with another white stone, until it sparked, while Yanni held dry grass against it and blew on it to help it ignite.

By noon our potatoes were done. We devoured them with great relish, cracking them open while they were still hot and licking our burning fingers between each bite. Then we fell asleep before the smoldering embers of the fire.

I thought I dreamed a doleful procession of women in black flashing white palms at the sky. And men with bowed heads, trailed along, their hands clasped before them. Voices wailed mournfully, riding the hills like dozing whales on the rolling swell of the sea. A dead man, bound in his shroud to sticks and straw, was carried by six companions.

I opened my eyes. A feeling of oppression was heavy on my chest. There in the distance, the ragged black line of the procession moved against the green of the pasture. I pinned them with my eyes, and carried them along to the small stone house waiting in the valley.

"Cristodula!" I whispered, nudging her with my elbow.

She rubbed her eyes and sat up slowly. "What is it? What do you want?"

I pointed to the procession.

"What are they doing?" she asked, not yet understanding the scene.

The mourners reached the small house and brought the corpse inside.

"They're carrying a dead person," I said softly as if they could hear. We sat mesmerized, staring at the house, trying to see through the stone wall.

"What do you think they're doing in there?" Cristodula whispered.

"I don't know. Do you want to go look?"

"No!" she answered quickly. "Maybe they'll catch us and put us in there with it."

"If we're really quiet, they won't see us," I said, almost afraid to convince her. "And the tall grass will hide us if they come out."

She thought for a long moment calculating our odds. "We could go down by the cows and sit in the grass if they come out. We could just pretend we're tending the herd."

We woke Yanni and explained the drama taking place in the valley below. But as we prepared to leave, the mourners filed out again and worked their way over the ridge from where they had come. From their dress we knew they were Turks. The corpse was not with them.

When they were out of sight we ran down the hill toward the house and crept up to a small window on the east side. Cristodula, the tallest of the three of us, stood on tiptoes to peer into the window, but she could not reach above the sill.

"I can't see," she whispered.

"Let me try," I said.

I climbed the stones that jutted out as Cristodula pushed my behind up toward the window. Yanni stood anxiously keeping guard so we wouldn't be surprised.

"Remember what the old woman said," Cristodula whispered.

"What?" I said.

"She said, 'Don't let the Turkish ghosts steal your spirit.' Do you think she meant this?"

I finally cleared the sill with my chin and used it to prop myself up until I could get my elbows over the edge. Then I peered in, adjusting my eyes to the light streaming through the small window where I stood.

The corpse lay on a table wrapped in white cloth. Its shroud glowed in the dim light, as if the light were radiating from within the serene being that lay there, so cold and silent. I was so intent on the corpse, I didn't notice the man sitting on a stool beside it. He sat as still as his lifeless companion. At first I thought he had also died and had frozen in his sentry's seat, but every so often his head jerked up anxiously to stare at the corpse.

I lowered myself down again and whispered what I saw. Cristodula and Yanni also looked. Then we raced down the hill. We went into the forest and collected twigs for kindling and tied them to our backs, then we rounded up the cows and headed for home. The glowing corpse floated before me.

"Come in children," the old woman whose cows we had taken to pasture said. "I have some little gifts for you."

When we entered her home, a pot of stew was bubbling on the tripod in the fireplace. Its fragrance filled the air. The old woman wiped her hands on her apron as she shuffled over to a little basket that hung on the wall. She took out some thin trinkets: bracelets and rings.

"Take these for your trouble with my cows," she said, handing each of us a gift.

"We saw a dead man," I blurted out. "And a man was sitting with him in a little stone house."

The old woman opened her eyes wide.

"Oh! Then you've seen something no one else I know in the village has ever seen. And I see you are all still in one piece. They say the man guarding the dead must sit there the entire night to see if the dead one is really dead. If the dead man awakens, the man guarding him must bring him home again. If the dead man is truly dead and the man guarding him survives the night, they will know he is very brave. That is the Turkish way in these mountains I've been told. But," she added, "they say they are not always fortunate enough to survive the night."

When we returned home, Father was playing his viol by the fire.

Grandfather was playing his flute. A pot of stew hung from a chain in our fireplace also, where Mother stirred it every so often.

As always, it was comforting to be home. My legs were tired from the long journey and my sleepy eyes still saw the glowing corpse lying there on the table. I could see it in the steam rising from my bowl of stew. And that night, as I lay in my bed in the dark, it floated on the wall.

9.

BATTLES AND BELLS

GIRLS IN MY country never married at fifteen. Not Greek girls at least. The Greeks waited until they were older. There were two young people in my village who married early, but not because their parents wished it. In fact, their parents tried for years to stop them, but they were determined.

Merlina and Dmitri were their names. I used to see them in different parts of the village, leaning against a barn wall or sitting on a rock, holding hands and staring down at their feet. They rarely talked, at least not when I caught sight of them.

I first spotted their flirtation in the Cathedral of Iondone that last summer. As the congregation stood in worship, my child's eyes were wandering over the cathedral. It always fascinated me. I loved the vaulted ceiling, the wooden balconies, the crossed trusses, the rafters, and the long line of the stone walls. As my eyes roamed from rafters to worshipers, they fixed like a magnet on a finger jutting out to where another strained to find its mate. Merlina, all cream and vermilion, lifted her voice in song to camouflage her flirtation. Her amber eyes glinted from the flames of the candles and her thick black curls cascaded down her back to a waist still full with the roundness of youth. Dmitri stood beside her, tall and lean and handsome as a god.

Behind them I could see by the disapproving eyes of Merlina's mother, their flirtation had been discovered. She pressed her plump body between the pair and scowled at Dmitri. Merlina stiffened and retrieved her hand. Dmitri fidgeted with his sash. At the end of the service, with great exaggeration, Merlina's mother grabbed her daughter's hand and pulled her home.

It was after church one day at the end of that summer that I saw them again. We kids were playing our favorite game out in the field. It was like baseball, but we didn't have a ball, and we didn't have a bat. For a bat we used a straight branch of a tree that we made smooth, and for a ball we used a twig. We'd dig a little hole in the ground about three inches by five inches and about five inches deep. Then we placed the twig over the hole and slipped the stick we used for a bat under it. With a quick jerk, we'd flip the twig up in the air and give it a whack. It would go flying and the other team would try to catch it before it hit the ground. If they did, it was an out. If they didn't, they'd pick it up and run after the batter as he or she ran from home to first, second, and third bases, and then home again. Just like baseball. We used stones for bases, but it was really the same. I don't know how we learned to play it. I don't know whether we learned it from others, or others learned it from us. The only contact we had with the outside world was when villagers went to the towns to buy supplies or sell their goods. The world seemed much bigger then. But our world, as vast as it sometimes appeared to our eyes, was very, very small.

One of the boys had just been to bat. He had flipped the stick up and had given it a whack. It somersaulted through the air as twenty pairs of eyes, both boys and girls, of various ages, watched it tumble along.

"Come back here!" a woman's voice shot through the playing field. "Come back here, or you'll never go out again."

Merlina's mother ran as fast as her plump body would carry her, shouting and puffing as she ran. Before her, Merlina and Dmitri were fleeing down the hillside.

My friend, Marigoula, reached for the flying stick and grabbed it before it touched the ground, but the rest of us froze in our places to watch the scene unfolding before us.

"They went that way!" someone shouted.

"Come back!" Merlina's mother shouted again and again.

Her breath came heavily as her heels crashed against the ground. The young lovers ran past our game, looking neither left nor right. Merlina stumbled, but Dmitri caught her before she fell, and grabbing her by the hand, pulled her along.

"Catch them," Merlina's mother cried.

We watched grown-up after grown-up get caught up in the chase, until it seemed the whole village was racing down the hillside after the fleeing pair. In a spontaneous explosion of racing feet and flailing arms, we children joined in the chase, laughing and skipping and running along. We ran through the meadows and pear orchards. We ran through wheat fields and past the rows of corn. We ran down into the valley and all the way to Iondone, but we couldn't catch them. They had disappeared as if into the air itself. One moment they were there, running and stumbling before us, and in the next they were gone.

I stopped running and looked around bewildered. A smile was still engraved on my face and my heart was pounding. Then, out of the corner of my eye, I saw a flutter of white; just a small piece of her dress under a bush by the side of the road. It rippled in the breeze for only an instant before a hand gathered it up and pulled it out of sight. I opened my mouth to shout that I had found them when Dmitri's face peered out at me with a look so pleading, that my mouth froze still wide open.

By evening the chase was abandoned. People went back to their homes and night fell without their return. But Merlina's mother continued walking through the village and down into the field to look for her daughter, calling out her name again and again. The next day was the same, and even the day after that. Tongues wagged.

"Why are they still looking for them?" I asked my mother a few days later.

"Because they have run off without her parents' consent," Mother said. She leaned forward to grasp another handful of clothing she was washing under the porch and rubbed the cloth against itself.

"Why did they run away? Were her parents mean to her?"

"I don't think so. They want to get married and her parents won't allow it."

"But if she wants to marry?" I said. I wondered if I had done the right thing by keeping their secret.

"They are too young to marry," Mother said. "Her parents want them to wait until Merlina is at least twenty-one. That's our way."

On the fourth day, early in the morning, I heard a commotion farther down the road. The agitated sound of a woman screaming and crying cut through the sound of rain pattering softly on the roof, and a man's voice, husky with emotion, spat out angry, incoherent abuses.

Cristodula and I ran down the road to find the lovers standing silently in the rain before her parents. Their heads were bowed as they watched the drops of rain shatter the gray sky in puddles gathering at their feet. Dmitri had begged Merlina's parents for over a year to let him marry their daughter, but they would not consent. Now it was no longer a question of obedience, but one of honor.

"Son of a mule!" Merlina's father shouted. "I will tear out your heart with my own hands if you don't marry my daughter now."

"And you! Stupid girl!" her mother added. "If you don't consent you will never leave the house again."

Merlina's shoulders shuddered with a sob, but her eyes, hidden from her parents by her bowed head, found her mate's, as a sweet, sly smile crept across their lips.

🕊 🕊 🕊

The day of Merlina's wedding was the first time since the war ended that things began to change. Not all at once, but we heard Pontians were being killed again along the coast, and strange men began to lurk about the edges of our villages.

The first time I noticed them was on the morning of Merlina's wedding. That morning Mother and I walked down to our garden to begin collecting the produce for drying and curing for the long winter ahead. The pumpkins had to be picked and split, then laid in the sun to soften their skins so the flesh could be peeled more easily. They were then sliced in long, continuous strands and hung up to dry. The *lahana* had to be dipped in a huge pot of boiling water and also hung to dry in the sun. Cabbage was pickled in large vats and all the grains, corn, wheat, and barley were dried or thrashed. They were then placed in the supply room of our home in huge bins that took up the entire wall.

When the weather turned colder, an animal was slaughtered. I never watched the process, but a portion of the meat was always given to neighbors. The rest was boiled for many hours in huge pots and then stored in vats for winter to be used as flavoring for soups and stews. On top, the thick coating of fat that formed protected the meat and broth.

Mother and I moved slowly through the garden, bending now and then to pull a clump of grass or pluck a tomato that had ripened on its vine. The day was sunny and warm, the sky clear with just a hint of autumn in the dry, still air. An occasional beetle crashed from leaf to leaf, and a fly buzzed about my head. I stood watching Mother's bent figure, her hair escaping from her scarf.

"For as far back as I can remember, Dmitri has loved Merlina," Mother said. "Even when he was a small boy he would bring her wildflowers and stand by her side without a care in the world who knew of his love for her."

Mother snapped a few more beans from the vine, then straightened and placed her hand on her arched back and looked up at the sky.

"It's a good day for a wedding," she said. "I remember when your uncle Nikolas married. The day was overcast and dark. He and his wife had many disappointments."

"Mama. Why do we call Uncle Nikolas uncle?" I said.

The day before a boy told me Nikolas must be my cousin if he is the son of my grandfather's brother. I told Mother of my new found information. Mother smiled.

"Your uncle Nikolas is not your cousin. He's not really the son of your grandfather's brother. He's your grandfather's son. Your father's true brother."

"Then why does he live with Grygorio and why does Grygorio call him his son?" I asked, more puzzled by this new twist.

"Grygorio and his wife couldn't have children," Mother said. "They tried many times but each time the child died before it was born or died soon after. So when Nikolas was born, your grandfather's third son, he gave Nikolas to his brother to raise as his own."

Mother bent again to snap a few more beans from the vine. "How strange life is sometimes," she said as she worked. "When Nikolas married they also wanted many children but they had no luck either." Mother dropped the beans into my basket.

"Where are their children?" I said. I remembered a number of times when they had a child, but then it was gone.

"His poor wife had many children, just like Grygorio's wife, but they also died right before they came into the world, or they died a short time later. No one knows why."

I also bent to pull a small clump of grass. A worm squirmed frantically to dig itself back into the earth. An ant tugged on the carcass of a bug three times its size, and little green worms worked the tender edges of a cabbage leaf, depositing their little green droppings along the way. Everywhere I looked, the earth teamed with life.

Mother told me of a ritual performed on my aunt to save her further pain and despair. It was a ritual that would prevent her from conceiving any more children because they never survived. The women took a round thing with a hole in the middle and placed a scissors across it. Then they melted beeswax and poured it through the opening into a pan of water below. When it formed into a "frog," it was taken into the woods and buried. From then on my aunt would never conceive again.

Out of the corner of my eye I saw something at the edge of the garden. A crouched figure dressed in a way I had not seen before. He waited silently, motionless but for his eyes, which followed our every move as if bound to us by a cord that pulled them up and down, left and right. Even as we moved away and headed for home I could feel his eyes follow us, eerily, like those of a creature of prey, long after we were out of sight.

Merlina's wedding was held in the Cathedral of Iondone. I had never seen anything more beautiful. Candles were everywhere, competing softly with the stream of sunlight shooting down from an upper portal. The priest chanted the ceremonial vows as the congregation, teary-eyed, stood in worship. But Yiorgos, the groom's father, glanced about nervously. Both pride and fear seemed to alternate in quick succession on his face. Dmitri's mother stood beside him with her head bowed, drawing the sign of the cross across her breast again and again like someone performing a ritual to ward off evil.

Merlina wore a little black hat with a small lace veil, as was the custom for brides. Dmitri wore high black boots with his pant legs tucked inside, and a vest neatly hugged his slim chest. Around his waist he wore a wide band of cloth and a small round hat sat on his head. Merlina's mother wiped her eyes continuously and dabbed at her plump cheeks. But Merlina's smile never left her lips as she stared into the eyes of her betrothed.

After the wedding the traditional tray of wheat, sprinkled with honey and nuts, was brought outdoors to offer to the crowd. The children jumped around holding up their skirts or cupping their hands to receive their share. Even the grown-ups held out their hands for the bridal offering, while the proud groom pranced about, and the bride smiled demurely surrounded by her friends.

"Varidimei!" Yiorgos shouted to Grandfather.

Grandfather looked around as Dmitri's father rushed toward him.

"Call the others to meet tonight. There's trouble," Yiorgos said.

"What is it?" Grandfather said.

"The Turks are attacking Greek villagers again along the Black Sea coast."

"But why? The war is over." Grandfather said.

"I will tell you all I know tonight when the others have assembled."

That night after dinner, a group of men came to our house and sat around our long table.

"Come, Yiorgos!" Grandfather started impatiently. "Tell us what you have heard."

"Only that the Turks along the coastal towns have been attacking Greek villagers there. They have killed many."

"But why? What is the fight about?" one of the men asked.

"There is no fight with the Pontians. But there is anger over the signing of the treaty. The Sultan is complying with the demands of the Allies and the people resent it. Turkey is to be stripped of all its European territory. Only a small portion surrounding Constantinople will be left; and in Asia, only Anatolia. Greek forces have landed at Smyrna."

"But what has that got to do with the Pontians along the coast?" one man demanded. "This is our country too. We were born here. Our parents and grandparents were born here, and their grandparents before them."

"I don't know if they are angry at all Christians, or at the Greeks because Greece finally entered the war with the Allies. Maybe they blame all Greeks, even the Pontians," Yiorgos said.

"No!" the man shouted. "Don't make excuses for them. This is not the first time they have slaughtered our people. This is only one of many times. The last time the Greeks were not in the war and still they slaughtered our people. And when they weren't slaughtering them outright, they were driving them from their homes, or enslaving them in those filthy labor camps, leaving them to starve to death without proper food or shelter."

"Greece has protested the treatment of the Pontic Greeks and demanded they be protected," Yiorgos said. "The sultan has sent a general called Mustafa Kemal. He fought in the war. He is to come and dismantle the army here and protect the Pontians. And the British have sent a commission to oversee the disarmament of the Turkish troops."

"Kemal has a fierce reputation," Grandfather said. "Will he really protect us?"

"I don't know. He fought bravely in the war and won most of his battles. But they want to be rid of him in Constantinople. He is a nuisance to them there. He is proud and does not want the sultan to comply with Allied demands."

"He will kill us like the rest," the angry one shouted.

"How can you know these things?" another man asked Yiorgos.

"My cousin is a guard for the sultan in Constantinople. And another works at the telegraph office in Ankara. When I send my goods to Ankara they send back news."

"Is there danger to us here?" Grandfather asked. "What about the *Andartes*? Will they protect us?"

"I don't know if they can. They spoke only of the Black Sea villages. Fatsa. Ordu. Samsun. But we are not so far away."

Because of slaughters of Pontic Greeks and other Christian minorities by the Turks in 1915, the first Pontic *Andartes* began to appear. They were made up initially of a few thousand Greek deserters from the Turkish army, and were joined by men, women, and children fleeing the persecution. Their mission was to defend the lives and honor of the Pontic Greek people, some of whom had been able to escape to the mountains.

Grandmother rocked back and forth without looking up, but her fingers worked the wool around the knitting needles with a fierce determination. She had family who still lived on the coast. Mother stoked the fire and the shadows of the men danced on the walls and ceiling, accenting their ominous expressions with dark crevices.

"I should be going," Yiorgos said, rising from his stool. "Perhaps there is nothing for us to worry about here. We have always had good relations with the Turks. I just thought you should know what's going on so we can be prepared if there is trouble."

With a clatter of stools the other men rose also and followed him out the door.

"What do you think?" Father asked Grandfather when the others were gone.

Grandfather shook his head slowly and stared at the table.

"I don't know," he said. "I don't know."

10

THE YEAR OF THE SNAKE

MAYBE MOTHER KNEW she would never see me again when she gave me away, but I didn't know. I never would have let her go. I would have crawled on my hands and knees for a thousand miles, and faced death a thousand times to stay by her side if I knew. When she said, "Maybe you should stay with that woman for a while," I said yes, but only because I never said no to my mother. I loved her too much to say no. Even the Turks loved her. My mother's name was Barthena, but the Turks always called her *Küzel*, which means beautiful, and that she was. Just being near her was like breathing. I loved her even more than that. I loved her more than my own breath.

I know she gave me away to save my life. I did almost die once, but that was when I was nine, before the exile. It was in early autumn. I was sitting in the field playing quietly by myself when I felt a sharp stinging on my leg. I screamed and felt another sting. I sat screaming, stunned by the sharp pain. I heard voices shouting. My mother and father came running. Then Father scooped me up and carried me home.

Grandfather tended me night and day. He was the doctor in our village. People came to him because no real doctor was near. Once a woman from our village came with a big cyst on her breast. Grandfather cut it open for her and cleaned it and soon she was well. Grandfather was even the dentist.

I was unconscious for three days. But on the third day, I heard Mother speaking softly as if she spoke in a dream, and I could feel her smooth hand stroking my forehead.

"My little Themía," she said in her gentle voice. "My sweet, sweet Themía, open your eyes."

I opened my eyes to find her kneeling beside me. A worried look troubled her lovely face. Grandfather stood beside her looking down at me, ready to dissolve in tears. He closed his eyes when I opened mine, perhaps to say a silent prayer, or maybe to hide the emotion he felt for his favorite child.

Some say a snake bit me, but nobody knew for sure. There were two small marks left on my leg that formed into scars; the only mementos I have from a time when life promised to spread out before me in endless cycles of happy seasons with the people I loved by my side.

Mother prepared a bed for me near the fire so I could be near her while she worked. I watched as she prepared a special bread that day, the kind she would bake in the fireplace instead of the oven.

"There's a story about this kind of bread," Mother said.

My heart was filled with a love for her I have never been able to fully express.

"There once were two sisters," she began. "One was very rich and the other very poor. One day, the poor sister decided to make bread, but she was so poor that she took some ashes to mix with the flour to make it go further. She kneaded it together, then swept a place on the stone floor of the fireplace and placed the dough there. On top of the dough she put leaves of the rubber plant to cover it and let it bake. When she was finished, a knock came at the door. She opened it to find a poor old man who looked tired and worn.

"'Please,' he said. 'Could you spare something to eat? I am very hungry and have no food.'

"'Oh!' said the poor sister. 'I just baked bread, but I mixed the flour with ashes because I didn't have enough flour to bake a loaf without it. You are welcome to share it with me if you wish.'

"And so she gave the old man some of her bread and he ate and went on his way. He then went again to ask for food. This time he went to the house of the rich sister who had also just finished baking bread. She didn't have to use ashes with her flour because she was very, very rich. But when the knock came at the door she hid the bread she had just baked.

"'Please,' the old man said when she opened the door. 'Could you spare something to eat? I am very hungry and have nothing.'

"'Oh!' said the rich sister. 'I'm so sorry, but I have nothing to offer you. I'm hungry also and I'm afraid I can't help.'

"So the old man went on his way without anything. But little by little the rich sister became poorer and poorer and became ill, and the poor sister became richer and richer."

After the first days of my convalescing, my recovery was swift. I sat outside on warm autumn days staring at the blueness of the clear skies. I had watched the pear trees lining the slope of the mountain in springtime adorn themselves with soft white blossoms above their pale green leaves. I had watched the frail green of spring deepen to the indolent green of summer. And now I watched again, as the orchards and forests surrendered their greens for the reds and golds of autumn, as if dressed for one last spree before the frosty winds of winter blew their finery to the ground and covered it with snow.

Mother sat beside me on a rocker, gently rocking back and forth as she cleaned beans for the evening meal, as two Turkish women from a nearby village strolled up to our house. They had come to have Grandfather repair some old metal pots, and he had invited them to have coffee at our home while they waited, as was our custom.

"How are you *Küzel*?" one woman called out as they mounted our porch.

"I am well," Mother answered with her usual warm smile. "And how are you on this beautiful day?"

"We are well, thanks to God," they both answered in unison.

"Oh, *Küzel*, I see you will have twins this time," the older woman said. She clasped her hands together and shook them approvingly. Mother laughed and picked up her apron. Nastasía, only three years old, peeked out laughing from underneath, her head resting on Mother's lap.

"Oh!" The women laughed, enjoying the joke. "But," the older woman continued with a smile. "You will have twins, *Küzel*."

Cristodula brought them coffee while I sat on the steps of the porch, leaning my head against the logs that made up our home. I closed my eyes and listened to the sound of the women talking. Their long black dresses and white scarves glowed red behind my closed eyes. They talked of the children and the crops and premonitions of hard times in the coming year. The autumn sun cloaked my flesh in a thin, warm, protective shell, as the sound of my mother's voice, soft and melodious, cloaked my soul.

A winter chill was just beginning to fill the autumn air, and a sailor's moon brightened the fields, marking the edge of the mountains against the sky. We children sat by the fire reading our books for school while Mother baked bread in the fireplace on the large curved griddle we called a *sedge*. She had just lined the base of the *sedge* with wet ashes to keep it from getting too hot, and she was laying the flat loaves on its convex face when the village exploded in pops and cracks and shouting voices.

Father put down the new viol he had made for himself and ran for his rifle. Uncle Constantine bolted through the door of his room, stared at Father for only a moment, then grabbed his rifle also. In an instant, they were out the door.

For what seemed an eternity, the sound of shots rang out. It was strange to hear shots in our village. Even the crickets were silent at that time of year. I ran to the window to decipher in the moonlight what was taking place. A white, ghostlike form flew along the hillside. Figures wove in and out of the moonlight, and crying and shouts ricocheted with the bullets against the ridges of the mountains.

"Come away from the window," Mother called. "You could be injured there."

I squinted my eyes to see through the darkness one last time before reluctantly coming back to the fire. Cristodula sat quietly in its glow, her foot propped on a stool. Only the violent shaking of her leg gave evidence to the fright she felt sitting there.

"Are you all right?" Mother asked her.

But Cristodula only stared into the fire not hearing, as if trying to suspend reality; as if hearing and speaking would make the events more real. Her body shook more and more violently with each shot. It reminded me of how I had felt when I was left in that town with my aunt and her family during the famine when the war was raging and shots rang out every day and every night.

Mother placed the loaves on the *sedge,* sat beside Cristodula, and enclosed her in her arms. But Cristodula still stared into the fire and her legs still shook violently. Finally the shots and shouting stopped. The village quieted down. Then Father bolted through the door and shouted for Grandfather to follow him, and they both ran out again.

"What was it?" Mother asked when Father came home again. "What happened?"

"A robbery," Father said.

"A robbery? Here?"

He leaned his rifle against the wall, then came to the fire and sat down heavily on his stool.

"They shot Yiorgos," he said.

"But who? Why? What did they want? Is he all right?"

"They were robbers," Father said. "They came to steal Merlina's hope chest. Perhaps they heard of the wedding. How I cannot say. They stole into the house while the family gathered around the fire. They were about to leave with the chest when Yiorgos saw them. He shouted for them to stop. One of the robbers fired his rifle. Yiorgos was hit in the leg and his wife began to scream for help.

"His brother ran for his rifle as the robbers ran out the door still carrying the chest. Stavros tried to grab hold of the chest as they ran by, but was kicked to the ground. Clothing flew in all directions, bouncing out of the chest as the thieves ran down the hill. By then the whole village came with their guns, shooting. I don't think we hit them. The chest was too heavy to carry while running, so they finally dropped it further down the slope and disappeared in the darkness, leaving a trail of clothing strewn along the field."

We sat glued to our seats, mouths agape, and eyes child-wide. The palms of my hands stung from squeezing my fists so tight that my fingernails left little half-moon grooves in a row on my palms.

"Who were these people?" Grandmother asked.

"I don't know. They weren't from our villages, and they weren't Turks. It was hard to see in the dark, but I think they were Kurds."

More and more of those strange people had begun to inhabit our villages. Everywhere one looked, there was one or two sitting in a field or at the edge of the forest, as if they knew something about our fate that we ourselves did not know. They were always watching. Always waiting.

It was a few weeks after that, that we got the greatest shock of all.

11

THE TAKING OF FATHER

I STILL REMEMBER the sound of that woman's voice as she ran toward our home shouting.

"Barthena! Barthena!" Mother was in our kitchen preparing the midday meal. The frantic banging at our door made her jump.

"Barthena!" the woman said when Mother opened the door. "They have taken Lumbo."

Mother's eyes opened wide, and the undisguised fear in her voice jerked us to attention.

"Who has taken Lumbo?" Mother cried.

"The soldiers. They've taken all the men they could find and marched them away."

Without waiting for further explanation Mother pushed past her and ran out the door, still holding the knife she was using to cut vegetables. She ran down the road toward the center of the village and we chased after her.

"Lumbo!" she called out, looking frantically in every direction. "Lumbo!" But the men and soldiers were gone.

Women of the village were rushing about, crying and shouting.

"Where have they taken them?" Mother cried.

"To a work camp," an old woman said between sobs. She rubbed her eyes with her apron and shouted to the sky. "They've taken my son. They'll kill him there. They'll kill him."

"My husband was in one of their work camps," another woman said. "It's true. My husband was so weak when he escaped. There was no food or decent housing."

When her husband was taken she had stood on the road every day waiting for him to come home. "I'll make a new dress for the first person who comes to tell me my husband is home," she had said. And one day there he was coming up the road. I ran to tell her, hoping to be the first to bring her the good news.

"But the war is over," Mother said. "The war is over."

Every day we expected to see him at the door, but each day passed as the day before. More and more, Grandfather went to his shop in the Turkish town at the foot of the mountain. The house was quiet without them. Sometimes I'd go and stand outside their shop and listen for the familiar *clink, clink, clink* of metal striking metal and the *whush, ahhh, whush* of the giant bellows. And when there was only silence, which there always was, I'd go in slowly with my eyes closed, then open them quickly, hoping to catch father standing there, holding a horseshoe or an old iron tool, his face glowing red from the hot embers of the fire, while Grandfather blew noisy gusts of air from the huge bellows inserted into the fire.

A few months after Father was taken I went to the mill with my friend, Marigoula, to grind the wheat. There was no time to stop, even for grief, or winter would come and find us unprepared.

The mill was crowded. We sat in the sun, bundled up to keep warm and waited our turn. I leaned my head against the cool stone wall of the mill, and listened to the water rush and gurgle as the giant wooden wheel went 'round and 'round, its long wooden vessels scooping the water up and pouring the water out. Inside the mill a huge round stone lying flat on top of another like it, also turned 'round and 'round, grinding against the one below.

"Wouldn't it be fun to sit in one of those bowls and ride it 'round and 'round?" Marigoula said and smiled. Her eyes crinkled and the little gap that showed between her lips where a tooth once sat gave her sweet, impish face an added touch of mischief.

"Yes. Wouldn't it be nice," I said.

"Has your father come home yet?" a woman called to me from her place at the grinding stone.

I shook my head. No. He had not returned and with each passing day our hope faded a little more. The woman clucked her tongue and shook her head, then turned again to attend to her grinding. She lifted the hem of her dress and tucked it in at her waist to keep it out of the way. Her matronly flesh spilled over the edges of her apron ties as she poured her wheat into a hole near the center of the large top stone, sending the ground flour out a spout on the outer edge into her waiting sack. She hummed as she worked, flowing about the mill efficiently from long years of practice. Other women also bustled about as their children tugged at their aprons. Grandfather and his sons had built that mill for all who wished to use it, and I was proud of its sturdy walls and giant, magical wheel.

By the time I arrived home, the air had turned frosty again. I went to the fireplace to warm my chilled hands and feet. Mother took my sack of ground flour and poured it into the large wooden vat she used to make dough. Inside she formed a little fortress of flour around an empty well cleared at its edge. The leftover dough from the previous batch, which would be used to help the new dough rise, was already soaking in warm water to make it soft.

Little by little she watered the well with the dough water and pushed down a portion of the wall of flour, working it into the wet with her hands. Again she watered the well, and again pushed down part of the wall, over and over until the wall was gone, the well was dry, and a large smooth ball, enough for a dozen loaves, was formed. She added the leftover dough and worked that in also. Then she covered it with a cloth and let it rise in a warm place.

It was Mother's turn to fire the oven and her day to supply the wood. We made a pile of wood ready for her. Mother built a fire inside the oven below its arched ceiling to get it hot while the dough was rising. When the oven was hot, she moved the fire out to sit by its doorway and placed the fresh, plump loaves she had formed, inside to bake, slipping them off the large wooden paddle she used to slide them in. When her baking was done, the other women came to use the remaining heat from the oven for their bread, adding more fire as need be.

As I lay in my bed that night, breathing in the sweet scent of the warm bread that filled the house, I heard Mother crying in the next room. I got up to see what was the matter. Cristodula was right behind me.

Father stood at the door half-frozen. His feet were bleeding from cuts that were raw. Mother quickly closed the door behind him and stood crying at the sight of him. His clothes were torn and his hair was matted and foul.

"Don't touch me," he said to her as she drew near. "I'm covered with lice."

"How did you come? Did they let you go? What can I get you?"

She rushed to pull a stool to the fire.

"Come sit by the fire and warm yourself. I'll bring you something to eat."

He limped over to the fire and let himself down slowly, as if each move was a painful burden.

"No. They didn't let me go," Father said. "I escaped. You must tell no one I'm home. If the neighbors find out they might tell the soldiers. Too many of their men are still imprisoned in those filthy labor camps."

Mother poured hot soup into a bowl and brought it to him.

"The camps are cold and full of vermin. We're worked day and night without enough food to eat or a decent place to sleep or wash," Father said. "In some camps the Greeks are just left to die with nothing at all. Even when the war was still being fought, the Turks left the Greeks behind to be killed without arms to defend themselves or food to eat. I think that's what they want, for all of us to die."

Mother covered her face with her apron and her shoulders shook with sobs. "How can this be happening?" she said.

We stood mesmerized at the door of the bedroom. I could feel the tears welling up in my own eyes. He looked as I had never seen him before, like a stranger in his bloody rags and matted hair.

"Papa?" I said.

Mother dried her eyes quickly.

"Bring the washtub, Themía. And Cristodula, bring water so your father can bathe. Then run along to bed. You can see your father in the morning."

We ran about dutifully bringing the water and the tub.

"Are you all right, Papa?" I asked when we were finished, my eyes glued to his bloody feet.

"I'm all right now," he said, "now that I'm here where I belong. Go to sleep now. You have school in the morning. Go to sleep and dream sweet dreams."

It was a long night. I fought sleep as best I could, afraid he might not be there in the morning.

Our school was built of logs like our homes, but without the animal stalls underneath. It had just one large room. A big potbellied stove sat in one corner. Each student brought a small bundle of wood each day to help heat it.

For the little ones, like Yanni, who were in kindergarten at that time, Grandfather burned the alphabet into a wooden plank with a hot iron rod. The plank had a handle to carry it to school. With this we learned our alphabet. For the older kids he bought a large sheet of paper with words and pictures on it. I'm not sure where he got it, probably from one of the towns he traveled to for supplies, since there were no stores of any kind in our villages. He folded the sheet many times in a special way. Then he stitched it together in the center and cut open the folds on the outside edges to form a book.

Sometimes, when our teacher wasn't in the room, we'd take one of the little books with pictures in it and lay one of its pictures on the hot potbellied stove. Then we'd lay a clean piece of paper on top of it and rub it with a walnut back and forth until the oil from the walnut transferred the image of the picture onto the clean sheet.

There was one girl who especially loved school. Despina was her name. She was one of the older girls. She always ran to the center of the room and took her seat directly in front of the teacher. The older kids sat up front. The younger grades sat behind so that in each row the kids were younger and younger. The littlest ones sat in the back. Despina didn't get distracted like the rest of us. She listened to the teacher almost reverently. She loved to read. She read everything she could find. "You will go far," people would tell her, sure that one day her love of knowledge would bring her to great things. Her sweet face would sparkle with pride and enthusiasm.

But most of us kids, myself included, only half listened to the teacher as the sun peeked through the window. When we heard a child's laughter out on the road, we longed to join him.

"What is it?" the teacher would ask to a raised hand near the back row.

"Can I go out to the toilet?" the thin voice would ask timidly.

When our teacher consented, the child would dash out the door, but the journey back was never as swift as it was when leaving. He'd drag himself back again as slowly as a turtle wading through molasses. But usually I, or others who used this excuse, would race out as if sprung from prison, not to be seen again for the rest of the day.

At other times, we'd run out and stand in the sun and look down at the ground at our feet. If we could stand on our shadow without it springing out, we knew it was noontime. We'd race back in again beaming with the good news.

"Excuse me," we'd say, struggling to keep our enthusiasm to a minimum. "It's noontime. Time to go home to eat."

A patient smile would creep across our teacher's young face. She'd slowly reach into her pocket, and even more slowly, pull out her little gold watch. She'd flip open the cover to look at the time underneath, then slowly look around the room.

"All right, one hour for lunch."

The exodus was swift and reckless.

If my memory serves me, we attended school all year long, except in summer. Grandfather also tried to teach us our ABCs and the Lord's Prayer at home. We'd sit and listen patiently until it was time to stand and repeat after him. Then our shyness would double us over with childish laughter. He'd try again and again with the same result. Finally, he would also pull out his beautiful gold watch, pop open the cover to expose the little hands and numbers on its face, then he'd shake his frosty head forlornly and leave us to our giggles. I still remember that watch with its three tiny knobs and a gold chain that started in one pocket of his vest, then traveled across his belly to another pocket on the other side.

How often since then I've sat reciting the Lord's Prayer silently to myself.

౿   ౿   ౿

Except for the strange people who were hanging around our villages more and more, we heard no more news of trouble that autumn. Mother was standing under the porch making butter when my father and uncle came out of the forest carrying their great prize between them.

"Mama!" I shouted. "They're coming. I think they caught something."

She stopped shaking the butter and sheltered her eyes from the sun with her hand.

"Yes," she said, turning again to her task. "It looks like they caught something. They will be tired. Go bring cool water for them to drink."

I took the water jug and ran to the village water spout. A group of children ran with me. When we returned, lugging the heavy jug of water, Mother was in the kitchen warming stew for them to eat, and Father and Uncle were heading toward the barn. Between them, a huge, scary-looking animal, with coarse, scraggly hair, hung by its ankles from a thin log. Two giant teeth, one on each side of its jaws, came out of its mouth and curled up toward the sky. I handed my father the first dipper of water absentmindedly as I stared at the beast. Father drank a long deep gulp.

"What is it?" I asked, mesmerized.

"It's a wild boar," Father said. He laughed, probably at the looks on our faces.

"What's a wild boar?" one little boy asked.

"It's a kind of pig, only much more dangerous."

"Will it attack you?" my friend Marigoula wanted to know.

"Yes," Father said.

I gave my uncle a dipper of water to drink also. Then they hoisted the boar up, balancing it on two posts to make it ready to be divided for our family and our closest neighbors as was our custom. Larger animals were divided more widely among the villagers. It was a gesture of friend-ship that had probably been practiced for thousands of years, since meat was precious. We were lucky to have a few scraps in our food. It was mostly used for flavoring.

"Come wash my hands, Themía," Father said. He knelt down and held his cupped hands out to me low to the ground. I ladled the cool water and poured it over his hands as he rubbed them together. Uncle Constantine knelt next and did the same. Then we walked home together with Father's strong hand resting on the nape of my neck.

The other children stared at the boar for a few moments longer, then ran to their homes with their eyes still wide.

By the light of the fire, Father told of his adventure; of seeing a wild animal he thought was very small until it sprang up, becoming so large that it frightened him. Then he picked up his viol and perched it on his knee. With his sturdy blacksmith's hand he skimmed the delicate bow across the viol's frail, taut strings. On his face there was a combination of exhaustion and contentment. Grandfather joined him on the flute he kept cradled in a small niche of the great stone chimney to keep it warm and ready. Then my father closed his eyes and his mellow voice effortlessly filled the room. It was a Turkish song he sang often.

Eh sini, sini, sini
Galailarum eh sini nanagigum
Senesever Turkidamam
Banaina alduda hedge guremaim
Aski halima savedamaim nanegigum
Senesaver Turkidamam

A few weeks after that night, two other men from our village went out to hunt the wild boar. When they didn't return, men from the village went to look for them. They found them dead, torn to pieces by the boar they were hunting.

12

THE YEAR OF FAMINE

W E   W E R E N ' T   R I C H people, but neither were we poor. We owned three houses: our main home, one in the Turkish town, and a house higher in the mountains we used for summer vacations. And we had two black-smith shops, one in our village and one in the Turkish town below. My family were the only blacksmiths in the area, so they made a good living, even though they did some of the work for barter. It was a way of letting the poorer people still have the services they needed even when they had no money. They'd come to help us with our fields in spring, or give what-ever else they had to offer. That's how the Turks, and even our neighbors, sometimes paid us, by helping in the fields.

There was only once when we were very poor, but most of the people were poor that year. It was the year of the Great Famine. I must have been about six years old at the time. It was 1916 I think. That meant the First World War was still in full force. That was a terrible year for my people.

For the first few years of the war, Turkey was victorious, but by 1916, the tide had turned. In the beginning of the war, a sporadic reign of terror by the Young Turks and faction groups were carried out against the Pontians and other Christian minorities, but after the 1915 massacre of the Armenians, the persecutions became more pronounced. Mass depor-tations took place under the cruelest conditions. Thousands died on long death marches, and as part of a military mobilization, all men between the ages of twenty and fifty were asked to report for duty or be sentenced to death. Most of the Christians were assigned to the infamous *Amele Tabourou,* which were labor battalions used to break stones and open roads for the Turkish army throughout Turkey. Some were sent as far away as Baghdad, Mesopotamia, and the Caucasus Mountains where they were literally worked to death without enough food, clothing, or shelter.

In the summer of 1916, the entire Greek population of Sinop, a town on the Black Sea, had been wiped out, and the same fate was reported of the Greeks from Samsun, another coastal town. On a pretext of searching for Pontic deserters, eighty-eight Pontic Greek villages were put to the torch. A campaign of intimidation, rape, theft, and murder left 100,000 Pontic Greeks slaughtered between 1914–1918. Many others fled the country.

When the Great Famine swept over the land, many of our cows got sick. We brought the sick cows higher into the mountains to keep the healthy ones safe, but some simply fell over dead in the fields. Huge buzzards would appear in an instant—flapping their massive wings like claps of thunder—and tear into the carcasses of fallen beasts.

The fields had not produced. The parched grass, stripped of its luscious green, pointed broken, russet shafts in no particular direction. Where once our garden stood, only churned clumps of soil, accented here and there by a wilted stalk, yawned impotently at the sky.

There was another Nastasía then. Three years old at the time. She had been ill from lack of nourishment as were many children in the village that year. Children became sick and died at an alarming rate, and because of the war, food and medicine was scarce everywhere. One day Grandfather came from his shop and saw Nastasía sitting on the grass outside our home chewing on the hoof of a cow she found on the ground. Grandfather told her to put it down, but her glazed eyes stared at him blankly. So he picked up a small stone and tossed it in her direction to get her attention. It hit her foot. Not very hard. The next day she died.

Because of tragedies such as ours, families in the villages who had greater supplies opened their homes to children who might otherwise not have enough to eat. The children stayed for a week at a time in a host home to help them through this difficult time. I was sent to Iondone to a large house near the cathedral. They were fabric merchants I think, and although their intentions were good and I remember them to be kind, I don't ever remember being as hungry as I was when I was in their home. I would lie on my little mat at night with other children lying beside me and my stomach would churn with hunger. I'd twist and turn unable to sleep, listening to the sound of the others breathing, wondering if they also felt the pain.

One night I rose from my bed as silently as I could while everyone else was sleeping and tiptoed to the room where they kept their supplies, terrified someone would wake and find me. The house was dark except for the light that glowed from the embers of the fire and the moonlight filtering through the windows. I found the door and opened it gently. My heart pounded in my throat. I made my way to the flour bin and dipped my hand in, bringing out a fistfull of flour. There I stood, eating it little by little. I could have choked to death, but such was my hunger and desperation at the time. When the pain in my stomach stopped, I again found my way through the darkened rooms to the little mat and fell asleep. How happy I was when my parents came to take me home.

One day Grandfather came home with the head of a calf. With famine in the land it was quite a luxury. He gave it to my mother to cook for the family and then went off to his shop. She placed the head in a huge pot and covered it with water. Then she placed it in the fireplace to cook. When the head was done, Mother put it on the table, and Cristodula, Mother, and I went off to the woods to forage for greens. Mother would grind the greens with the flour to make it go further when she made the bread. Each of us gathered a bundle of greens, tied them on our backs and headed for home. When we arrived, the calf's head was still sitting on the table, but the best part, which were the cheeks, was gone.

"Why didn't you wait for the family to eat together before you ate from the calf head?" Grandfather shouted at my mother.

"But I didn't take it," she said to my father. "It was already eaten when we came from the woods."

"I know you took it to give to your children," Grandfather said.

My mother bowed her head and began to cry.

"No," she said.

"If she says she didn't take it," Father said, "then she didn't take it. She doesn't lie."

"I will not have people under my roof who steal food while others go hungry. Take your family and leave this house."

"But where will we go?" Father protested. "How do you know someone else didn't take it?"

"Because she has children. I know she gave it to them," Grandfather said. "Who else would do such a thing?"

"Why don't you ask Constantine and his wife?"

Of course they said no, but to this day I believe they did eat a portion of the calf head but were too afraid or embarrassed to admit it.

The next morning my mother and father packed our belongings and we left the house. The villagers watched as we passed. Because my mother was pregnant and had to walk slowly, the trip down the mountain seemed an eternity.

While my parents looked for a place to live, they left me with my aunt who lived with her husband and in-laws in a large town where both Greeks and Turks lived side by side. With the war going on, tensions between Greeks and Turks had become violent in that town. Bullets flew through the streets almost every night. I felt awkward left with people I didn't know, and when a Greek man was shot just behind the house, I also became afraid. Only a few days after my arrival my aunt's father-in-law came to me when no one else was around.

"You have to pay for the food you eat here," he scolded. "What do you think? Your parents just leave you here and we have to pay to feed you?"

I looked at him with astonishment.

"But I don't have any money," I said, not knowing what else to say or do.

"Well let your parents come and get you then. Or tell them they must pay to let you stay here."

I ran from the house in horror, then sat down and cried.

"What is it," a voice said. "Why are you crying?"

I looked up and through the blur of my tears, found my aunt's husband staring down at me.

"Has someone hurt you?"

"Your father said I must pay for my food, but . . . I . . . don't . . . have . . . any . . . money," I cried, choking on every word.

"He has no right to say that to you. You are our guest. We want you to stay with us," he said. He gently patted my tiny, heaving shoulder. "You mustn't worry about such things. I will speak to him. He won't bother you again."

He went into the house then. Soon the sound of his angry voice came through the open window.

"How dare you talk to a six-year-old child like that? She is our guest, not yours. I pay for her food and you will never speak to her like that again. Do you hear me?"

"All right. All right," the old man tried to calm his son.

Soon after, my parents came to take me to their new home. My father had opened a blacksmith shop in a Turkish town where the streets were wide and the buildings low. Each day the Turks brought us food to welcome us among them as was their custom. Each morning, scarcely before the sun had a chance to brighten the sky, the sound of my father's hammer, crashing against iron, could be heard throughout the quarter. The Turks loved him for it, and because he was a musician, they loved him more.

"Lumbo!" they would call to him each night after dinner. "Come play something." And my father, to be kind to those who were kind to us, would pick up his viol and go out to play.

Sometimes at three in the morning he would drag himself home to bed only to rise again in a few hours time.

"No!" he shouted one night when we heard them calling. "I can't go on like this. They want me to play every night. I never get any sleep or have time to spend with my family."

He rose from his chair, and taking his viol, smashed it against the wall and threw it into the fire.

"Now maybe we can have some peace."

We lived in that town about five months, I think. The second Nastasía was born there. It was our custom to name a child after someone who was deceased.

Cristodula was quite a beautiful girl, and although she was still a child, the young Turks began to look at her in the way a man looks at a woman.

"She's too young for them to think of her in that way," Father said to Mother one day. "It's time to go home."

"Will your father take us back?" Mother asked.

"He will take us back. Spring planting is coming soon and he won't be angry any longer anyway. Time enough has passed for him to cool down."

And so we packed our things and headed for home. When Grandfather saw us coming up the road, he cried.

13.

WINTER TALES

THE SNOW PILED high in big drifts that last winter. The pines on the hillside were draped in white like Cinderella in her gown going to the ball. Occasional gusts of wind grabbed at the white ledges of snow and whirled them about like tiny tornadoes, then whipped them into a fine spray to dissipate against a cobalt sky.

The first snowfalls were exciting for us children. We'd race out of our home barefoot to lay down in the snow. We'd flail our arms to make angels, or just lie there with outstretched arms to leave our ghostly image imbedded in the fluffy white cradle made by our warm bodies. Then we'd race again indoors laughing to sit by the fire, our toes tingling from the cold. But as cold as the winds blew outside, inside was cozy and warm.

Grandmother rarely took part in the daily routines of survival. She seemed above such menial tasks. Perhaps that's why it's hard for me to remember too much about her. It was a comfort to me to watch Mother kneading dough, baking bread, or standing before the fire stirring a pot of winter stew, her face glowing red from the flames. Her movements never seemed rushed or awkward. She flowed about the room or in the field with ease and efficiency.

When Grandfather came home from his work in the evening, Mother washed his feet. Even then she moved with grace and dignity, touching her lips to his feet lightly when she had finished their cleaning. She never spoke to Grandfather directly. When there was something to say to him, she said it through Father. It was the place of the daughter-in-law to treat her husband's father with such respect. I suppose one could call it a token of thanks for providing a roof and warmth and the daily bread. But it was the women who always seemed to work the hardest.

We children also helped with chores, not so much in the home, but with the cows and chickens; little things that were fun as well. Sometimes we would go to the village with a large five-gallon jug to bring back water. The men of the town had installed a pipe through which the water flowed from the mountain into a waiting jug. The excess water fell into a huge tub made of stone or cement that sat beneath the pipe, where the animals could come to drink. Water was scarce and precious.

On occasion, we also went into the forest to bring bundles of wood on our backs for the fire, but usually the men went with their wagons for great loads.

The fireplace was such an important part of our existence. It supplied the heat, cooked our meals, and even gave us the light we lived by when the sun went down. Perhaps we also had a lantern, but I don't remember one. To go out at night, one lit a piece of pine that was thick with sap to carry like a torch. The sap acted as fuel to keep the fire burning longer.

Although they lived under the same roof, Uncle Constantine and his wife rarely joined the rest of the family. Being young, he was usually out or keeping house with his wife and small child in the other room.

Around that time, one night in particular stands out in my mind. Nastasía, Cristodula, and I were sitting on the floor near the fire playing with the dolls we had made of rags and sticks and pieces of tar from the sap of a tree. We used old buttons for their heads, then wrapped them with cloth. Twigs, which branched out, were used for legs, and for feet we formed the tar into high-heeled shoes. I don't know why we made high-heeled shoes. I had never seen such shoes before, but that's what we made. We painted the faces with charcoal and with the dyes we made from plants we found in the forest.

Mother, already big with another child, sat near the fire crocheting a tiny sweater. Father and Grandfather sat at their usual places. Grandmother sat quietly like a princess in her fine clothes, and Yanni lay on the floor fast asleep, curled like a cat.

It was a moment of reprieve, a time when our little ship resumed its ancient course. These were seductive, hope-filled moments that defied any sense of pending doom.

"There were once two very stupid brothers," Grandfather began.
He leaned forward, rested his elbows on his knees, clasped his

hands, and stared into the fire. My hands were busy with my little rag doll, but my ears perked up, recognizing the beginning of a tale.

"Even though there were so few men in the little village where they lived, their mother could not find them brides. No one would consent to marry them. They had their hearts set on the two most beautiful young maidens in the village. But when they asked for the young girls' hands in marriage, they were told by the girls' father they would soon be wed to two handsome young men from the large town on the other mountain. So one day the two brothers decided to travel to that far-off town to look for wives of their own.

"'What should we take with us,' the younger brother asked, since they had never taken a journey before.

"'I don't know,' said the other brother.

"'You will need an ax,' said their mother, 'so you can use it to chop wood for a fire.'

"'Good,' said the brothers.

"'And you should take a lantern to see where you walk if you must travel in the dark,' said the mother.

"'Good,' the brothers said again.

"'And don't forget to take blankets and food and matches to build a fire,' said the mother. She was the only smart one of the three.

"And so they made their provisions ready the day before they were to travel and wrapped them up in small sacks to carry on their backs.

"The day they chose to travel was calm and quiet when they started out, but no sooner had they crossed the wooden bridge hanging over the deep ravine that separated their village from the outside world, then the wind began to howl. It whistled through the crevices between the rocks and it whistled through the branches of the trees.

"'What was that noise?' the younger brother asked. The further they got from home, the more frightened he became.

"'What noise?' asked the other. 'It's only the wind in the trees,' he said. But he was also afraid.

"They walked on, jumping at every sound along the way. Finally they decided to stop near a small stream to prepare their evening meal. The sky was growing dark and the wind howled louder. They built a fire and ate and then lay down on their mats to sleep.

"'Do you believe in ghosts?' asked the younger brother.

"'No!' said the older one. But he looked around to see if anything could hear him.

"'Then what was that that touched my ear?'

"'I don't know,' said the older brother. 'What did it feel like?'

"'Like the cold finger of death,' he said, and his voice shook with a shiver as he spoke.

"'It was just the wind,' said the older brother. But his eyes grew wider, and he looked around in the dark again to see if anything was near.

"'What was that?' cried the young one again.

"'What?' said the other.

"'Something licked my elbow.'

"'It was the wind,' his brother said. But this time he was not so sure.

"The older brother pulled the covers up over his head to hide, and when he did, his big toe stuck out the other side. The wind whistled louder and louder.

"'What was that?' cried the older brother this time, pulling in his toe and sitting up.

"The younger one jumped to his feet. 'What?' he almost screamed.

"'Something licked my toe,' said the older brother. And he also jumped to his feet. By now his hair was standing on end.

"The brothers quickly wrapped up their things and tied them on their backs. Then they lit the lantern so they could see to travel in the dark. But no sooner had they lit the lantern when a huge giant loomed before them.

"'What's that?' cried the younger brother.

"'I don't know,' cried the other.

"They turned in another direction but another giant sprang up there as well. At that they dropped the lantern and started running for home. They ran and ran stumbling over rocks and branches that lay on the ground, afraid to look back. They thought the ghost would catch them if they did. Finally they came to the bridge that separated their village from the rest of the world and raced across.

"'Give me the ax,' cried the older brother as soon as they had crossed to the other side. 'I'll cut down the bridge and then we'll be safe at last.'

"'Yes,' said the young one. 'Then the ghost can't follow us home.'

"And so the older brother chopped and chopped at the ropes that held the bridge, until it finally fell with a great crash into the deep ravine.

"The brothers arrived home in the early morning before anyone in the village was awake. They went straight to their beds and did not rise again for almost a year. Their mother was so embarrassed when she heard their story, she told no one they were home.

"Finally one day, the brothers decided to leave their beds and walk through the village. The villagers were very impressed that they had been to the big town and returned again after so long. They made a big party to welcome the brothers home as if they were heroes. They even celebrated for three days. The two brothers were also so embarrassed that they told no one of their adventure.

"On the third day, the father of the beautiful young girls came to the brothers and asked if they still wanted to marry his daughters.

"'Yes!' they both shouted. 'But why have you changed your mind?'

"'Well,' said the father, pretending to be casual. 'Now that you are both worldly men, it would be an honor if you married my daughters.'

"But what the father didn't tell, was that the handsome young men who were coming to marry his daughters never came. And, of course, the two fools never mentioned they had destroyed the only bridge the young men could cross.

"And so it was that the two village fools married the two village beauties."

Everyone laughed. I giggled and pulled on the arms of my little rag doll. "Oh, Grandpa," I said. "There are no ghosts."

". . . are there?" I added when something crashed against the outer door.

Again they all laughed, and Father rose still chuckling and went to the door.

"Give me only Themía," Grandfather said.

He pulled me toward him and wrapped his arms around me affectionately. Then he nuzzled his stubby chin against my cheek until I dissolved in laughter.

"You can have all the rest," Grandfather said. "Only give me Themía."

When the door opened, a cold wind whipped around the room. My two uncles, Constantine and Nikolas stood frozen in the doorway holding up a man who could barely move.

"Bring him to the fire," Father said.

He quickly helped them with the stranger as Grandfather added another log to the fire, making the sparks fly about. My uncles struggled with the man. The tips of their fingers were blue and stiff with cold and, like the man's, their hair and clothing were almost a sheet of ice. Mother rushed into the supply room and brought back syrup in three cups. Then she filled the cups with hot water from the kettle that hung over the fire and offered Uncle Constantine and Uncle Nikolas each a cup to warm them. Father took off the man's shoes and rubbed his feet gently, while mother threw a blanket over him and put a cushion under his head. They removed his gloves and rubbed his hands and cheeks until finally he began to move. I was mesmerized by the strange frozen man stretched out on our floor, his large bare feet slowly turning pink again by the fire.

"What big feet he has," I blurted out.

"Shhh," Mother reprimanded gently. "That isn't nice to say."

When the man moved enough to show he was conscious, mother helped him drink the hot syrup while Father held his head and shoulders.

"Where does he come from?" Father asked.

"I don't know from which village," Uncle Constantine said. "He's a Turk. We found him in the snow, too cold to go on, so he just lay down to die. He must have gotten lost in the storm."

"It's good you made him walk," Grandfather said. "It kept his blood moving."

They helped the stranger out of his wet clothes while we left the room. Then they made a bed for him by the fire where he spent the night. My uncles had frostbite on their toes they said later, but in time they were fine.

My dream that night was of a frigid landscape
of whirling snow tossing two men about.
They leaned on the wind with frozen faces,
their clothing became a thin shell of ice.

Behind them loomed a ghostly cadaver
shooting Arctic fingers that prodded them on,

when they came upon a sleeping figure
tucked in a snow drift as if cozy and warm.

A Turk with a mask of glacial stillness
lay silent and frozen in his soft bed of white.
They flanked the man and made him stand upright,
then marched him toward home,
through the blue breath of night.

When they came to a fissure on top of the mountain,
it opened its jaws to yawn at their feet.
A frail bridge of snow lay lightly across it,
a venue to safety for their valorous deed.

But when they traversed it, it crashed down behind them,
then spat from its depths a great mass of white;
a luminous plume of shimmering snowflakes
that scattered like stars in the cavernous night.

ॐ　　ॐ　　ॐ

Our Christmas was a reverent time, our gifts simple; a handful of nuts and raisins given with great love. Mother even wrapped seeds and grain in a kerchief for Yanni and me to take down to the ravine to scatter for the birds. We'd sprinkle them along the water's edge where it flowed through the mill. Then we'd stand back, our little noses glowing red from the cold, to see if any birds came to peck at our Christmas gift.

A pine branch was hung in the back of the fireplace where the fire only warmed the little green needles and the sap of the branch, sending out a sweet perfume that filled the rooms.

It was soon after Christmas that mother went into labor. We had just come home from school when I heard Mother moaning in the room where we usually slept. The midwife was already there rushing about. Grandmother was busy stoking the fire and boiling water. Father paced back and forth, back and forth. The commotion and the sound of Mother's distress frightened me.

"What's wrong?" I said.

"Shhh!" the midwife said and gently pushed Cristodula and me back out the door. "Sit down outside and be quiet."

We did as the midwife told us. Cristodula and I stared at each other and sobbed. With each new sound of distress squeezing through the door, I thought my heart would just stop beating. I closed my eyes tight to shut out the sound as if that small act of defiance could make my mother's pain cease.

There was another time, a few years before, when Mother was to have a child. It was summer then and we kids were out playing on the grass. Mother kneeled on the porch washing the dishes from the afternoon meal when one of the cows became agitated and started running toward us. Mother's panicked cry pierced the mountain air. I looked up from my doll to see her bolt toward us with a pot still in her hand. We hadn't realized we were in danger. Her cries stunned us and we froze, staring at her misshapen figure racing toward us. I turned to look behind me at what she feared. A cow was moving in our direction. We jumped up, but as Mother ran she tripped, crashing headlong onto the grass. She tried to get up again to continue on her mission, but she couldn't. Then the cow changed direction and settled down as we ran to Mother. She lay there moaning then also in the same mournful way, holding her broad stomach with both her hands. Cristodula ran for help while I sat beside Mother, crying and stroking her hair. Father came and carried her home and put her to bed as Cristodula ran to call the midwife. I stood crying outside the bedroom door, listening to Father's voice comforting Mother and feeling every shock of pain that passed through her. When the midwife arrived, then as now, Cristodula and I were sent to stand on the porch with only our tears as consolation. We hadn't known Mother was pregnant. Pregnancy wasn't talked about in those days. Only later, when we were older, did Mother tell us she had lost a child.

Now we listened to the midwife scurry about. I pressed my forehead against the door and shut my eyes tight to see with my ears what was denied to my eyes. I heard the midwife's voice encouraging and consoling Mother. I heard Mother's tired voice and her occasional moans. And finally, after what seemed an eternity, a third voice entered the room through some magic portal all its own. A baby's voice.

My eyes sprang open and my heart leapt into my throat at the realization of the sound. Mother sighed and her faint laughter drifted out to where we stood. Cristodula and I stared at each other through our tears. Then Mother's moans began again.

"Oh!" the midwife said. "There's another one coming." And soon, a fourth voice joined the other three.

Mother must have only been a few months pregnant when the two Turkish women had come to our home to repair their pots in the fall. It was hard to imagine how anyone could have known she was pregnant, yet the Turkish woman knew at a glance, not only that she was pregnant, but that she would have twins.

The day after my sisters were born—Mathea and Maria—Mother was back at her chores. My father made a wonderful cradle for the babies. It was about three feet high, oval in shape, with rockers on the bottom. A little below the center on the bed, there was a hole through which the babies' waste could flow without soiling the bed of the cradle when they relieved themselves. They slept under a blanket without diapers. Broad plant leaves were placed under each baby and between their legs, then into the hole, where a container waited to catch the babies' waste.

To nurse, Mother knelt beside the cradle and tilted it on the edge of its rockers toward her to offer her breast to the babies one at a time, first on one side of the cradle, then on the other. Even then, her hands were busy doing other chores. There was no time to just relax and hold a baby in her arms. There was always something that had to be done.

14.

THE DROWNED MAN

F OR SOME, the Easter of 1920 came without the joy it usually brought. The Turkish soldiers had carted off all the men they could find during the war and then again on the roundup that had taken my father from us the previous fall. Those who were fortunate enough to be away or who hid when they saw the soldiers coming, escaped the roundup. And those like my father, who had escaped, were just beginning to come out of hiding. Spring was a time for planting, and each hand was needed to assure a proper harvest for the long winter ahead. For those left in our villages, life again began to resume its normal rhythm. No one expected what lay ahead.

Even though each village had its own small church, on Good Friday evening the inhabitants of all three villages went to give worship in the Cathedral of Iondone. It was a tradition to hold Easter in our beautiful cathedral. The intricate woodwork of its balconies and trusses made us feel proud. Homemade candles of beeswax were everywhere. They were twinkling on every altar, on stands, on the ground, and in the hands of each worshiper. Everyone from all three villages marched down the slopes to Iondone bringing their candles with them.

We didn't sit in church, but rather stood in prayer, bending periodically to touch the ground with our first three fingers tripoded together. Then we rose and touched our foreheads and breasts in the sign of the cross. In the evening, we formed a procession and circled the outside of the cathedral three times with our candles lit. Our priest led the way, chanting as we prayed, the glow of the candles illuminating each face in the dark as we walked around and around the cathedral. The absence of many of the men at church that year gave the holy day a very personal meaning for us all. Mothers had lost their sons, wives and children had lost their husbands and fathers. The sadness on their faces, illuminated by the light of the candles they held, was almost as sorrowful as that of the Virgin herself.

When the services were over, the people made a glowing path of candlelight to their homes, branching out to the other two villages midway down the slope. The worshipers became a procession of twinkling lights in the dark, twinkling to the contour of the land, floating in the star-studded night.

For the three-day Easter celebration, it was the children's job to collect the eggs our chickens laid. Cristodula, Yanni, and I, and even little Nastasía, searched for the eggs. One of our chickens had a habit of hiding her eggs, and sometimes we couldn't find them. So I hid myself behind the barn door and waited. The ancient Romans thought the chicken was a wise bird because it announced the laying of an egg, but on that Easter morning, I thought just the opposite. The hen looked around to see if anyone was near, then she sneaked off to lay her egg. But when she was through, she couldn't help bragging about her accomplishment. I went to look in the area where she had been, and there, tucked inside a hollow she made in the haystack, was a whole pile of eggs. Mother boiled and colored them red with onion skins and dyes made of plants. She also boiled corn to give to children who came to sing at the door on Easter morning.

> *Ella, ella, kalispera*
> *Galgevado mula robo*
> *yabia crió neró*
> *Kali sas espera erhone*
> *Anine erismosa*

> Come, come on, hello, how are you?
> Let's ride the little mule
> and drink cool water.
> It's a good day to come
> if the fates allow.

When they were finished singing, the woman of the house gave each child a scoop of boiled corn in their baskets and a colored egg if they had some to offer. The men, especially the young men, prepared their own eggs in a special way. They placed their eggs in the fireplace propped up with ashes, then covered them with a bowl so when the eggs cooked from the heat of the fire, they filled the entire shell instead of leaving a pocket of air as they do when boiled. When their eggs were done, they went from home to home during the three days of festivities, challenging any sport to an egg-breaking contest. It was a fine opportunity to visit and have a good time after the long winter.

"Ah," Father said. He tapped one of the eggs he had cooked against his front teeth. By the sound it made he knew whether it was good enough for a challenge. "This is a good one. You won't beat this egg," he said to my uncles. "It's cooked just right."

Uncle Constantine laughed "No! You will not beat me. Mine is much harder; a real champion." He also tapped his egg on his front teeth.

"You are both wrong," Uncle Nikolas joined in. "Mine is the best today."

And so the spring began innocently enough, but it would be the end of everything.

꿩   꿩   꿩

On one of those days when overnight the mountains had traded their drab ocher and rust for the frail green and crimson of springtime, and the late afternoon sun played on the summit, leaving parts of the valley immersed in shadow, my friend, Marigoula, and I walked along the road to Iondone. At times we skipped along, stopping now and then to pick some leaves from a bush, which we shoved into our pockets. It was a special bush. The leaves made a dye that children used to color their fingernails red.

"Look!" I called to Marigoula.

Some paper money lay in the road. We both ran to it, but just before I bent to pick it up, two Turkish soldiers on horseback trotted toward us. I straightened instinctively and put my foot on top of the note to hide it. It was unusual to see soldiers in our villages.

"Where are you going?" one soldier asked.

We both stood still, my foot still shielding the money beneath it.

"We're only going to pick leaves," I answered in my broken Turkish.

"It's late," the soldier said. "You should go to your homes."

"All right," I said, but I kept my foot over the money.

As they trotted off, I looked around nervously and there, sitting against a tree, were two men wearing a kind of dress I first saw in the summer past. They had begun to appear in our villages more and more. Their language was new to us and they sat around always on the edge, away from the village, waiting and staring like birds of prey. It was eerie how they hung around all of a sudden, coming from nowhere and occupying our village. They slept in the woods or in a field, appearing wherever one cast an eye.

During the famine, the vultures used to appear from nowhere the instant a sick animal fell. Then they'd swoop down on their prey screaming, their giant wings beating wildly. They'd tear the flesh of the newly fallen beast without mercy—sometimes even before it took its last breath—and fight among themselves for the best bite. At times we'd see them sitting in a tree silently waiting for the weakened animal to fall, just as these strange people silently waited now.

I stared at the strangers for a few moments wondering what they would do. They sat quietly. Only after the soldiers were at a distance, did I bend to pick up the money. It was fun to have money all my own even though there was no place to spend it.

The evening light was fading as Marigoula and I finished collecting our leaves and headed for our homes. We walked quickly, passing the strange people waiting in every corner.

On the way home we stopped and, with a stone, crushed the leaves we had collected, then spat on them and stirred them around to make a paste. Then we painted our fingernails with the bright red dye and pranced home showing off our beautiful red nails.

Marigoula and I had just gotten home when we heard men and women crying further down the road. We raced to see what the commotion was and found Uncle Nikolas and two other men standing with bowed heads before wailing men and women.

"There was nothing we could do," one of the men was saying. "We tried our best to save him but couldn't. By the time we got a log over to him he was already going down for the fourth or fifth time."

"None of us can swim," the other man said. "We would have jumped in after him if we could."

"Why?" the drowned man's father shouted. "Why? What was he doing in the water?"

We stood with eyes and mouths wide open trying to take in the details, feeling that mysterious, dreamlike suspension of reality that death always brings with it.

"He saw a flower on the other side of the pond," Uncle Nikolas said in obvious pain. "He wanted to pick it because it was so beautiful. So he took a log he found there and put it across the water to get to the other side. But when he walked on it, the log broke and he fell in."

"It's very deep in that part of the pond," the first man said. "He couldn't touch the bottom and he couldn't swim."

The men shifted nervously as the drowned man's mother lifted her tear-stained face to the heavens and wailed her grief, shaking the palms of her hands at the sky.

I looked down at my newly painted fingernails and thought of the brightly colored flower, its image reflecting in the still water of the pond as it innocently stood in the sun, oblivious to the sorrow its treacherous beauty had caused.

They had tried for a long time to help their friend, they said. But after pushing to the surface and gasping for air again and again between plunges to the depths, he had finally sunk like a stone. After the last time the men waited for many hours for him to come back up, but he never came. Finally, they headed for home.

The next day men from the village, my uncles included, went back to the pond to look for the body of their friend. They stretched a log across the pond where he went down, but each day they returned without him.

It was three or four days later that the wailing could be heard again. We raced out in our childish curiosity to see. The man had come to the surface again, this time calm, his lungs no longer struggling for air and his limbs no longer flailing about. He caught himself on a branch of the log, then waited patiently for them to return, face down in the still water.

They said he would have sunk again after a few days if they hadn't come for him, as if the pond would give his kin one last chance to claim him before claiming him for its own and sinking him forever to its muddy bosom below.

The men carried the drowned man through the village on a stretcher with sticks and straw. His face and arms, the only parts exposed, were shriveled like a prune, as if all his life fluid had been sucked out, leaving only this soggy, wrinkled shell behind. It didn't seem right that someone should die in springtime when everything else was coming to life. But God, how small we all looked by his side!

It was our custom to bury the dead on the very next day. The drowned man was laid out in a white shroud surrounded by many lighted candles. The mourners wept and prayed and knelt before him. Then they carried him to the cemetery on the edge of our village and placed him in the ground. A headstone would later be carved and placed on his grave. The traditional wheat for the funeral was boiled and sprinkled with nuts and sugar by the drowned man's family, then placed on a large tray, called a *sini*, with an apple or pear in the center. Perhaps the wheat was a symbol of the cycles of life. After the funeral, the priest blessed the wheat and stood outside on a kind of ladder, holding the large tray for anyone who wished to share it. Mourners held open their aprons to form a pocket or cupped their hands to receive the offering.

That evening, our whole family assembled by the fire and talked of the drowned man. Even Uncle Constantine and his wife and Uncle Nikolas and his wife were there.

"There is a place in the sky where people live," Grandfather began. "They have eyes on top of their heads and they can see in all directions at once. If you shake hands with one of them, your hand will stick to theirs and you can never let go. One day a young man was walking through the forest when a wild beast leaped out from behind a bush to attack him. The man was frightened and jumped back and then started to run. The beast chased him and got closer and closer. Finally, the man came to a tree and climbed up to escape the beast. But the beast began to climb also.

"'Help me,' the man cried, looking up to the sky. "And all of a sudden a hand reached down from the sky and the man took hold of it. His hand stuck to the other and he was pulled to safety just when the beast was about to tear him to pieces."

It was soon after that, that Grandfather was at his blacksmith shop in the Turkish town. Soldiers still marched through the streets in the towns.

"Varidimei! Varidimei!" a woman outside his shop called to him. "Come out and see what's going on!"

He walked out of the shop to see what the commotion was and before he understood what was happening, the soldiers grabbed him and took him away. News of his capture came to us in our village. It was as if he had been swallowed up and where he had once walked and sat and slept, a huge empty space existed instead. Each day Grandmother watched the hillside for the sight of his familiar figure coming home. And each evening the sun went down as it had the evening before without Grandfather playing his flute by the fire.

Soon after, Grandmother took down her precious linens and towels and spread them out on the floor. Then she called each of us children to stand before her to measure us for something to wear.

"What are you doing?" Mother said as Grandmother began to cut the fine cloth.

"I'm making clothing for the children," she said.

"But your fine linen," Mother said.

"What good are they now?" Grandmother said. "All is finished. Better to put them to some good use. There is no need for finery now."

15

FROM THE
BEGINNING OF TIME

W E N E V E R T H O U G H T that one day we would be forced to leave
our paradise. Our history went back too far to believe that, and we had
survived invasion after invasion for 3,000 years. By the time of Alexander the Great's short rule between 336 and 323 B.C., Greeks had already
been living in Asia Minor, or Ionia as they called it, for over 800 years.
Alexander's conquest of the Persian Empire brought the influence of
Greek and Near Eastern thought and culture to the vast territories that
stretched from the Mediterranean to India. After Alexander's death the
Hellenized Persian ruler, Mithridates the Builder, took advantage of the
turmoil and in 302 B.C., established the independent kingdom of Pontus—the area of the Pontic Mountains and southern shores of the Black
Sea. Pontus flourished as a great commercial and educational center. After decades of war, the Romans finally conquered the kingdom of Pontus
in 63 B.C. But the Greek culture continued to have great influence. The
conquered gave culture to the conqueror.

The Roman emperor Hadrian, a great lover of the Greeks, spent
long periods in Asia Minor and the Black Sea area, and for a time even
made the city of Byzantium, later called Constantinople, his official government seat. It was there in Nicomedia, in Asia Minor, during his travels around A.D. 125, that he met a beautiful young Greek boy named
Antinous. Antinous became devoted to him and Hadrian took Antinous
with him on his many travels as a cherished lover and companion. He
commissioned many statues of Antinous, and when, at the tender age of
twenty-two, Antinous drowned during their trip to Egypt, the grieving
Hadrian built a city in Egypt, which he called Antinoöpolis, as a monu-

ment to his young friend. He built Antinous a tomb, and even minted coins with his likeness, often to the dismay of Hadrian's compatriots.

The Greeks and Romans worshipped many gods in those days, but as early as A.D. 35, the Apostle Andreas (Andrew) brought Christianity to Pontus. Around 312, an angel came to the Roman emperor Constantine in a dream and told him he would win the war against Maxentius if he would embrace Christianity. Constantine had all his soldier's shields fixed with the letters XP, which was a symbol of Christianity, and soon Constantine's army defeated Maxentius; the whole Roman Empire was his. In gratitude, in 313, Constantine became the first Roman emperor to allow Christians full religious freedom. In 330, Constantine established the city of Byzantium as the new capital of the Christian Roman Empire and renamed the city Constantinople after himself. St. Nicholas, also known as Santa Claus, was a Greek from Asia Minor.

Although the Pontos was part of the Byzantine Empire, in the eleventh and twelfth centuries, local Greek feudal lords ruled. In the early part of the eleventh century the Seljuk Turks attempted to invade Pontos after sweeping through the Caucasus Mountain region, but the Pontos held firm. The Seljuks turned their energies to central Asia Minor, achieving victory over the Byzantine army in the Battle of Mantzikert in 1071, and establishing the Sultanate of Iconium, known today as Konya. Pontos still held firm.

In 1204, the Byzantine imperial family of the Comneni created the independent Pontian Empire of Trebizond—a bastion of Hellenism on the shores of the Black Sea near the Russian border—which lasted for 257 years.

With the coming of the Turkish tribal leader "Timur Lang" (Timur the Lame), better known as Tamurlane, in 1369, a new reign of terror began against the Christian population. Tamurlane, who claimed to be descended from Genghis Khan, was fanatical in his hatred of everything Christian. When Tamurlane moved his troops to Persia in 1380, he had his men build a pyramid of 70,000 human heads in Isfahan, and in Baghdad a pyramid of 90,000 human heads, to warn the people not to resist. The Assyrian city of Tikrit was besieged and its inhabitants slaughtered. Before his reign of terror was over in 1404, the Christian population of Persia, Central Asia, and China were all but annihilated.

The Ottoman Turks invaded in the late 1200s. But even after

Constantinople fell to the Ottoman Turks in 1453, the Pontos held out for another eight years, until 1461. It was the last Greek territory to fall to the Ottoman Turks.

Massacres and mass kidnappings of male children were common practices, to force the Christian population to convert to Islam. Through it all Pontos still held fast to its Hellenistic roots, and during the next 450 years, numerous churches, cathedrals, monasteries, and schools were established.

After a mighty reign by Süleyman the Magnificent from 1520 to 1566, the Ottoman Empire saw a steady decline that eventually ended Ottoman military supremacy. Under weak sultans and corrupt bureaucrats, governmental administrations began to crumble. By the 1800s, the Ottoman Empire had become known as the "Sick Man of Europe."

It wasn't until 1840 that the rule of the ruthless Muslim *derebeys*, also known as the *lords of the valley*, came to an end, and Hellenism in Pontus and elsewhere in Asia Minor began to enjoy a period of extraordinary revival. From 1839 to 1856 the central government asserted its authority, made reforms, and restored order, which provided relief for both minority nationalities and Muslims alike. Historic trade routes from Trebizond to Tabriz were reopened between 1829–1869. International markets for the Turkish tobacco of Pontos were expanded, and new trade routes opened, extending from the Black Sea town of Samsun all the way to Baghdad. The closing of the mines of Argyroupolis (Gumushane), a region of Pontos, led to a large-scale Greek migration. Pontic Greeks from many of the mountain regions, where they had settled to be secure from tyranny, moved back to the coastal regions along the Black Sea, and from eastern to western Pontos. They also migrated to the Russian-held Caucasus Mountains and to the newly acquired Russian territories along the Black Sea, and back again.

During this period, Pontic Greek society saw an extraordinary cultural, political, social, and economic renewal. Over 1,000 churches were constructed. The Ecumenical Patriarchate recognized the growing importance of the Pontic society and created seven church districts in the Pontos, each headed by a Metropolitan. One thousand Greek schools were also built that had 85,000 students enrolled in 1900. Numerous newspapers, journals, and books were published in the Pontos and scientific and cultural societies also emerged. Within a brief period of fifty years, the Pontians had achieved economic superiority in their homeland.

In 1876 Abdul-al-Hamid II became ruler, initiating a series of reforms and a new liberal constitution, which again gave the era a cultural and literary renewal. But Hamid II soon revoked his new constitution and once again periods of oppression resumed. He abused his subjects, especially the minorities, and his ill-conceived wars resulted in great losses.

For 3,000 years, the Pontians had survived it all; all the upheavals and tyranny; the changing faces of the conquerors. How could we know we would not survive this?

16

ORDERS OF EXILE

T HE TAKING OF Grandfather had signaled the end of even those moments of reprieve. Plans and preparations for the Festival of Panagia—when Mary, the mother of Jesus, was assumed into heaven—had already been started, but they would be abandoned before the spring planting was done.

Panagia was a beautiful festival, different from the Harvest Festival in a number of ways. The Harvest Festival was held on the threshing floor near our homes in autumn. An animal was killed to be shared with other villagers as part of the year's supply of meat. It was a time to give thanks for the harvest, and a time to prepare for the long winter ahead; to preserve the meat, vegetables, and grains.

Panagia, which came in August, was held higher in the mountains. People from all three villages came for services, to pray to the Virgin Mary, and then to dance, sing, and feast. Even people from far away came and spent days enjoying the festivities. A cow was chosen for slaughter; breads and pastries were baked, and candles were made to light on the Virgin's altar.

On the day of the festival, each of us kids ran to the village spring to get a pail of water. Mother warmed it on the fire, then stood each of us, one at a time, on a stool to bathe us before the fire. She rubbed us with a soapy cloth and poured the warm water over us to rinse us down. I loved it when she bathed me. I loved feeling the soap suds squish between my toes and in every crevice, and the warm water roll down my body like a sheet of silk before the warmth of the fire. I loved her touch. Her gentle, gentle touch.

In the late morning on the day of the festival, the whole village would troop up the mountain to the little chapel on top. Inside the chapel, paintings of the Virgin sat on the altar. The villagers lit candles and placed them all around, then knelt to say a prayer.

The men of the village brought the cow up the mountain. They dug a huge pit about six feet long by two feet wide and two feet deep. There they built the fire, and above it they hung the cow to roast on a spit for all the people to come and enjoy.

It was a grand festival. Father always played his viol and Grandfather played his flute while the people of all three villages danced and sang and carried on until long after the sun went down. And children ran about playing tag or "baseball" or other favorite games.

I remember the festival of the year before; my mother's beautiful face drenched in sunlight as she laid our few things out on the grass: a blanket to sit on, bread and a platter for our portion of the roasted cow. She hummed with the music and smiled down at me sitting beside her.

"Come dance, Themía," Cristodula had called out.

I looked up to see her and Yanni, and other children, dancing and laughing, matching the steps of the grown-ups. Even little Nastasía was jumping about, trying to snap her tiny fingers and kick her feet. I ran to join them as firecrackers erupted in a string of small explosions, and the startled laughter of the dancing crowd also erupted in small explosions as firecrackers were tossed throughout the hillside, crackling, sputtering, and popping.

My friend Marigoula was there too, and a merchant's son danced beside me. As my friends and I danced, kicking our feet and shaking our skinny hips in time with the music, and laughing all the time we danced, the merchant teased me about his boy. He was a robust man with a stout belly, who lived in a very large home that was painted white. He smiled at me approvingly and nodded his head up and down.

"You're going to marry my son one day," the merchant called out to me. Then he laughed boisterously and added, "You will make a good match for him."

"Oh, no I won't," I said, embarrassed even at the thought of marrying. I ran off through the dancers with my friends and we giggled and giggled until we could hardly stand.

"Yes, you will," he shouted after us and laughed some more. "You mark my words. You will marry my son one day."

But it only made us giggle all the more.

Our hopes for the festival of 1920 had also been high. The crops from the year before had been good, and the weather promised to be fine. But without warning, everything would change. There would be no dancing, no children laughing, no bonfires licking at the clouds.

The day the soldiers came, my father and uncles, and local Greeks and Turks, were out in the field preparing our land for planting. The Greek and Turkish farm workers came early in the morning with huge baskets slung over their broad shoulders, ready to work off the services done for them during the year. They trooped to the pile of manure and filled their baskets, then marched back down the hillside to scatter it on the earth. Back and forth they went collecting and spreading, collecting and spreading, without stopping to gaze at the sky or wipe the sweat that formed on their brows.

Where the men had already fertilized the field, my father walked behind the bulls in the deep furrows that opened there, guiding the great plow that cut and peeled back the earth. Long, straight grooves, one beside the other, ran the length of the field until it met a wall, or another span of furrows shot across its path; a patchwork of lines cut into the earth, ending only when they reached the stones that marked the borders of our land.

My mother sorted the seeds for planting, and we children helped with her chore. Even the chickens worked, clucking and scratching and pecking at the feast of worms and little bugs released from the ground, as the army of workers picked up their hoelike tools to also peck at the earth. They broke the clumps of soil into soft grains, and leveled the ground from border to border. And on those borders, along the roads or leaning against a tree, the vacant eyes of the strangers stared out at us.

With stunned disbelief in her eyes, and Mathea clutched to her breast, Mother shouted to my father at work in the field. "Lumbo!"

My father and uncles looked up from their plows to see a soldier at the door of our home. His rifle was pointing at my mother's heart. Constantine's wife stood in the doorway with her little girl clutching her apron, and Grandmother stood at the window holding Maria, our other twin. The men dropped the reins and raced to Mother's side.

Father tried to catch his breath. "What's going on?" he asked the soldier.

The soldier knitted his brow and kept his rifle aimed at Mother's breast. As fiercely as he could, the soldier said, "Take your family to the village and you will be told what to do."

Father again tried to calm his heavy breathing and compose his face. "But what is the problem?" he said.

"We've done nothing wrong," Uncle Constantine said.

"Go!" the soldier shouted. He raised his rifle in a gesture to strike my uncle.

"No!" Constantine's wife cried from the doorway.

Uncle Constantine drew back and raised his hands to show he meant no fight.

"Go!" the soldier shouted again.

Mother carried Mathea. Nastasía held Mother's skirt and stared up at the soldier with frightened eyes. Her little brown curls bounced on her head as she ran along trying to keep up. My father put his hand on the nape of Yanni's neck and we all walked slowly to the center of the village as we were told.

In the center, we found other soldiers with rifles in hand. There was something different about this invasion into our little village; different from when soldiers had come to take our men to labor camps. They banged on doors with the butts of their rifles while other soldiers stood sentry around the village, as if they expected resistance to their presence. Their eyes were expressionless. We didn't know why they had come, but their presence was ominous.

The soldiers shouted to the people to come out of their homes. Old eyes peered from windows and doorways. Others came out tentatively, and clustered together. Even the children assembled to listen to the proclamation of an officer who stood stiffly beside his horse, while other soldiers, their rifles held in readiness, surrounded the villagers.

"You are to leave this place," the officer shouted. "You will have three days to gather your things. You will take only what you can carry."

"Where are we to go?" an old man asked.

"You are to leave this place," the officer repeated, this time more fiercely. "I am not here to answer your questions. Be ready when the soldiers come to take you away."

"But this is our home," a woman cried as the officer and his men mounted their horses and trotted down the road toward Iondone.

"This is our home," the woman shouted after them. "You can't take us from our homes and send us away like vagabonds or beggars with our belongings on our backs. We belong here. This is our country too. This is our home! This is our home!"

I looked from stunned face to stunned face, and then spotted the strangers. They peered out from behind the houses or sat on their haunches in the field waiting. Always waiting.

17.

WAIT FOR ME

For the next few days Mother worked without stopping, taking each of us in turn to prepare a few pieces of clothing, moving from room to room without complaint. She tied up some wheat in a large cloth and placed it near the pile of cooked corn and barley she had already prepared, and she spent part of the day baking bread to take on our mysterious journey. The soft rosy color had drained from her face, and a new crease gathered up the delicate skin between her brows.

Father dug a deep pit beside our home and buried our pots and pans for the day we'd come back home again. My calf Mata nuzzle against her mother in the field. In the distance dull clouds churned over the mountains as the sun flitted in and out of clouds above my head.

For my part, I ran down to the mill in the ravine to grind the wheat. I poured it into the hole in the top stone and watched the fine beige powder fall into the open sack I had placed at its edge. I used to love to go to the mill. I loved to watch the ever-turning wheel with its vessels that scooped the water up and poured the water out, with always another vessel to scoop behind it, and another and another, on and on and on. It was comforting to watch its endless cycles, stopping neither for war nor death nor birth nor sorrow, as if life would go on in the same sweet way forever. Even now when my heart was breaking, it still went 'round and 'round.

"What's a vagabond, Mama?" I asked when I returned home.

"They are people without a home," Mother said when her voice was steady.

"Will we come back?" I asked.

"I don't know," she said, almost in whisper.

That night we sat before the fire staring into the flames. It was hard to believe we would be leaving in the morning. It seemed that our family had been on this land for thousands of years; that we had sprung from the earth, born of its flesh like a tree or a flower, deep-rooted, not by our feet, but by our hearts.

I stared into the flames of the fire, and my mind played again at the Festival of Panagia. Father laughed as he sat with the other men on the area cleared for dance. His big black mustache accented his wide smile. He played his viol while people danced. Even Mother danced, holding the end of a scarf in each upraised hand. My aunt held the other end and another woman held the end my aunt extended. Seven women dancing in a row, gently swaying their hips and lifting their feet like dancers on a Grecian urn. In my imagination, even Grandfather moved about the threshing floor. His graceful figure barely showed his age. His arms twined around those of two companions whose arms twined around two more. They moved to the left and to the right, dipping and lifting their knees slow and steady, then clicking their heels to the grounds. Even little Nastasía danced. Her head and shoulders bounced up and down while she randomly stamped her feet and stared into Mother's eyes.

Cristodula, barely beginning to bud into a woman, stood shyly to one side with her friends, stealing glances at a group of boys, while young men strutted like peacocks, their thick black hair falling into their eyes and their broad shoulders pressed back to swell their proud chests. Yanni ran around them playing tag. The air smelled of wood burning and a cow roasting on a spit. The sun beat down but a cool breeze ruffled the women's dresses and tousled their hair.

"We'd better go to sleep," Mother said, jolting me from my reverie. "We will need all our strength tomorrow."

It was a few moments longer before anyone moved. Only little Nastasía and the twins slept peacefully by the fire. It was as if crawling into our beds would acknowledge the end of our stay; the end of roaming the fields and forests and breathing the fresh mountain air we all loved so well; the end of curling up by a cozy fire to listen to stories and songs; the end of a world that would never come again.

I crawled onto my mat in the darkened room and listened to the sweet, sharp, monotonous song of the little spring frogs that serenaded us through the open window. I forced my eyes wide open and stared at the spots and squiggly forms that swam before them. I made them dance to the rhythm of Father's viol and Grandfather's flute. I made them dip and turn and sway gracefully in the dark. I made them laugh and run and strut before budding maidens, until the image that crept into my mind of our long mournful procession, trudging down the road like vagabonds or beggars with our bundles on our backs, was crowded out again.

The rain came in waves just before I drifted off to sleep. It pounded the rooftop and beat against the windowpane. Veins of lightning shattered the blackness and a great rumbling rolled across the night.

By morning there was calm. The gray light skulked about the room with barely a trace of shadow, and the fog drifted down the face of the mountains like smoke, blending the ridges into the brooding sky. In the other room Mother moved about methodically preparing the morning meal. Our things sat by the door in a sorry pile of bundles wrapped in cloth.

"Wake the others," Mother said when I entered the room. "We don't know when the soldiers will come."

She stood at the table pouring melted butter over the bread. Father sat at the table drinking his coffee, and Grandmother tended the twins.

"Why must we leave Mama?" I said.

She rested the pitcher of butter on the table and turned her head to hide the tears that sprang to her eyes. I looked to my father for an answer, but he clenched his teeth until the muscles stood out in ridges on his jaw. Then he closed his eyes to shut out the sound of his own helplessness.

"Because they will kill us if we don't," Mother said finally, in an almost even voice. "Run along now and wake the others."

I went back into our room and looked down at my brother and sisters sleeping. Nastasía was curled in the cradle of Cristodula's curved body, her little back against Cristodula's chest. Yanni slept with abandon, his arms and legs scattered about.

As I reached down to touch Cristodula's shoulder to wake her, the boards beneath my feet vibrated. The sound of boots stomping across the floor in the next room made Cristodula jump and her eyes sprang open. I ran back to see who had come. Uncle Nikolas stood there. He carried a bundle and his breath came heavily.

"I'm not going," he announced. "My wife is waiting at the foot of the orchard. We're not going."

Mother's face was a mixture of hope and alarm. "What do you mean you're not going?" she said.

"What do you mean?" Father said.

"I'm not going. And you should not go either."

"But how can you stay?" Father said. "They will kill you if you stay."

"I will not leave my land. This is our land. This is where we belong. I will not let them drive me from my home."

"Damn it! They will kill you," Father said. "They will kill you."

"No! I will go among the Turks until it's safe," Uncle Nikolas said. "They will protect me and my wife. We have always been friendly with the Turks here. They will protect you too if you stay."

Mother looked at Father for the first time with hope in her eyes.

"Do you think we could?" she said.

"They will kill him," Father shouted. He stood up and threw his cup into the fire.

"How can you leave?" Uncle Nikolas also shouted. "How can you leave everything behind?"

Mother looked from one to the other as my father stood staring into the fire. In the doorway to the bedroom, Cristodula, Yanni, and Nastasía also stood silently staring.

"How?" Uncle Nikolas shouted louder when he got no reply.

"You are alone," Father finally shouted in return. "You are alone and can hide among the Turks perhaps. But we are many. How can I hide an old woman and a wife and six small children? Tell me and I'll do it. Just tell me how."

The hope vanished from Mother's eyes then and she cried for the first time. I ran to her and threw my arms around her to crush out the pain.

"It will be all right, Mama," I said, trying to fight my own tears and the thick saliva that choked my speech. "We will come back one day. You'll see."

She wrapped her arms around me and leaned her head on mine. I could feel her warm tears fall on my hair and soak down onto my scalp as she pressed my face against her breast.

"Tell me and I'll do it," Father said more gently now. "Just tell me."

Father and Uncle Nikolas stood staring at each other. Then Uncle Nikolas lowered his eyes.

THEA HALO

"I don't want to leave you," he said, "but I can't go."

"Then don't go. Stay if you think you can make it. Stay and God be with you."

My father held out his arms to Uncle Nikolas and Uncle Nikolas threw his arms around him.

"See if you can find out about our father," my father said when they finally pulled apart. "He is old and the camps are cruel. More than likely he can't survive. Listen for news of him."

Uncle Constantine and his wife came from their room and stood staring at Uncle Nikolas.

"So you are staying for sure then?" Uncle Constantine said.

"Yes. We're staying."

"You'd better go before the soldiers come," Father said. "Say good-bye to your uncle, children."

We ran to him and he wrapped his arms around us all at once. He kissed Mother on the forehead. Then he kissed my aunt, embraced Uncle Constantine, and in the next instant he was gone.

I ran out onto the porch to watch him go. In only a moment he had disappeared between the pear trees lining the slope of the mountain. The fog had lifted and the sky had cleared. Overnight, the apple tree by our home was laced in frail pink blossoms and the pear trees were dressed in a glory of white. My little calf Mata stood tied to the apple tree beside our home. Her furry coat had become more sleek. I went to her and put my arms around her neck. I pressed my cheek against her brown furry face. Her coat was warm against my skin.

"I'll be back," I said. "Wait for me."

Mata gave a long, low reply.

Then I lay on the ground with my face pressed against the cool grass, and stretched out my arms to hug the earth. I wanted to suck it all inside me, to remember its smell, its cool feel against my face, and the sound of its music rippling through the trees. I wanted to turn back time and look up to find Father working in the field and Mother rocking on the porch with little Nastasía tugging at her hem. I wanted to race down the slopes with my little calf and see Cristodula and Yanni chasing behind. But when I did look up, they were standing on the porch, stacking our bundles helter-skelter in the sun.

I went indoors and through the house one more time to fix it in my mind. All the rooms were in perfect order. In Grandfather's room, our living room, the embers still smoldered in the hearth. The large pot, blackened from years on the fire, still hung from its chain. The dishes were perched on their shelves, lining the wall with their shiny faces staring out. And the long wooden table and stools sat neatly in their places. Even the rug mother made lounged by the fire. It looked like any other day. Mother had tidied the rooms as if we were only leaving for a holiday to our summer home.

I realized then that I had never seen my home without someone inside; Mother kneading dough, or stirring a pot of stew hanging over the fire; Grandmother crocheting or caring for the twins while Grandfather played his flute. I had never seen it barren of people as it was now, except perhaps for a moment on those days when we returned from holiday at our summer home, and I was the first to burst through the door. I'd find it quiet then, with the sun streaming through the windows and everything in its proper place just as it was now, and I'd feel that strange, uneasy feeling that something was amiss. Then, in an instant, it would be full again of the sights and sounds of family life, of children laughing, a baby crying, pots and pans being readied for the evening meal. Then I would breath again, and my dis-ease would disappear.

The soldiers had come. We could hear the horses and many voices further down the road, and the sound of a woman crying floated toward us.

"Come, Themía," Mother called from the porch. "We must go."

I closed the door to Grandfather's room gently as if someone lay asleep; as if I were afraid to disturb the memories so they'd wait for us to return; so they'd remember that this was our house, even if someone else crawled into bed where I once slept, or sat on Father's stool where he closed his eyes and lifted his voice in song, or stood before the fire where my mother stood in all the memories of my life.

Mother wrapped little Maria in a small blanket and tied her on Cristodula's back. She tied Mathea on my back. Maria was a slight child with delicate health, but Mathea was full of laughter. I could feel her nuzzle her sweet face against my ear, and rub her tiny nose on my shoulder as I descended the stairs. They were no more than four months old. Cristodula was twelve then, I think; Yanni was eight; Nastasía was four. It was the spring of 1920. I don't know if I was ten by then.

Mother closed the door of our home slowly, then leaned her forehead against the panels and closed her eyes, as if in prayer. She bent to touch the floor of the porch with the tripod her three joined fingers made, then touched them to her forehead and breast in the sign of the cross. Then she slowly turned to join us as Nastasía, her thin legs and tiny feet peeking out from under her long flowered dress, held Mother's shirt.

Almost all the villagers were already gathered when we arrived in the center of the village. They had formed a long line, two and three abreast, over 3,000 people from all three villages. They flowed along the winding road, rising and falling in a jagged stream down the valleys and up the hills, all the way to Iondone and beyond.

The sound of babies crying mingled with the singing of the birds. The old woman, whose cows we often took to pasture, jutted out from the procession, bent and bony like an old twig in her long black dress; her frail, knobby hand clutched the arm of her son.

While soldiers ran from home to home, pushing in doors with the butts of their rifles and looking inside, other soldiers on horseback shouted orders to the people as they shuffled nervously in the sun. Then the moment came when the soldiers on horseback shouted for us to move.

Was it in total silence that we picked up our bundles and began our journey? That first traumatic step has been wiped from my mind.

We descended the road to Iondone with the sun behind us. An eerie silence settled over Iondone. No children played near their homes. No women hung out their wash. No smoke rose from the chimneys and no men worked in the fields. Only the haunting figure of a hunched Kurd crouching by a tree or peering out from behind a building with his vacant eyes, gave any evidence of life, which was hardly life at all. They had come closer than they had ever come before. They were poor people by the look of their dress. Hardship showed clearly in the coldness of their eyes. I wondered why the soldiers didn't ask them to march also; why they were left behind in a village that didn't belong to them while we were pushed from our homes.

On the far side of Iondone where the forest met the edge of the road, the air was still moist. The rains of the night before had soaked the rotting leaves that lay on the ground, giving off a sweet, mellow scent I would not smell again for many, many years. I inhaled deeply to fill my lungs. Birds flitted in and out of the sun and shadows through the trees as the long procession snaked down the road before me, and dipped into another valley.

Just before we descended that final slope that would hide our villages from view forever, I turned to look one last time at the landscape that I loved. I looked at the flowering orchards and rust-colored earth; the grassy pasture dotted with wildflowers glistening in the sun. I followed the line of graying log cabins with their neighboring barns winding along the contour of the road, and the pale green mountains against a clear blue sky. Then I closed my eyes to remember their colors and fix them clearly in my mind. But the greens had turned to red, the blues to yellow. I saw lavender hills and an orange sky.

Book Three

THE EXILE

On my long travels
I saw so many lives unravel on the road,
as if each life was like a knitted scarf.
And time and time again
I even saw that first knot
from which one begins one's own design,
slip its bind and fall away,
its weaver in the dust.
I watched the fabric of my own life
uncouple link from link,
until all the precious pieces of my world
lay behind me on the road
like a useless, curling strand.
But my master knot, my God's knot,
held fast to let me weave again.
God's plans for me remained a mystery.

In 1908 a new revolutionary party was formed popularly known as the Young Turks. They were greatly welcomed by all segments of Ottoman society, and with the help of the army, they forced Sultan Abdul-al-Hamid II to grant a new constitution in place of the one he had revoked. The Young Turks vision for the Ottoman Empire was to improve its military power, reverse the economic dominance of the non-Muslim minorities—Greeks, Armenians, and Jews—and create a Turkish Muslim bourgeois class. In the beginning, they also made an attempt to unite all ethnic and religious groups into a multiethnic, multinational federation with representation in parliament. The more liberal environment in Turkey, even with periodic setbacks of renewed repression, after hundreds of years of Ottoman oppression, encouraged a Pontic Greek renaissance. With promises of justice, freedom, and dignity, Pontians gained a new sense of identity and self-worth. But their hopes, along with their cultural and economic renewal, would come to a cruel end. By 1915 a faction of the Young Turks took control of the government and began ordering the wholesale slaughter and exile of the Greek, Armenian, and Assyrian minorities, and the confiscation of their property.

In 1914, the alliance between Germany and Turkey deepened, and Germany's declaration of war began World War I. When the Russians occupied the Trebizond region in 1916, the Turkish governor Mehmet Cemal Azmi Bey, turned the city over to Metropolitan Chrysanthos, a local Greek notable, with the statement, "From the Greeks we took the city and to them we return it." But Pontian control was short-lived. By 1917, an exhausted Russia withdrew from the war. The tzar abdicated and the Bolsheviks, led by Lenin, took charge of the government. Pontians who had fled to Russia had organized to address the plight of Pontic Hellenism, passing resolutions that would enable Pontians, including those who had settled in Russia, to return to their homeland. In February 1918, the first Pan-Pontian Congress was held in Marseilles bringing together Pontians from as far away as the United States. Constantine Constantinides, a wealthy Pontian merchant of Marseilles, was elected president. The congress sent a cable to Trotsky asking his support for the development of an independent Pontic Greek state. It claimed that guarantees for minorities in Turkey were meaningless, and called for full autonomy as the only way to safeguard the future of Pontic Hellenism. Other Pontian groups in Constantinople, Thessaloníki, and Athens put together similar resolutions.

By 1918, great losses, economic failure, and President Woodrow Wilson's proposal known as the "fourteen points," brought Germany to cede defeat, bringing World War I to an end. On October 30, 1918 an armistice was granted to Turkey by the Principal Allied Powers. At the 1919 Peace Conferences, Britain, France, Greece, Italy, Bulgaria, the Serbs, Croats, Azerbaijanis, Armenians, Arabs, Kurds and Zionist Jews, all came to lay their claims to the Ottoman Empire. The result was a series of disputes, promises, and betrayals that led to disaster for some of the participating parties, and set the stage for conflicts between nations and peoples that still exist today.

Two months after the Paris Peace Conference, Italy began landing troops in southern Anatolia in March 1919. In response, Britain, France, and finally the United States asked Greece to land troops at Smyrna, which it did on May 15, 1919. This began the Greek–Turkish war of 1919–1922. For Greece the mission for the invasion was clear; to take back territories lost centuries earlier. For her allies, it was to deter an Italian takeover of parts of Anatolia that it had been promised in an unimplemented agreement of 1917.

As promised by President Wilson, the Treaty of Sèvres, signed on August 10, 1920, gave the minorities of Turkey, such as the Armenians and Kurds, independence, territory, and statehood, and Greece was given Eastern Thrace and most of the islands in the Aegean Sea. The treaty also recognized Greece's right to occupy Smyrna and its environs in Turkey for five years, after which the Council of the League of Nations could grant the area to the Kingdom of Greece permanently or order a plebiscite by the inhabitants in which they could choose Greece as its permanent ruler.

Greece had already won its independence from the Ottoman Empire, beginning with a countrywide rebellion on March 25, 1821 in which Greek guerrilla forces won control of much of Greece, and ending with Russia's own war with Turkey. The Treaty of Adrianople, following Russia's defeat of Turkey in August 1829, made a provision for Greece's independence and ceded to Greece the Peloponnesus, the Cyclades, and Central Greece. In the first Balkan War of 1912–13, Greece again won back ancient Greek territories from Turkey, such as Crete, when Greece's premier, Venizélos, backed by an alliance with Bulgaria and Serbia, declared war on Turkey. In the second Balkan War of 1913, Greece won back parts of Macedonia from Bulgaria.

The Greek invasion of 1919 was to play a decisive role in Mustafa Kemal's successful victory over rival political factions in Turkey, and would eventually bring him the title of Atatürk, literally "father of the Turks." The Greeks made surprising progress with their offensive, winning battle after battle. Even with a series of setbacks after the change of government in Greece, in an amazingly short period of time the Greek army reached to within a short distance of Ankara—the future seat of the Turkish government in central Turkey. With Greece's army near victory in reaching Ankara, Mustafa Kemal took over as commander of the Turkish army. In a clever political maneuver, Kemal called for a secret session of the National Assembly at which he proposed to be appointed dictator for a period of three months during which time he promised to drive the Greek army out. Although there was some dissent, the National Assembly complied with Kemal's request, setting the stage for Mustafa Kemal's rise to power.

Although President Wilson had been in favor of protecting the Christians and the missionary colleges of Turkey, and had a policy that the peoples of the Middle East should be allowed to establish governments of their choice, his successor, President Warren Gamaliel Harding, was not sympathetic to these concerns. Other intrigues had developed, such as oil interests and trade with Turkey, that took precedence over the more humane policies of Wilson.

Instead of pleasing her allies, Greece's victory frightened them. The Allies had not expected Greece to be so swift or so complete in her advances. Afraid Greece would expect to keep the lands she won from the Turks, cutting the Allies out, the Allies became leery of the encouragement they had given Greece for the invasion. When support was needed most, Britain, France, and Italy abandoned Greece, thereby insuring her defeat. In fact, France and Italy began to supply the Turks with money and arms. Greece's change of government in 1920, in the midst of the war, which voted out Premier Venizélos and restored King Constantine to the throne, also had major negative effects on Greece.

Overextended, and without proper supplies to continue the fight, the Greek army abandoned the territory it had gained in Anatolia and retreated. King Constantine attempted a new tactic. By withdrawing three regimens from Anatolia and assembling them opposite Constantinople in Thrace, Constantine hoped his announcement that Greece intended to occupy Constantinople would cause the Allies to intervene in the Greek-

Turkish war and bring some resolution. At the least, King Constantine assumed his troops could pass through Constantinople and join his troops in Anatolia. Although the Allies would later complain bitterly that they would appear weak if Turkey succeeded in driving the Allies out of Constantinople, at the time the Greek army stood at its gates, the Allies blockaded the Greek army from entering the city.

The abandonment of Greece by her allies gave Kemal's forces the momentum to reclaim Turkey's strength and push the Greeks back to Smyrna, their port of entry, and finally off Turkish soil, leaving a burning city in its wake. The Turks blamed the Greeks for the burning of Smyrna, but a correspondent of the Chicago Daily News reported from the scene of the catastrophe in 1922:

> Except for the squalid Turkish quarter, Smyrna has ceased to exist.
> No doubt remains as to the origin of the fire. . . . The torch was
> applied by Turkish regular soldiers.

When American church groups, such as the Methodist Episcopal Church, implored the American government to send troops to stop the resulting massacres of the Christians of Turkey, few Americans understood the effect of President Harding's callous desire to commence trade with Turkey. Harding complained to Secretary of State, Charles Evans Hughes:

> Frankly, it is difficult for me to be consistently patient with our
> good friends of the Church who are properly and earnestly zealous
> in promoting peace until it comes to making warfare on someone of
> the contending religion . . .

In a desperate plea, the Archbishop of Smyrna wrote to ousted Prime Minister Venizélos of Greece who was without means to offer assistance:

> Hellenism in Asia Minor, the Greek state and the entire Greek
> Nation are descending now to a Hell from which no power will be
> able to raise them up and save them . . . out of the flames of catas-
> trophe in which the Greek people of Asia Minor are suffering—and
> it is a real question whether when Your Excellency reads this letter

*of mine we shall still be alive, destined as we are . . . for sacrifice
and martyrdom . . . to direct this last appeal to you.*

A few days later, the archbishop was arrested by one of Atatürk's generals and turned over to a Turkish mob who first tortured, then murdered him.

As Smyrna burned, American, British, Italian, and French navy vessels came to evacuate the inhabitants. At first both the Americans and the British refused to evacuate anyone other than their own nationals. The Italians accepted on board anyone who could reach their ships. The French accepted anyone claiming to be French if they could say it in French. Finally, even the American and British ships began to accept refugees. In the following weeks, during which Greece evacuated its troops, Greece and the Allies evacuated thousands of Greek and Armenian Nationals of Turkey in response to threats from Atatürk that he would treat the men of military age as prisoners of war.

In the Black Sea area the British commissions—which had been sent to safeguard the return of the Pontians to their homes—were abandoned when other concerns took priority, leaving the Pontians to fend for themselves. During the slaughters, Russian ships had periodically evacuated some of the Pontians along the Black Sea coast, but many more were killed by the Turks or sent on long death marches.

Each Allied country blamed the others for the failures in Turkey. Although Britain placed blame on Italy, France, and Russia, it cast the heaviest blame on the United States, claiming that the Allies could have imposed a settlement in 1919 but had deferred to the United States to secure its cooperation. Britain accused the United States of failing to live up to its agreement to occupy and safeguard Constantinople, the Dardanelles, and Armenia, those agreements made when Wilson was president. Secretary of State Hughes responded to these recriminations for the United States by saying he would not for a moment assent to the view:

> that this Government was in any way responsible for the existing
> condition . . . The United States had not sought to parcel out
> spheres of influence . . . had not engaged in intrigues at Constan-

tinople . . . was not responsible for the catastrophe of the Greek armies during the last year and a half . . . diplomacy in Europe for the last year and a half was responsible for the late disaster.

A biographer of Mustafa Kemal Atatürk asserted that Atatürk gave orders that no Turkish soldier was to kill any Greek National during their march to exile. It is doubtful that Atatürk truly gave such an order because there is no doubt that the genocide of the Greek and Armenian populations of Turkey was systematic and deliberate. According to American diplomatic reports, Atatürk himself was directly involved in the slaughter of thousands of innocent Greek and Armenian civilians and was present in Smyrna as his troops torched the city. It was reported that Atatürk held congresses in Erzerum and Sivas, which are in Eastern Anatolia, in the summer of 1919, where a decision was made to attack "all people from Rumeli and all Hellenes." During the time Atatürk set up his provisional government in Ankara in 1919–1920, and prior to his successful ousting of the sultan, Cemal Musket, legal advisor of the sultan, collected various documents from the sultan's archive and wrote a report. It was found in the archives of the Foreign Ministry of Greece.

> *The government of Ankara decided that the Greeks of the regions Atabazar and Kaltras, first, and later the Greeks of the Pontos would be slaughtered and eliminated. He assigned Yavur Ali to burn down the Greek village which is near Geive and to kill all of its inhabitants. The tragedy lasted two days. The village with its twelve factories and its nice buildings became a dump site. Ninety percent of the population was slaughtered and burnt. The few who were able to escape in order to save their lives went to the mountains. In order to preserve his Chets, Mustafa Kemal had to find an area which he could attack. For this purpose he went to the area of the Pontos. The slaughter, looting, and general elimination in this area lasted from February to August. These displacements and killings were conducted with the semiofficial participation of military and civic personnel . . . The Turkish authorities and the Turkish governments of 1919–20, including at the Peace Conference in Paris, attempt not to deny their actions but they attempt to put all*

*responsibilities to the Young Turks; in other words to the govern-
ment.*

*Six thousand men, women, and children of the Bafra area were burned
alive as they took refuge in churches, and their valuables were stolen. In the
town of Alajam another 2,500 Christians were slaughtered. Of the 25,000
inhabitants of the Bafra region, 90 percent were eliminated by mass slay-
ings or by sending them on long death marches where they were often
raped and robbed and left to die of disease and starvation.*

*Although it may be tempting to blame the Greek-Turkish war of 1919
for the slaughter and exile of the Greeks of Turkey—here collectively
known as the Pontians—according to German and Austrian archives,
which have now been made public, a series of communiqués attest to
Turkey's brutal intentions long before Greece invaded. In fact, the communiqués attest to Turkey's brutal intentions against its ancient Christian population, which included Greeks, Armenians, and Assyrians, even before
Greece entered the war on the side of the Allies in 1917; even long before
the Balkan War. Unfortunately, neither the German nor the Austrian authorities did anything to prevent Turkey from carrying out its plan of genocide.*

*24 July 1909 German Ambassador in Athens Wangenheim to
Chancellor Bulow quoting Turkish Prime Minister Sefker Pasha:
"The Turks have decided upon a war of extermination against their
Christian subjects."*

*26 July 1909 Sefker Pasha to Patriarch Ioakeim III: ". . . we will
cut off your heads, we will make you disappear. It is either you or
us who will survive. . . ."*

*14 May 1914 Official document from Talaat Bey, Minister of the
Interior to Prefect of Smyrna: The Greeks, who are Ottoman subjects, and form the majority of inhabitants in your district, take advantage of the circumstances in order to provoke a revolutionary
current, favourable to the intervention of the Great Powers. Conse-
quently, it is urgently necessary that the Greeks occupying the*

coastline of Asia Minor be compelled to evacuate their villages and install themselves in the vilayets of Erzerum and Chaldea. If they should refuse to be transported to the appointed places, kindly give instructions to our Moslem brothers, so that they shall induce the Greeks, through excesses of all sorts, to leave their native places of their own accord. Do not forget to obtain, in such cases, from the emigrants certificates stating that they leave their homes on their own initiative, so that we shall not have political complications ensuing from their displacement.

31 July 1915 German priest J. Lepsius: "The anti-Greek and anti-Armenian persecutions are two phases of one programme—the extermination of the Christian element from Turkey."

16 July 1916 German Consul Kuchhoff from Amisos to Berlin: "The entire Greek population of Sinope and the coastal region of the county of Kastanomu has been exiled. Exile and extermination in Turkish are the same, for whoever is not murdered, will die from hunger or illness."

30 November 1916 Austrian consul at Amisos Kwiatkowski to Austrian Foreign Minister Baron Burian: "on 26 November Rafet Bey told me: "we must finish off the Greeks as we did with the Armenians . . ." on 28 November Rafet Bey told me: 'today I sent squads to the interior to kill every Greek on sight.' I fear for the elimination of the entire Greek population and a repeat of what occurred last year." (the Armenian genocide).

13 December 1916 German Ambassador Kuhlman to Chancellor Hollweg in Berlin: "Consuls Bergfeld in Samsun and Schede in Kerasun report of displacement of local population and murders. Prisoners are not kept. Villages reduced to ashes. Greek refugee families consisting mostly of women and children being marched from the coasts to Sebastea. The need is great."

19 December 1916 Austrian Ambassador to Turkey Pallavicini to Vienna lists the villages in the region of Amisos that were being burned to the ground and their inhabitants raped, murdered or dispersed.

20 January 1917 Austrian Ambassador Pallavicini: "the situation for the displaced is desperate. Death awaits them all. I spoke to the Grand Vizier and told him that it would be sad if the persecution of the Greek element took the same scope and dimension as the Armenia persecution. The Grand Vizier promised that he would influence Talaat Bey and Emver Pasha."

31 January 1917 Austrian Chancellor Hollweg's report: ". . . the indications are that the Turks plan to eliminate the Greek element as enemies of the state, as they did earlier with the Armenians. The strategy implemented by the Turks is of displacing people to the interior without taking measures for their survival by exposing them to death, hunger, and illness. The abandoned homes are then looted and burnt or destroyed. Whatever was done to the Armenians is being repeated with the Greeks."

By 1923, Kemal Atatürk had successfully driven the Allies out and, in the Treaty of Lausanne, forced the Allies to recognize the sovereignty of Turkey in Asia Minor and eastern Thrace, thus nullifying the Treaty of Sèvres in which the Greeks, Armenians, and Kurds were awarded territories.

History has been written by so few disinterested authorities that, depending on the nationality or loyalties of the writer, the facts have been slanted, or even twisted, to cast the events in a very calculated light. Numerous scandals have surfaced concerning the Turkish government's policy of paying American universities, such as Princeton, endowments to insure that a history is taught that is favorable to Turkey; one that excludes reference to the Armenian, Greek, and Assyrian genocides. With many chairs for Turkish studies at American universities, Turkey's revisionist history has a chance of reaching a large segment of the American student body.

On October 27, 1995, The Chronicle of Higher Education, *in a report by Amy Magaro Rubin, stated that a petition was being circulated by American scholars that accused the Turkish government of using United States academics in universities to manipulate its history by excluding reference to its genocide of the Armenians.* The Boston Globe *followed suit on*

November 25, 1995, affirming that gifts with strings attached from foreign governments were causing great concern in U.S. colleges. On November 30, 1995, the Philadelphia Inquirer *reported on Princeton University's unethical use of funds from Turkey. The* New York Times *followed with an article on May 22, 1996 stating that Princeton was "fronting for the Turkish Government." And on Sunday, November 30, 1997, The* Los Angeles Times *reported an offer of a $1 million endowment to UCLA by the Turkish government, which UCLA rejected in the aftermath of Princeton's scandal. Even an On-line Encyclopedia called the* Free Concise Encyclopedia, *in its brief account of the history of Turkey fails to mention the Greeks, Armenians, or Assyrians as inhabitants. It refers only to the Hittites and then to the "Invaders known as the Sea Peoples" who came in 1200 B.C. The entry fails to mention that these "Sea Peoples," the Greeks, were there for over 2,000 years before the first invasion of the Turkish tribes.*

Because of these systematic attempts of various governments and interested individuals to hide their country's atrocities, and to create a fictional history, survivors' testimonies, as well as eye-witness accounts from disinterested bystanders, including European and American diplomats, often provide the most authentic and legitimate sources of truth. As with the Holocaust, these firsthand accounts by survivors who lived through the horrors, such as my mother, offer us authentic ways of understanding the events, and have provided historians with their most important sources for their writing of history. My mother's story is such a firsthand account of the hell that Secretary of State, Charles Evans Hughes, attributed to "the barbaric cruelty of the Turks."

Armenian deaths are estimated at 1.5 million. The Assyrians, another historically Christian group who have inhabited the land for thousands of years, were also subjected to wholesale slaughter and exile. The 750,000 Assyrian deaths represented an astounding two-thirds of the entire population of Assyrians. As to the Pontians, in the final analysis, approximately 360,000 Pontians were killed, and about 1.5 million exiled.

There were three separate groups of Greeks in Turkey: the Ionians, who lived in the western coastal regions facing Greece; the Kappadokians, those from the area of the ancient Greek cities of central Anatolia now known as Cappadocia; and the Pontians, who lived in the Pontic Mountains below the Black Sea and on its southern shores. But the term Pontian has come to encompass the struggles and tragedies of all the Greeks of Turkey.

In the spring of 1920, Mustafa Kemal Atatürk ordered the people of my mother's villages in the Pontic Mountains to be sent on a death march to exile into the Syrian desert. They were marched south for seven to eight months, through the mountainous regions of northern Turkey and the arid plains of the south without concern for food, water, or shelter.

During those cruel death marches, countless other Pontians lost their lives, for, as intended, there are ways of killing without knives or guns. My mother's story attests to such ways.

18

THE LONG ROAD TO HELL

IT TOOK MANY hours just to reach the Turkish town below. As we passed, the people of the town stood on the side of the road to watch us. It was hard to tell what they were thinking as we passed. They had known us all our lives, as we had known them. Father's shop was in that town. He and Grandfather had forged their plows and made new shoes for their animals. They had fixed their pots, mended their tools, and sat together in the afternoons sharing a glass of tea.

"Lumbo," a voice whispered as we passed. Father turned to find a man standing with bowed head.

"Your father is dead," the man said. "He died in the camps. I'm sorry."

We kept walking. The soldiers carrying whips, skidded around on horseback keeping a close eye on the exiles. Mother crossed herself and reached out to hold Grandmother's hand. Father closed his eyes and clenched his teeth but walked on like the rest.

I could feel the tears rolling down my cheeks. I had missed my grandfather. I missed his warm mustachioed smile and soothing voice telling tales by the fire. I missed standing before him when he tried to teach us our ABCs and the Lord's Prayer. I missed the patient way he clasped his hands and rested his elbows on his knees to wait for us to finish our shy laughter. I was his favorite child. I could tell by the way he patted my head when he came home at night, or the little necklaces of roasted chestnuts he slipped only around my neck. Or the way he let me spring open the face on his beautiful gold watch when I tugged on its chain. I don't know how they knew Grandfather had died, but it seemed they always knew what had happened to a person no matter where he was.

As we passed the Turks standing along the road, Father motioned to a man.

"Please," Father said as we walked by. "I want to buy a donkey. Could you bring me one?"

The man left without a word and we kept walking. When we reached the end of the town the man was back with another man who was leading a donkey by a halter. Father paid him and took the reins, but the first man continued to walk with us.

"Don't you remember me?" the first man asked my father and Uncle Constantine who walked nearby.

"No," Father said. Uncle Constantine looked at him intently, then shook his head.

"You saved my life in the snow," he said to Uncle Constantine, "and I slept by your fire." Tears came to his eyes then.

Father reached out his hand to the man as a soldier on horseback shouted and trotted up alongside to force the man away. We left the town behind with his words still echoing in my ears.

I remembered the night my uncles brought the frozen man to our house, as Grandfather told us the story about the two fools. I remembered the man's frozen body lying by the fire with his big frozen feet turning pink as they warmed. How cozy and secure it had felt to be warm inside when the winds whistled and the snow beat against the windowpane.

There was another time my uncles had risked their own lives to save the life of a Turk. They were walking home past a small Turkish village when they saw smoke and fire coming from a house. A woman stood in the road crying and screaming that her husband was still inside. Without a thought to their own safety, my uncles ran inside and carried the man out. Grandfather had even saved a Turk who had been bitten by a snake.

As the town receded behind us, I remembered the other story Grandfather told us. The one about the man who cries out for help to the people in the sky, then reaches up and takes hold of a hand that pulls him to safety. I wondered if Grandfather had also cried out from the camps, and reaching up to grab a hand, got stuck to it and was pulled to a life beyond; a safe life where he could sit by a fire and play his flute and teach little children their ABCs.

We walked the whole day, stopping only briefly now and then, more for the soldiers to lay out their mats and kneel in prayer, than for any consideration for our well-being. Father piled the bundles on the donkey's back to ease our burden. Mother nursed the babies one at a time, and sometimes we ate a piece of bread along the road as we walked. The soldiers on horseback shouted every now and then to keep us moving. My arms ached from holding them behind me to support Mathea on my back, and my legs felt stiff from the added weight. But I just kept walking like the others, with everything blurred before me through my tears.

𝒴   𝒴   𝒴

When the sun was just setting the soldiers shouted for us to halt. I dropped my bundles gratefully, but my cramped fingers were barely able to let go. Nastasía's limp body was draped over Father's shoulder as she lay asleep in his arms.

The temperature had dropped drastically, and I was grateful for the cowhide moccasins grandfather had made for me the year before. In our villages we children often ran barefoot in late spring and summer. We enjoyed the feel of the cool grass tickling our toes. But on the roads, for hours on end while carrying our heavy loads, it was difficult.

Our first night on the road was spent outside a small Turkish town south of the villages we came from. Father made a simple tent to cover us for the night with one of the blankets and a few sticks. Mother prepared a simple meal, which we could hardly eat without falling asleep between bites. All the greens of the landscape melted together as the red glow of the sunset faded and the sky deepened to a mysterious blue.

And then it was growing light again in a twinkling of an eye. The pink reappeared above the mountains and the sky became pale. Maria was sucking at Mother's breast and Mathea sat contentedly sucking on her tiny fist when I opened my eyes. My first sensation was the feeling that my body had melted into the ground like hot wax that had then frozen. I could feel the aching and the stiffness of my arms and legs. Only by sheer will did I release my body from its bond to the earth as the sound of the Muslim call to prayer drifted on the morning air.

We had bread for breakfast as the sun peeked over the mountain and the throng of uneasy exiles stirred about. Fires smoldered here and there, and a few little children, too young to understand the significance of their journey, raced about playing tag.

Each day the soldiers were replaced with other soldiers from the closest town. As they changed the guard, we folded our blankets and packed our things to continue our journey. The donkey Father bought helped us have some small comforts by lightening our loads. At least we had a few blankets with which to cover ourselves at night when the air was cold, but we also snuggled against one another to help keep warm. But even with the donkey, we each carried a heavy load.

As we set off again, Father tried to load one more thing onto the donkey's back. Its hee-hawing complaint was so noisy and swift, one would think we had cut off its ear. The poor beast sat down then and refused to move until Father unburdened it of some of its bundles.

In the beginning, each day was like the last. We still had food, even though it was meager, and we still had our health. The landscape was lush and green and the fruit and nut trees were in full bloom. Men worked in the fields, carving the earth to prepare it for planting while the women, in their balloon pants, walked behind them scattering seeds or bending to stuff them into the ground. Birds were building their nests, and an occasional stream trickled from a stony crevice in the mountain. So normal and sweet, for everyone but us.

We spent one night in a soldier barracks. The walls were painted white. They herded us in like sheep and let us spread our blankets on the ground. The sound of old people moaning and babies crying could be heard all night, while others fell asleep before their heads touched the ground. The old ones suffered most in the beginning. Later, everyone suffered alike as one day melted into the next.

The old woman whose cows we used to take to pasture didn't last very long. Her frail body gave way in the middle of nowhere. Her son had carried her on and off as best he could but finally sat her on the edge of the road leaning on a rock. She looked dazed as we passed, staring past us with unblinking eyes. One bony hand rested in her lap, the other lay lifeless on the ground beside her, and the soles of her crusty feet gaped at us through the worn-out soles of her shoes.

Almost without noticing, the landscape changed. The trees grew smaller, the rocks grew taller, and the colors changed from green to sand. Little by little, jagged cliffs and parched, coarse earth stretched out before us as far as the eye could see. The sun beat down on us all day without the relief of a saving breeze coming from a tree-lined hillside. At night we lay in our sweaty clothes pressed together to keep warm under our little blanket tents.

We had been on the road for about four months when my shoes wore out completely. Walking through this barren land with bare feet was like walking on pitted glass. The food we had brought was also gone. Each day brought another death, another body left to decompose on the side of the road. Some simply fell dead in their tracks. Their crumpled bodies littered the road like pieces of trash flung from a passing cart, left for buzzards and wolves.

It was good fortune if victims died in the evening when we had stopped for the night. Then the victim's kin could try to cover the body with a few grains of soil, using a spoon or stick to scratch the earth. But in the daytime the soldiers kept our death march moving, ready with their whips to prod us on with a swift, stinging lash.

When our food was gone, Father bought something in the small towns we passed through when the soldiers allowed it or were not looking, but often there was nothing. The sound of crying was a constant companion for the first few months, but even that had diminished as our bodies grew weaker, our minds numbed, and our eyes focused only on the road ahead.

19.

BABIES AND BUZZARDS

THE MARCH WAS a nightmare I have partially wiped from my mind so I could survive. The day-by-day events have disappeared, blended together much the way days blend one into the other in the lands of the midnight sun in summer. Our nights seemed no more than a cloud passing across the dazzling blue of the sky, when we could close our eyes before the sun would begin to shine again, as if time were a continuous stream not divided into zones. Each sweltering day ended not by night and calm, or an evening meal with family gathered around the fire, but by another death, another corpse, another wail of grief tearing a gaping hole in my heart.

Only certain memories come back, but those memories come with a reality that's frightening. I find myself standing before the scene again with glazed eyes. The years are wiped away, and I am ten years old again, seeing and smelling and hearing everything, as if it were before me now. Even with my eyes wide-open, all of my present surroundings disappear, and I am back again on that scabby road to hell. Corpses are lying on stone walls or on the road, lined up like targets at a shooting gallery, while the buzzards that follow us wherever we go, hang like grotesque prizes pinned to the sky.

By the time we reached central Turkey, the weather was so hot, even moving was a chore. Water was scarce, and the sun beat down and sucked the moisture from our lips, splitting them open to bleed against our swollen tongues. Sometimes in the distance, great clear pools of water lay in our path. They would draw our shriveled bodies on, our minds filled with the vision of falling headlong into a cool oasis to replenish our bodies lost sea of sweat and tears. Those who still could, quickened their steps with arms outstretched, grasping toward the moist, wavy air rising from the pool, their bodies falling forward with each step.

But time and again as we drew near, as if by some devil's dirty deed, the pool would grow smaller and smaller and we'd arrive in time to watch the last drops suck together and disappear, only to appear further down the road.

Each day Mathea was heavier on my back, and my clammy, long-sleeved dress, thick with dust and perspiration, stuck to me like wet glue. With each passing day, Mother seemed more debilitated, perhaps from the extra strain of nursing the twins without proper food or water. At the edge of a small town, there was a water fountain with water flowing continuously, spilling its cool treasure into a stone bowl, then overflowing onto the ground, turning the stones around it black.

I had never seen Mother so in need of anything before. She had always been the graceful, patient jewel the Turks rightly named *Küzel*. But Mother left the file to stumble to the fountain. The exiles stopped and watched expectantly, ready to race for the fountain also if she succeeded in her quest. But just before she reached it, a Turkish soldier trotted up on his horse spitting out commands. He raised his whip and gave her a lash like one would an ox or a donkey. She fell to her knees as my feet rooted to the earth and my heart slit open. Father threw down his bundles and ran to her.

"Water, please," Mother said to the soldier.

Father tried to raise Mother to her feet.

"Please."

The soldier raised his whip again, spitting out more abuse. He would have hit her again but Father threw his arm around her shoulder and pulled her away.

The disappointment on the marchers' dirt-streaked faces was barely noticeable. It was more like numbness that showed in their eyes, the numbness that comes from deprivation and prolonged defeat. Mother stumbled back to her place as the others turned like robots to continue their march.

Was it on that day that little Maria died? I don't remember. I only remember her little body tied to Cristodula's back like a papoose, her little head bobbing back and forth, and the realization that something was wrong crept up my hot body with a cold, clammy, panic.

"Mama!" I said as calmly as I could, hoping my calmness would make everything all right. "Maria looks funny."

Mother looked up and burst into tears. Maria's face had turned ashen. Her eyes stared out at nothing like little doll eyes that were broken in an open position, and her head rolled back and forth with each step.

"What's wrong?" Cristodula demanded in a panic. "What is it?"

We stopped in the road like a pile of stones in a river; the weary exiles ruptured out around us and continued their march. Mother took Maria from Cristodula's back and cradled her in her arms as her tears washed Maria's lifeless face.

"Move!" a soldier shouted as he trotted up to where we stood.

"My baby," Mother said.

She held out Maria for the soldier to see, as if her shock and grief could also be his.

"My baby."

"Throw it away if it's dead!" he shouted. "Move!"

"Let me bury her," Mother pleaded, sobbing.

"Throw it away!" He shouted again, raising his whip. "Throw it away!"

Mother clutched Maria's body to her breast as we stood staring up at him. Her face was gripped with a torment I had never seen before. Father reached for Maria, to put her down I suppose, but Mother clutched her even more tightly. Then she walked over to the high stone wall that separated the road from the town and lifted Maria up to lay her on the wall's top as if on an altar before the Almighty.

That night Mother cried herself to sleep. And each time I closed my own eyes, I saw her holding Maria up to the heavens like an offering. The image of her lifeless body lying on the wall, like some gift in a pagan ritual, followed me even into my dreams and all through the next days. Each time I thought of my little sister left lying there alone in the burning sun, with the buzzards flying about waiting for us to pass, the sobs would come without my ability to control them.

It was always with great relief each day when the call to prayer halted our march. We all secretly prayed it would come in or near a town so we could try to find food and water. The soldiers got down from their horses then and knelt on their little mats facing east. They bowed to touch their foreheads to the ground in supplication, steadying themselves with their hands. Their rifles and whips rested on the ground by their sides as a mullah's voice called out from a minaret: *"Allahu akbar."* "God is great."

20.

HOLDING DEATH IN MY ARMS

W<small>E HAD BEEN</small> on the road for so long that our money was gone. Clothes and household things were strewn on the road behind us, left because their owners had died or were just too weak to carry them further. People had taken to begging when we passed villages or towns. Some of the Turks along the way took pity, stuffing a piece of bread into an outstretched hand as we passed. Others just stared.

On one of our stops, I took the beautifully colored beads from around my neck that Grandfather had brought me from Fatsa and held them out to sell for something to eat. But before I could try to exchange them for a piece of bread or cheese, a boy appeared from under the arm of a man who stood nearby. He grabbed the beads from my hand, then disappeared again. I stood staring down at my empty hand in disbelief, my country heart unused to treachery of that kind.

If it rained at night, Father dug a little trench around our makeshift tent with a stick or spoon to keep the rain from soaking onto our blanket and our bodies. It was good when it rained. The soft pattering on the blanket above our heads at night was a small comfort to the scorching heat of the day.

One morning, after rain had pelted our tent throughout the night, we woke to a clear sky and a loud cry of anguish that rivaled the brilliance of the morning. Not far from where we stood, a boy lay on the ground. He lay on his side with his legs drawn up and his body curled as if in sleep. His father bent over him sobbing, his huge graying mustache dripping tears. I recognized him at once. His voice shot through my memory.

"You will marry my son one day! You mark my words. You will marry my son one day."

Through his sobbing, the dead boy's father tried to shake his son awake. Then he lifted his son's stiff and frozen body off the ground to cradle the boy's head in his arms. The boy's parents dug a shallow grave on the side of the road with only their hands to use as tools. The father tried to straighten his son's legs to lay him to rest, but they were already frozen in place. We left him lying there in his shallow grave covered with a few grains of soil as if he were still asleep.

Further down the road we saw Despina, the beautiful, promising girl who read so well, lying dead under a bush. Her arms had been carefully folded over her breast. Her soiled dress was pulled down to cover her swollen legs. Her bare, blood-stained toes pointed to the sky. Tucked beneath her folded arms was a book, her constant companion.

All along the road, one haunting image after another assaulted my eyes, and as we got further south they were more and more numerous. A newborn baby, dropped from her mother's womb, lay in the dust, still covered with its skin of blood. Patches of soil clung to it to form a gruesome shell. Its mother lay beside it in a pool of her own blood.

And each day the heat increased. Father sold the donkey to buy food. Most of our things were then left behind because we were too weak to carry them. North of Diyarbakir, French relief workers stood on the side of the road handing out bread to the exiles. Maybe they gave us more. I don't remember. Maybe there were other countries that also sent aid, but for some reason, only the French stand out in my mind.

Some of the exiles walked on the scorching, desert crust surrounding Diyarbakir with only their calluses to protect their torn feet from the gritty soil. The air was stiflingly hot and when the wind blew, the air became even hotter. Mud-brick houses clustering together in groups of four or five near a lone, dusty tree, occasionally dotted the barren landscape. They sat in the blinding sun like children's castles on a dry beach after the waves had washed away the fancy peaks. Only the wide, white-painted borders accenting their windows and doors gave them distinction.

I don't remember if we crossed the river near Diyarbakir. Maybe we walked across in a shallow spot. And I don't remember which of its four gates we entered through, whether we came from the north or west. But in the evening, we stumbled through a giant door and passed through that sprawling city of heat and dust with barely the strength to place one foot before the other. The huge stone wall surrounding the city towered over us.

In Karabahçe, a town on the other side of Diyarbakir, they let us sleep in a church that night. Our family was given a small closet of a room to lay down our blanket on the floor. Father went out to sell his gold watch to buy us food. Nastasía had fallen ill. Her eyes were lusterless and she slept most of the time, waking only to relieve her running bowels. I lay her across my body to keep her warm and off the ground. Yanni slept soundly. Mother held Mathea to her breast. Cristodula was also sick.

"Themía," Cristodula asked in a pitiful voice. "Please get me some water?"

"No," I said. "I don't want to."

I would have had to go into the town to look around for water. It wasn't a simple thing of going to a sink and turning a faucet. I was so tired. In my ten short years of life, I had walked enough for a lifetime. But to this day, I wish I could take back my answer. I would gladly walk a hundred miles to bring her water now.

Nastasía was up and down all evening. She'd open her eyes and ask me to take her to relieve herself. Her bowels had been running for many days. I will never forget the last time I took her out, then came back again to lay her across my chest and cradle her sweet curly head on my arm. Her head fell back and her eyes began to roll, and from her throat came such an eerie, gurgling sound.

"Why is she making that noise, Mama?" I asked. The pain and defeat in my mother's face was heartbreaking.

"Because she's dying," was all my mother could answer before she burst into tears.

I froze. My arm stiffened. My heart stopped beating and I couldn't take a breath. With bulging eyes and open mouth I stared down at little Nastasía, torn between my love for her, and the terror of holding death in my arms.

Then, in only a moment, she was gone. I lay there, afraid to take my arm from under her lifeless head, my own body rigid as a corpse, until Mother took her from my arms, crying a sea of tears.

Each time I closed my eyes to sleep that night, the sight of Nastasía's head rolling on my arm replayed itself before my closed eyes. The sound of her dying mingled with the sound of Mother's grief, until I lay almost in a trance, suspended between two realities: the cold stone floor on which I lay, with the sights and sounds of death and dying, hunger and tears constantly before my eyes and in my ears, and the dreamlike reality of our lush mountain home.

With each new sound of death, so like the last and yet so different, I found myself slipping away in my mind on my own secret journey to the life I had loved. I carried those memories with me like a child carries a rattle, shaking it now and then to shut out the sadness, and shaking it even harder each time I was struck by another insult to my senses.

I had finally surrendered to sleep when we heard the soldier's command. "We will move out in twenty minutes!"

I tried to rub the sleep from my eyes. I felt again as if my body were glued to the floor, a feeling I had become accustomed to on our seven-month march. But each time I tried to raise myself from my new spot on the earth, I felt as if I had never been so tired before. My spirit was willing to obey if it had to, but my body would not rise to the soldier's command. It just lay there fused to the cold, hard ground. My eyes too, found it difficult to focus. The lids kept sliding shut if I dared let go the thought of rising, even for a moment.

"Come, Themía," Mother's voice said softly, slipping in between me and the floor of the church. Almost in a dream her voice came to me, but the power of that gentle voice lifted my head and moved my shoulders up until I found myself standing, not sure how I had arrived on my feet.

Church bells tolled, a deep, resonant sound. Outside the gray walls of the church, the sun peered over the edge of Karabahçe like a huge flaming caldron. Long shadows clutched the bloody feet of the exiles as they stood waiting, shuffling about in the low morning sun. Then we began to move like a giant insect, rippling along the crusty earth, as the night's dew steamed from the surface of the road.

Corpses littered the way. They lay helter-skelter, bloated in the extreme heat, like abandoned balloons from a child's parade. The acrid odor was everywhere. It burned my throat and eyes and seeped into every crevice of my being.

Was it only a few short months ago that I used to awaken to the sound of crickets and the smell of lush, moist mountain air, instead of the constant wailing of mourners and babies crying?

I closed my eyes and walked along. But with my eyes closed, the stench brought the picture of the dead even more vividly to my mind. Mathea felt heavy on my back. I could feel her little head resting against my neck and her hair tickling my ear. Cristodula was ill but she bravely dragged herself along. Mother's face was swollen with tears and Father was saddled down with so many bundles, it seemed only a mule could have carried more.

As the sun rose higher in the clear blue sky, the heat rose up from the baked earth. It burned my skin; the hot, dry air mingled with the stench of death and burned my nostrils.

I felt as if I were floating above the surface of the ground, carried in a trance in slow motion. With each step I took I became lighter, until I felt I took no step at all; my body just glided along suspended. In the distance, water rippled on the road in a great pool that pulled me along like a magnet. I could hear children laughing and screaming with delight. I could even hear Grandfather's voice as if he were beside me.

"Rub it with more cow manure," Grandfather shouted. "That will make it go faster."

I picked up the slab of wood we used as a sled and ran over to a pile of fresh manure lying in the grass. I rubbed the underside of the sled over the manure, then on the grass again and again, working the manure into the wood more deeply with each application.

"Now try it," Grandfather shouted.

On the grassy knoll they were all assembled; Mother was there, and Father, and even Grandfather and Grandmother sat calmly watching as we children slid down the hillside on our slicked-up sled. I could hear their laughter as I raced to the top of the hill with my friend, Marigoula, and lay the sled on the soft grass.

Nastasía ran to me to jump into my lap. Yanni jumped aboard behind me. I clutched Nastasía to me tightly so she wouldn't fall, her back pressed against my chest, her curly head resting against my cheek. Yanni gave a push and we were off, gliding down so quickly I could barely catch my breath.

"Yea!" Yanni shouted. "Wahoo!"

"Wahoo!" Nastasía echoed, sucking in her breath half in fear.

"Me! I'm next!" Marigoula screamed with delight as we zipped by.

Our country house was perched on a hillside beside a beautiful lake higher in the mountains. I loved to watch the breeze ripple the surface of the water in rows of tiny finger waves. Water spiders skated where an inlet protected it from the wind, and the branches of the berry bushes were reflected in the water like deep tendrils, as white, billowy clouds floated on the surface.

"No!" a pitiful voice cried, and the deep wretched wail filled the sky and shattered my sweet reverie.

I looked around to find a young woman sitting on the ground. Her eyes were open but blank. She sat with one leg tucked beneath her and the other stretched out as though she were about to take another step when she fell. Her chest was still, as still as her lifeless eyes. Beside her a young man had thrown his head into her lap against her swollen, pregnant stomach. His body convulsed in great sobs.

"No!" her mother cried over and over again as she knelt before her child. She clutched the girl's head to her breast. "No!" and the sound reverberated through my whole being. It filled up my ears and my eyes and spread like a thick, heavy carpet over the vast, suffocating space before us.

I recognized the girl, and the young man too: Dmitri and Merlina, the young lovers in the church that day. The ones who had run away and finally married.

In the distance the church bells tolled again, and for a moment I again saw the yellow flicker of candlelight dance in my mother's eyes and heard the familiar, velvet voice of the priest chanting a prayer. The sun shot down a shaft of light that made merry with the particles that floated in the air while the lovers secretly stretched out their hands to steal a forbidden touch.

"No!" Merlina's mother cried, again shattering my reverie. "No!"

I longed to race down the hillside once more on our little patch of green by the cool water. I longed to see Merlina and Dmitri racing before me with the whole village running alongside.

"No!" I also shouted inside my brain. "No! No! No! No!" But no one heard except me.

21.

THE GREAT ESCAPE

By THE TIME we stopped for the night, and even through most of that day's march, I was only semiconscious some of the time. For the rest of the time I must have been lost in another world.

It's clear I arrived at the night's destination with the others, but I don't remember getting there. Even before my head touched the hard ground I was fast asleep. Great waves of heat and cold passed through me, and in my delirium, a great, barren mountain sprang up and threatened to topple over and crush me like a tiny insect. I stretched out my hands to hold it back, but it grew larger and larger until I fell backward on the ground and covered my face with my hands. I lay there expecting to be buried alive at any moment, but when I opened my eyes again, I found a road starting at my feet that went straight to the top of the mountain. I tried to rise but my limbs would not move. I pulled with all my strength, but still I could not move. With my head pressed against the ground I could hear a great thundering of horse's hooves crashing against the desert floor. The sound came from all directions like the sound of an army charging toward an enemy in battle. They drew nearer and nearer. My heart pounded inside my breast.

"Rise!" I told my body but it would not move. Long tendrils grew from my limbs and dug into the ground to root me like a tree. Again I pulled with all my might to free myself as the sound of the hooves grew nearer.

"Rise!" I shouted to myself again, but I could not rise. The roots kept growing and spreading and the more I pulled, the tighter they bound me to the earth.

In the distance I could see the soldiers galloping toward me with swords drawn. Their eyes were like black holes burned into their skulls above huge teeth that spread in hideous, evil grins across their faces.

"Help me, Grandpa," I finally whimpered. "Help me." And no sooner had the words fallen from my mouth then I felt something snap. My hand was free, then a knee. I felt a movement under me as if someone crawled about below the surface of the earth. Another snap and another limb was set free. I felt another movement on the other side, smaller than the first, and a sound like someone gnawing at my tendrils with tiny teeth. And yet another and another, each crawling below me, biting or snapping my bonds until little by little they were loosened. Then hands, little hands like a baby's, and child's hands, and great, strong, sturdy hands, and hands strong but gentle, pushed me to my feet.

"Run, Themía, run." Was it Nastasía's laugh I heard as I rose up and ran for the mountain? And Maria's?

I ran as fast as I could toward the top. I could feel the coal-black eyes of the soldiers envelope me from all sides as the horses started up the mountain so close behind me that their hot breath seared my back. My flesh burned. I ran faster and faster.

My mother. I must bring my mother.

I turned to find the earth crumbling beneath the horses' hooves as they struck the ground, as if it was being pulled out from under them from within. Mother stood below unable to move. Her feet too had grown tendrils that rooted her to the earth.

"Save her," I shouted. "Save her."

"Themía," Mother's plaintive voice came to me.

"Save her," I shouted again.

"Themía. Wake up, Themía."

I opened my eyes in terror, still sobbing from the nightmare. A cold, clammy sweat covered my burning body. Mother was kneeling beside me.

"Wake up, dear," she whispered again. "We're leaving."

The sky was still dark. Not even a flicker of light shown to indicate the rising of the sun. They all kneeled around me, Mother and Father, Cristodula, and Yanni.

"They were coming to get me Mama. Men on horses. And I couldn't move."

"Tell me later. There's no time now. Be really quiet and wrap up your blanket."

"But it's still dark. Where are we going?"

"Shhh. We're going away."

"But my dream, Mama. My dream."

She gently put her fingers to my lips to silence me.

"Later I will listen to it all," she said, "but right now we must be very quiet and we must hurry."

I got up and rolled up my blanket and tied it to carry on my back. We crouched down low and stole between the sleeping figures on the ground. The soldier that slept on the other side snored loudly as we passed. His hand clutched his rifle. Near the end of the mass of sleeping people, other soldiers sat together talking. An occasional laugh cut through the darkness, the only indication of where they were. There was no moon and the night was so dark it was difficult to see two feet in front of us. But we blessed the darkness as our only cover for escape.

As we approached closer to the soldiers, a horse whinnied. We dropped to the ground so quickly I was sure they heard. My heart pounded and my breath came in short, uncontrollable eruptions. A soldier looked around to search the darkness, then turned back to the others. Again they laughed. And after a moment, we again began to steal through the crowd. Near the end of the sleeping figures, just across from the soldiers, the horse whinnied again. This time the soldier rose and turned toward us. We hit the ground and lay as quietly as we could, but my heart was beating so loudly, I thought surely he could hear it. It banged in my ears with such a deafening sound that it was hard to believe it came from within my chest. It sounded like a drum beating out a monotonous message, announcing, "We are here. We are here. We are here."

And then, as the soldier again turned back to his comrades and we again rose to steal away, someone grabbed my leg. A scream welled up inside me. My heart stopped as I started to form a scream. But Father threw his hand across my mouth and pulled me to the ground. I trembled there locked in his arms, staring down at the hand that grabbed my leg. Only after some moments that seemed an eternity, did I realize the hand was not a hand at all, but only a piece of damp cloth hanging from Father's sack that had fallen across my leg.

Father held me close until I could breathe again.

"Are you all right now?" he whispered.

I tried to control my shaking.

"Yes," I said.

This time we made it past the sleepers and past the soldiers. Again we crouched down and waited to be safe before going on. And again the moments passed like an eternity until we finally rose again, and half-standing, slipped away.

It was a moonless night. The black sky above us was filled with a multitude of stars. Each twinkled so innocently in that vast chasm that reached to the ground in all directions. Not even a mound barred its descent. I could feel a tug like gravity on my chest; the vastness, the enormity of the universe enveloped me in blackness and lifted me up so powerfully, I could barely breath.

And then, "I think we are finally free," Father said, and the air suddenly rushed through me, filling every crevice. I felt I could embrace the whole world with my enormous arms, could hug it to my chest like a child's toy balloon and still have room to reach for more, all the way to the stars.

𝔜 𝔜 𝔜

We walked along in the dark stumbling on stones toward Karabahçe. Now and then we were assaulted by the stench of death deposited on the road. I was glad I couldn't see the corpses lying there in the darkness, but I clutched Mother's arm in mine to give me courage. She walked along silently. Only when I felt a tear fall on my arm did I realize she was weeping.

"If we go on, we will lose them all," Mother had told Father after Nastasía's death a few days earlier. It was then they had resolved to escape when we got the chance.

As we walked toward the north, the air began to feel suddenly cooler. The temperature seemed to drop twenty degrees. We found ourselves beside a small oasis covered with lush green trees, so odd in that desert.

"Let's rest here," Father said.

He led us off the road and under the trees to a pool of water. We threw down our bundles and almost fell on the cool ground. A wave of nostalgia swept over me as I closed my eyes and sucked into my lungs the fresh moist air. I filled them up again and again until I became light-headed and dizzy.

As I drifted into sleep, little lights flared behind my closed eyes like fireflies sparkling on black velvet. And in my dream I once again lay on my mat back home. The sound of my parents' voices were soothing in the dark. They lay together on the far side of the room. A cool breeze drifted through the open window, and Nastasía snuggled up against me. I felt her warm body against my chest and her curls tickling my chin. I wrapped my arms around her and we slept like two spoons tucked together on a shelf.

My parents' voices were soft but clear.

"I must go to her and say I'm sorry," Mother was saying.

"But you did no wrong," Father said.

"I must still go to her. I don't want to die with anger on my conscience."

"But she is the one who has a son who is a rapist. She raised him and you only told of your concern that her daughter should join our family. You were right in your concern," he said.

"What difference does it make who is wrong and who is right? Can we ever really know where life will lead us?" Mother said. "Can we ever be sure that ours will not go astray one day? It was not my place to say it. I said it without thinking in the heat of the moment. No. I was not right. I foolishly lay the burden of fate on her shoulders. She's a good woman who suffers the consequences each day just knowing of her son's misdeed. Who am I to add to her suffering? No," she said after a moment's reflection. "Tomorrow I will go to her and say I am sorry."

"Come, *Küzel*," Father said, using the name the Turks called her. And in my mind's eye I saw him wrap his arms around her and press her lovely head to his strong chest.

It seemed only a moment later that the sky began to brighten and birds begin to sing in the treetops. I opened my still-sleepy eyes just for an instant to find the green light that filtered through the trees washing over me, and a calmness filled my body. The cool air refreshed my mind as I slowly came to my senses.

I wondered why we had left our beds and chose to sleep in the forest for the night, but with a smile at the pleasure of being under the trees and feeling the fresh, moist air, I reached to pull Nastasía even closer. I could still feel her pressed against my chest. But my arms were empty. Confused, I opened my eyes and looked down to where I thought I'd find her, expecting to see with my eyes what my arms could not feel.

I remembered the conversation between Mother and Father, the one I had just dreamed, and remembered it had not only been a dream. It had once happened just as I dreamed it. But that was so long ago in another lifetime.

I thought again of Nastasía. Only the cool, fresh air that reminded me of home and the sound of Mother's voice kept me from being swept away by grief.

"We only have some small pieces of bread for the children when they wake," Mother was saying. "We must find food for them."

"Wake them," Father said.

"Mama," I said. "Can't we stay here?"

"No," she said. "This place doesn't belong to us. Wake your brother and sister. We must leave before someone finds us here."

"I'm awake," Yanni said.

He rubbed his eyes and gave a long stretch. "I'm hungry."

"Come! Get up and I'll give you some bread."

"I'm awake too," said Cristodula. "Mama, can't we go home now?"

"No. We're too far away," she said. "Come have some bread."

"Well can't we just walk and walk until we find our way back? I'm so tired of sleeping on the ground and seeing and smelling death and eating only bread and water. I'm tired Mama. I'm tired and I want to go home."

"I know," Mother said and began to cry. "We're all tired, and we all want to go home. But we can't. We don't have the strength or the food or money to buy food."

"But they said we would be going back."

"Yes I know," Mother said. "But they lied."

"It will be very hot again," Father said. "We must hurry before the heat increases."

"Come," Mother said, wiping her eyes. "Eat some bread to give you strength so we can leave."

We wrapped up our things and headed toward Karabahçe as the great blazing ball of the sun rose slowly above the horizon, and for an instant hesitated, and rested lightly on the ground.

Sano and Zohra (standing), Nana holding Arexine, and Hagop holding Sonja in Aleppo, Syria, 1925

Sano and Abraham on their wedding day, March 24, 1925

Circa 1915. Abraham in trolley car uniform. He added a sword and rifle and scratched a cigarette on his lip for fun.

Abraham (right) at age twenty-six with brother Amos in America in 1905

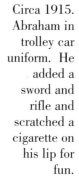

Circa 1921. Abraham and Farage

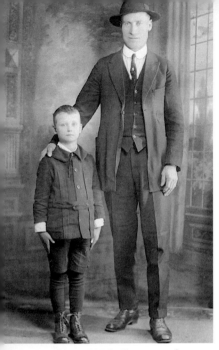

Circa 1922. Farage and Abraham

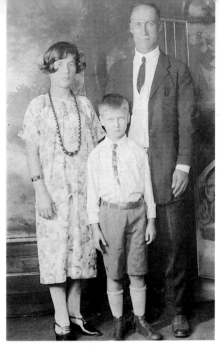

Sano, Abraham, and Farage in 1925

Farage, Sano holding Harton (Harty), Abraham, and (sitting) Mariam and Helyn in 1931

Circa 1938. Helyn, Harty, Jamie (Mitzi), Amos, David

Harty and Helyn with ducks, 1940

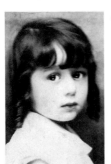

David, eight years old, 1944

Sano in her early twenties

Circa 1937. Amos at two and a half years

In Central Park, 1939. Mariam (standing in back); from left to right, Helyn, Jamie, Harty; and (in front) David, Amos, and Abraham holding Tim

Thea, one year old, wearing vest and shirt Sano made from a man's scarf

Back row from left to right: Jamie, Harty, Helyn, and (standing) Amos and David, and Sano holding Tim, with ducks in Central Park, 1940

Abraham, at around age sixty-five

Timothy, David, Adrian, and Thea on Halloween

Sano, Jonathan, and Thea

Thea, Henri, and Adrian, each wearing tiny dolls Sano crocheted clothes for and made into pins

Circa 1951. Abraham, Adrian, and Mariam's son, Henri

Adrian wearing an Alice in Wonderland dress Sano made; one for Adrian, one for Thea

Thea's sixth-grade graduation, wearing dress Sano made, in front of 153 West 102 Street

Sano with grandchildren Tasha and Cezanne (Helyn's children), 1960

Circa 1950. Sano and Mariam

Thea, one
year old, in
Spotswood,
New Jersey

Sano in Spotswood, New Jersey,
cooking over open fire

Thea and Tim, in Spotswood,
New Jersey

Adrian and Sano at beach

Adrian and Jonathan in Spotswood,
New Jersey

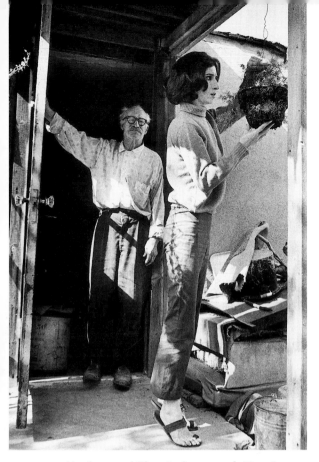

Circa 1945. Pop's house in Spotswood, New Jersey

Abraham and Thea in Spotswood, New Jersey, Thea wearing her "ten-minute pants" [photo by Gordon Parks, Jr.]

Adrian and Mariam in Spotswood, New Jersey. Elias's house is in the background

Adrian, Mariam holding her son Henri, and Thea, in Spotswood, New Jersey

Great-granddaughter Alexis (David's granddaughter), with Sano at age eighty-nine, in 1999

Sano and Thea (in mirror) in Spotswood, New Jersey [photo by Gordon Parks, Jr.]

Spotswood, New Jersey, firemen burning Abraham's house, 1974

Abraham at age ninety in front of his garden with grandchildren (Jamie's children) Lilli-ann and Alex, 1970

22.

THE GREAT GIVEAWAY

SOMETIME IN THE afternoon, when the sun had already heated the air so hot our breath evaporated even before it left our bodies, and the roads of hard, baked soil burned our feet through our calluses, we arrived at the edge of the town called Karabahçe. Nastasía had died in my arms there, and for the first time I looked around as we approached. The walls of many of the homes were broken down. Sometimes only a wall or two remained and, if one was lucky, part of a roof.

We moved into the same abandoned church we had slept in on the way south a few days before. To our surprise, other Greeks from our villages were already there occupying the ruins. Our priest was also there. Each family took a room, or at least a corner of a room.

As soon as we put down our bundles in the church, Mother said, "I must go to find food."

"Where will you find food?" Father said.

"I will go and beg for it. The children need food. And Mathea is sick."

"I'll come too," I said. I grabbed her arm and pressed myself close to her.

The houses we passed looked like they housed people almost as poor as we were. We walked on past them, perhaps not having the heart to knock on their doors to beg. We walked until we came to a field on the edge of the town. Mother ran to it and threw herself on the ground. She dug into the hard soil with her bare hands until she pulled from it a few roots. She stuffed them into her pockets and dug some more. How desperate that gesture of her body, bent over the ground, kneeling on both knees and clawing the hard, dry soil until her nails were filled with earth and her callused fingers assumed its color. She dug the ground with the devotion of a mother who is watching her offspring walk toward the gates of Hades as she frantically paddles across the river of death to get to them before they step forever into the abyss. Her dress was soaked with sweat. A look of fear mingled with a look of horror as she clawed the roots from their grave. Her own blood left little droplets of crimson on the tan earth. I knelt beside her to dig also, but my fingers couldn't break the earth's crust.

"Go to the field there, Themía," Mother said. "Collect the wheat along the edges where the ox has not passed to cut it."

And like Ruth in the Bible, I walked along the fringe of the wheat field breaking the abandoned stalks and laying them in the pouch I made of my scooped-up dress, until my hands were blistered from the unyielding shafts.

"Did you find food?" Father asked when we entered our little room in the church.

"Yes," Mother said. "It's not much, but it will help. But we must make a fire to cook it."

"I don't remember seeing wood here for a fire," Father said after some reflection. "How do they cook here?"

"I asked them in the village. They use cow manure baked in the sun until it's dry. Then they break it up and use it for fuel. Maybe someone will give us some to use until we can prepare some of our own," Mother said.

It was the first time we sat together without soldiers looming over us since we left our village, and for a moment, sitting by the fire and eating together, I forgot that there had ever been a march and the death along the way receded into the background. All I could see was the firelight once again on my mother's beautiful face as she knelt before it to blow on the flames.

"Tomorrow I will look for work," Father said. "Perhaps someone needs some labor to be done."

Mathea, who had always been such a healthy child, lay across Cristodula's lap sleeping peacefully for the first time that day. We slept again in the one little room we had slept in before, all tucked together on the few blankets we had left. Mathea was feverish and Mother tended her almost the whole night. In between sleeping and waking, I dreamt of a large group of people milling about. Someone was handing out food and they were all eating. It was one of those curious dreams that is so vivid one can actually taste the grain licked from one's open palm. The sound of the crowd murmuring and shuffling about still rang in my ears upon waking, and it was only with great astonishment that I found myself in another place, as if I had been transported by the wave of a magician's wand in that blink of an opening eye.

"What does it mean?" I asked Mother on rising.

It saddened her to hear my dream. She lowered her eyes and wiped her hands on her apron, weighing all the possibilities before answering me.

"My sister's baby must have died," she said.

And yes. It was a dying dream. People were eating like at a funeral, all milling about in a large crowd. We had lost touch with everyone. Even my step-grandmother and Uncle Constantine and his family were no longer with us.

"If we don't get better food for them we will lose these children too," Mother said. "I am afraid for Mathea."

Each day we went again to find food. We knocked on doors, no longer having the luxury of choosing not to when our digging in the field left us empty-handed. And each day we walked further from Karabahçe, until we came to a village, mud-brick like the others, only smaller, named Tlaraz. There too, the houses were the color of the earth, but the windows and doors were not painted white like in other villages. Some houses had a little courtyard around them. In the rear of the house the buildings seemed to grow out of the earth itself, using a mound of earth for the back wall.

The roof was mud too, a kind of clay-mud. When it rained, which was rare, they used a huge roller to roll out any cracks that had formed so the roof wouldn't leak. The embankment made it easy to climb to the roof without any trouble.

There were only five houses. We walked from house to house collecting little bits and pieces that some kind souls gave us.

"What a beautiful girl," a woman said when she opened her door to our knocking.

"We are hungry," Mother said. "I have children waiting in the next village with nothing to eat. Can you spare something for them?"

It amazed me how Mother could beg yet still hold her head high.

"Why don't you give me this one?" the woman said in reply. "You have enough to worry about and I will take good care of her. She can help me with my children."

"Oh, no!" Mother said. "I can't do that. She doesn't belong to me. I'm sorry."

"But she looks so much like you," the woman said. "Ah well, if you change your mind I will take her. At least then you won't have to worry about her anymore."

She gave us some grain then and we went on our way.

"Why did you say I wasn't yours?" I asked my mother.

"I didn't want to hurt her feelings," Mother said.

Then she stopped walking and looked into my face. Tears crept into her eyes and she threw her arms around me and held me to her breast.

"I couldn't bear to give you away," she said.

She held me tightly for some moments before letting me go. I could feel her chest heaving uncontrollably. She held my face against her breast so I couldn't see her tears but they fell on my head and cheek like crystallized drops of desert rain.

When the sun was low in the sky, Mother sat down on a stone and spread her apron to reveal the food we had gathered for that day. It was barely enough for two, let alone six. She stared down at it for a long time as if willing it to multiply. Then she closed her eyes and began to sob.

"Maybe you should stay with that woman for a while," she said. "She'll feed you and then you'll be safe, and I can come back to see you."

"All right," I said. I don't remember a time when I said no to my mother.

"Have you decided to leave her then?" the woman asked in Turkish when she opened the door.

"Yes," Mother said. "If you promise to take good care of her."

"Of course," the woman said.

Mother turned to me. "I will visit you," she said. "You must remember how much I love you; how much I love all of you."

She wrapped her arms around me and pulled me close, tucking my head between her breasts and kissing me on top of my head over and over again. She held me so tightly I could barely take a breath, but I melted into her until I couldn't tell where she ended and I began.

When she let go, she took the belt she had woven from around her own waist and wrapped it around mine. Again she pulled me to her breast and held me tight, imprinting my image onto her own body.

Again she let go and this time walked away without looking back.

I stood with the woman in the doorway of her home watching my mother walk away. Even when the woman went inside the house, I still stood there watching my mother grow smaller and smaller, until she was no more than a tiny line on the horizon that turned to vapor and disappeared in the waves of heat rising from the ground.

23.

RAVEN, RAVEN

THE HOUSE WAS dark inside, at least once you left the walled courtyard and entered the corridor that divided the house in two. It ran down
the center and ended in a room where the cows lived in winter. A low
wall, about eighteen inches high, ran across the front of the cow room to
keep them from roaming into the other quarters. Before the place where
the cows were kept, was a small room that served as a bathroom. A large
jug of water sat in one corner to pour over oneself to wash. There was a
hole in the ground like a Turkish toilet hole with a pipe that led the waste
to the back of the house and outside. Off the corridor to the left as you entered the house, was the room where the people lived. There too, a low
wall, which one had to step over to enter, ran the length of the room to
keep the cows out. On the other side of the corridor was the supply room,
again protected from the cows by a low wall.

"What is your name?" the woman asked me in Arabic.

I looked at her not understanding.

"Your name," she said again, this time in Turkish.

"Themía," I said.

"Th—Th," she struggled.

"The-mía," I said.

"Come. I will show you your new home," she said.

We turned off the hall into the small room on the left. The
floors were made of hardened clay, the walls of mud smoothed over then
dried to a hard surface. There was one window that let the brilliant sunlight fill the room and bounce around the dull clay walls. Against the
back wall there was a place to cook. It was a kind of indoor barbecue pit
where they burned the dried cow dung they used as fuel. A metal grill

rested on the built-up sides to the left and right, and hung over the flames.

"This is where we cook and sleep," she said in Turkish. "You can help me care for the children."

She shuffled about on leather slippers with the heels pushed down. Now and then, I peered up at her to get a better look. She was a short woman, somewhat stocky in build, with sturdy hands and feet. Her face was round with small eyes set deep into her skull, and when she spoke, her voice came sharp and piercing like a raven's, even when she was at peace.

Although she was not beautiful, she was not ugly either. She talked on and on but all my attention became fixed on the sound of her raven's voice and the way her thin lips moved when the words flew out of her mouth.

"Well? Why don't you answer me?"

I looked around in astonishment to see if she could be talking to someone else.

"I didn't hear you," I mumbled shyly when I found the room empty except for two small children sleeping in a corner of the room.

"You must learn to speak Arabic. That is our language here. We are not Turks in these villages. We are Assyrians. And there are also Kurds. You don't speak Turkish well either, do you?"

"No," I said. I kept my eyes glued to the ground.

"Do you know how to cook?"

"No," I said.

"Well, you will learn. Go into the storeroom and bring some bulgur," she said.

I took the clay bowl from her outstretched hand and crossed the corridor. In the supply room all the foodstuff was kept in barrels: wheat, barley, a pasta called orzo for pilaf, and bulgur. I filled the bowl and returned it to the woman. She stirred it into the pot of yogurt cooking in the fireplace. Her plump arm glowed with perspiration.

"I'm hungry," a man's voice said.

I looked up to find two men standing on the threshold.

"Come sit down," she said to them. "The soup is almost ready. What is your name again?"

"Themía," I said.

"Bring my husband and brother bread," she said. "It's over there on the wall."

Her husband was a kind-looking man, thin and tall with dark hair and eyes. His thick eyebrows drooped down on the outside edge of his eyes, which made him look like a man in constant despair. Her brother was also thin and dark, but shorter than her husband. He also seemed kind, even with the resigned expression he wore.

They spoke together in Arabic. I brought the bread and lay it on the mat on the floor where they sat for the evening meal. Then I cut the bread into pieces, and placed them in a pile near the large pot of yogurt and bulgur soup, trying not to notice that they glanced at me now and then as they spoke.

I also sat cross-legged on the cushion the woman pushed over to me. I kept my eyes down, looking at my hands on my lap, afraid they would talk to me and I would have to look at them to answer.

"What is your name?" the husband asked in Turkish as he turned to me.

A hot flash of shame ran through me. I looked at the woman hoping she would answer for me, but she also looked at me as if she saw me for the first time. I looked at her brother, but he stared at me too, waiting.

"Themía," I said.

"Themía?" he said. "So you are going to live with us."

I nodded my head. My hands nervously pulled at each other with a life of their own.

The children, a baby boy, and a five-year-old girl, had awakened. The little girl leaned against my leg and smiled sweetly up into my face, making me smile also.

"The-mía," she said.

Each person sat on a cushion around the pot the soup was cooked in, and reached into it with their spoon. They ate everything else with their hands, using a piece of bread to scoop up the food. In the north of Turkey where I came from, we had a table and stools and we each ate from our own dish with our own spoon. At least the Greeks lived like that. I guess the Turks up north lived the same way the people in the south of Turkey lived, but I didn't know much of that at the time. I had never been in a Turkish home.

And unlike our diet, their diet consisted only of the grains and orzo I found in the supply room, with yogurt and occasionally eggs. The only vegetable was a wild root.

Even though my stomach churned with hunger, each dab of bread soaked in soup that I took, got stuck in my mouth, and I found it difficult to swallow except by sheer will. At night the woman rolled up the eating mat and placed it on the shelf. Then she rolled out the sleeping mats side by side on the floor of the same room about two feet between each one.

"You will sleep here by my children," she said. She pointed to the mat closest to the entrance. "If they get up in the night you can take them to the bathroom."

"All right," I said.

I lay on my back in the dark that night staring at the ceiling, waiting for the murmuring sound of their breathing as in sleep. Each time the man began to snore, he'd jerk up, aroused by his own sound, then mumble and settle back into sleep again. The sound of their breathing, and even the sound of my own breath, and my heart beating, rushed against my ears and filled the room. I felt so big in that tiny room, conscious of every blink of my eyes and breath from my lungs. I fought sleep until I could barely keep my eyes from falling shut, until the whole room began to expand and contract as if it too breathed in and out, crushing and releasing me with each breath.

In the village a few days later, people stared at me as I passed by lugging the two huge jugs on my way to the well a quarter mile up the road. With only five families in the village, there were very few young people. There seemed to be no one my age in the village. They were either older or younger.

Other girls already waited at the well to fill their jugs. The water spilled slowly into a cistern from a pipe. The girls stared at me too as I took my place at the edge of the group to wait my turn. Even when a girl had filled her jugs she didn't leave, but stood staring at me, examining my every move, my every gesture.

I dipped my jugs into the cistern and stared down at the water as it slowly ran into the jugs. I stood with my head bowed. I could feel my cheeks burn with embarrassment as they stared at me. I tried concentrating on my hands holding the jugs. Each moment that passed stretched into eternity. Every move I made was more clumsy than I had ever noticed before. I felt like a thumb in the middle of a palm.

When my jugs were full I awkwardly lifted them out of the cistern one by one.

"Do you have breasts yet?" one girl asked.

I turned around to see if she could be talking to me.

"What?" I said.

"I said, do you have breasts yet?"

"No," I said.

"Let me see," she said.

I crossed my arms in front of me defensively, but before I had a chance to ward her off, she pulled at the collar of my thin dress and peered inside.

"No. You don't have any yet," she said and smirked. "I have some. They're beginning to grow. You want to see them?"

She began to untie the bib she wore that tied around her neck and again under her bosom to make her breasts appear larger than they were. The other girls wore them also.

"No!" I said. The girls giggled.

"Do you speak Kurdish?" she asked.

"No," I said.

"How old are you?" another one asked.

"Ten, I think," I said.

"You think? Don't you know?" she laughed.

I picked up my jugs and began to walk away. I would be glad to be free of them. They were so forward; so unlike the girls I had known in my village. I felt intimidated by their toughness.

"You don't know how to carry water," the first one said.

With each step the jugs banged against my legs. At times they nearly knocked me off my feet.

"I don't?" I said.

"No. The way you carry the jugs makes them too heavy."

"Oh," I said.

"Come, I'll show you," she said. "You must put your finger in the loop and hoist the jug over your shoulder onto your back like this. Then do the same with the other jug on the other side. You can even carry three jugs that way and it won't be too heavy. Watch!"

She hoisted one, then two, then holding the second with the same hand as the first, she hoisted a third on the other side, and balanced all three on her back.

"Oh! Let me try." I said.

For a moment I forgot my discomfort with them, truly impressed by the girl's ability. I hoisted one of the jugs up, but halfway to my back, the strength in my arm gave way and it fell down again, splashing me with water. It almost wrenched itself from my little fingers. The girls laughed.

"You must hoist it harder so it will reach over your shoulder in one step," the girl said.

Again I struggled, and again water splashed, soaking my dress. One girl leaned to another and spoke behind her hand, but loud enough for all to hear.

"Soon it will be lighter. When there's no water left she'll be able to lift them."

"Try again," the first girl said trying to restrain a laugh. "You'll get it."

"Use your knee," another called out.

She then stood back with the rest and watched expectantly as I struggled with the heavy jugs. I hoisted it again, this time to my knee and then over my shoulder in two almost-smooth stages. A great cry went up from the girls.

"I did it. I did it."

"Okay. You're not through yet. Don't get carried away. Now the other one," the girl said.

Again I felt awkward under their stares, but the challenge outweighed my discomfort and in two steps, I hoisted the second jug, spilling only a small amount of water. I wobbled under the weight, but only for an instant.

"I did it," I said again, this time more calmly.

I felt a blush of pride color my face as they stared at me.

"You see those trees?" one girl said, the jugs forgotten.

Five dusty trees sat in the field. There were no others for as far as the eye could see.

"Yes," I said.

"There's a story about those trees. They say each tree represents a person in a wedding. The tallest one is the minister. Then there's the bride, the groom, the best man, and the maid of honor," she said.

I suppose having only five trees made them precious. "Oh," I said and smiled, delighted at her friendliness. But she turned away, and as we walked back to the village together, the girls ignored me and laughed among themselves at things I didn't understand. They spoke in Kurdish to each other and again I felt alien and alone. By the time I arrived at the woman's house, my dress was soaked.

Father was standing in the room with the woman when I entered.

"She died last night," Father was saying.

"Who died, Papa?" I asked.

I held my breath waiting for his answer. Sadness and fatigue clouded his handsome eyes. He looked at me for a moment in silence, then spoke to me in Greek.

"Mathea has died," he said. "She was sick for a long time. She became worse and worse. Yesterday she died. Your mother wanted me to tell you. She is very upset or she would have come herself to see you."

I just stood staring at him not knowing what to say. The tears started falling from my eyes and a thick lump developed in my throat to choke any sound I might try to make.

"She is with your grandfather and Nastasía in heaven now," he said. He knelt down beside me and put his large hand on my shoulder. "And with her twin sister."

"Maybe you can come and cut tobacco for us," the woman said. "We can pay you something for the work."

"I could come tomorrow," he said, "or I can start right now."

He worked for the rest of the afternoon and came for the next few days to chop the tobacco for cigarettes and the water pipe.

"Do they treat you all right here?" he asked me one day when we were alone.

I stood watching his swift hands move with deftness as he slid the sharp knife over the tan leaves of tobacco, chopping them in fine, uniform pieces. *Do they treat me all right?* Most of the time the woman ignored me, only speaking to me when she wanted me to do some chore. She had stopped asking me how to pronounce my name soon after I arrived. It seemed to me she could have said my name if she wanted to, but had deliberately acted as if it was too difficult. After only a few tries, she began to call me *bint,* meaning girl in Arabic.

The men were kind but distant as was proper. The children were very young and full of life. I enjoyed taking care of them. I couldn't eat without feeding them first and sometimes when I got something special, I fed it to them instead. It made me remember my mother. I would never eat anything without offering her the first bite, insisting on sharing it with her no matter what it was.

For a moment in my mind, I sat once again in the silence of my mother's grace. I looked up at my father. I hadn't noticed how tired he looked, or how defeated.

"It's all right," I heard myself say.

"At least they feed you. You look better now," he said. "I'm finished with the tobacco so I won't come again tomorrow, but I will come to visit you one day."

My heart sank. Take me with you I wanted to shout.

"Will Mama come too?" I said.

A troubled look clouded his face.

"I don't know," he said. "She's not well. We'll see."

Each day I waited for him to come, but the days stretched to weeks, and the weeks to months. I watched for his familiar silhouette coming down the road. I watched for my mother too, but she didn't come either.

By Christmas they had still not come to visit. Ruth, the woman I lived with, handed out some raisins and nuts as a Christmas gift to the children and to me too. The holiday seemed so dreary without a branch of pine slowly burning in the fireplace to make a sweet scent. And the birds. Who was to feed the birds for Christmas?

"Here *bint*," Ruth had said when she handed me the gift.

I looked up at her with a smile, grateful for the kindness, which was so rare in her. But the dry look on her face told me she gave the gift only as her duty.

I stared down at the handful of nuts and raisins. Even though my time on earth was still so short, it seemed so long ago now, almost like another lifetime, when my mother had given us our simple gift at Christmas with such love.

I stood waiting in the road, watching, squinting in the sunlight toward the horizon, hoping to see my mother coming toward me out of the rising heat, so I could share my gift with her as I used to so long ago. I stood until the sun was low in the sky. Then I walked down to the place where the water filled the cistern, still clutching the raisins and nuts in my hand. One by one I threw them to the birds. I watched them peck and fly about. Then I sat on a stone to cry.

24

TOUCHING THE HAND OF GOD

C OME HELP MAKE the orzo," Ruth said as she carried a heavy pot of dough out to the courtyard. "Bring the trays and come outside."

I picked up the drying trays made of mesh and wood and followed her out to the yard wearing the new shoes her husband had brought me from Diyarbakir the day before. They were beautiful shoes, red with pointy toes that curled upward and a heel that was shaped like a horse-shoe. They clicked as I walked and Ruth eyed me enviously as she walked beside me.

"Take off those shoes!' she said as we got to the courtyard. "They're no good for you. You can take the other pair my husband brought. Give those to me."

I did as I was told and she kicked off the plain yellow slippers with backs that fold down and pushed them over to me. Then she slipped my shiny red shoes onto her swollen feet.

"Why do you give her those shoes and these plain ones to me?" she had scolded her husband when he presented us with the gifts.

"She's young," he had said. "They are shoes for a young girl."

"Young? Am I so old then? Am I too old for pretty things? Why should she get the prettier shoes?"

"They're not prettier. They're for a young girl."

"So I'm an old hag I suppose."

"Don't bother me with such nonsense," he said.

She had scowled at me for the rest of the night, and in the morning, had slipped her feet into the plain yellow slippers with disgust. Now, as she clicked along in my new red shoes, she smirked smugly to herself.

Other girls and the women of the village came with small mats to sit on the ground. They sat in a circle with their legs folded in front of them so their skirts formed a pocket into which the orzo, when it was formed, could fall from their nimble fingers.

I sat beside Ruth and watched as she yanked a hunk of dough out of the huge bowl and worked it between her fingers. They moved so quickly I could barely see what she was doing. Little oblong bits of pasta, only twice the size of a grain of rice, fell from her hands onto her open skirt as fast as rain falling on the ground.

"What are you waiting for?" Ruth demanded when she realized I only stared at her hands without working.

"I . . . I don't know how," I said.

"Just take a piece of dough. Roll it between your fingers until a small piece falls off. It's very easy," she said.

The bits continued to fly from her fingers.

"Like this?" I said, struggling with a chunk of dough.

"Oh! You're making a mess," Ruth said. "I thought you would be a help to me, but ahk! You're clumsy. You're no good at anything."

"You'll learn in time," another woman of the village said. "Watch my fingers and you'll see how it's done."

"She is just learning," another women offered. "You must be more patient with her, Ruth. She will learn."

"But look how much better she is already," a third woman said. "Already she is learning."

And even though I was slow, and my fingers stumbled, the little bits fell from my hands all the same. Ruth's little girl leaned against my arm and watched my fingers struggle with the dough.

"Why are yours all different sizes?" she said.

I looked around shyly at the other young girls to see if they were laughing at me, but they were busy working the dough.

"My mommy's are all the same size," the child said.

"I know," I said.

Again I looked around to see if the others heard.

"Don't you know how to do it?" she asked.

"I'm just learning," I said.

"She's clumsy," said Ruth. "That's why. Her fingers are stiff like an old woman's."

The little girl examined me intently.

"She doesn't look like an old woman."

"Who is that man who has come to the village and what is he building?" one woman asked no one in particular.

"He's building houses for chickens," another woman said. "They say he will build three of them. My husband is working for him."

"He must have a lot of chickens. The house he finished is six stories high. And where did he get so much wood to build the houses? He must be very rich."

Little by little, now that the conversation had been diverted away from my clumsy first attempts at making pasta, and had settled on other matters, my fingers worked more efficiently and by the end of the day, my grains were not nearly so bad. They fell from my fingers into my skirt with surprising ease. I listened to the voices of the other women as I worked, feeling the warmth of the sun on my back. It was the closest thing I had felt to a home since I had lost my own family, and I soaked up the comfort of their voices as a wilting flower drinks the rain.

The next day, as the orzo we made dried in the sun on the screens, the same group of girls and women assembled again at another home, and the process was repeated for that woman. By the fifth day, all the homes had orzo for the coming months. In time I learned to speak Arabic and even Kurdish. But I spent most of my time alone, always on the outside of things.

🕊   🕊   🕊

"Your father is coming," a girl of the village cried out to me as I swept the courtyard of Ruth's home.

My heart leapt and I ran outside to watch him walk toward the village. His shoulders drooped as if he carried a heavy weight. I raced toward him still carrying the broom and threw my arms around his neck as he knelt to receive me. I held him for a long time, not speaking, grateful to feel the warmth of his body and his embrace. There were so many things I wanted to tell him. I wanted to tell him that I had learned to make orzo with my own hands and even though I was not as good as the other girls who had done it much longer than I, I was not too bad either, and with time, I would be even better. I wanted to tell him how much I missed him and my mother. But as I opened my mouth to speak, he straightened and stared down at me. The look in his eyes told me he wouldn't be interested in my new ability to turn grain into little bits of pasta to thicken soup. A new crease had gathered up the skin in vertical ridges between his eyes. He stared down at me for a long time, his mustache pulling down the corners of his mouth, which he finally opened to speak, then closed again without making a sound.

A few moments passed. He struggled to clear his throat. Again he opened his mouth to speak. But again he closed it without speaking. I stood barefoot in the dusty road staring up at him, still clutching the broom, watching tears form in his eyes.

"Your mother touched the hand of God last night," he said at last with a raspy voice. Each word came with great difficulty as if he found it too painful to speak more plainly.

My mind searched to know what he meant, even though I knew. But I searched wildly through all my recollections to see if there wasn't some other explanation for his words, some other meaning; something less heartbreaking, like praying perhaps, or . . . or . . . but no other explanation came.

He knelt down beside me. I don't remember what I said. I don't even know if I said anything at all. I just stood there holding my broom with my mouth hanging open and my father kneeling by my side.

My mind and body were numb. Not even a tear came to my eyes. Only the wild pounding of my heart, beating against my chest like a frightened bird fighting to get free, told me I still existed at all; that I had not disintegrated into the dry, hot soil beneath my feet and turned to dust.

"She spoke of you last," he said. "She said, 'It's good Themía is not here. She loves me too much. She would lay down and die with me if she were here."

Each word that came from him brought new pain to his eyes and he stumbled over each one, forcing them from his lips by sheer will. I listened to his voice as if it came from a great distance; through a tunnel, or from under the sea. Its sound sifted through me like grains of sand falling through a sieve and scattering at my feet. "Loves me . . . God . . . Mother . . . Themía . . . die with me."

I tried to cry, but I couldn't. Even when he wrapped his arms around me and I felt him sobbing, I still could not cry. I could only stand like a tiny post for him to cry on.

"Ah, too bad," Ruth said with feigned pity when my father told her.

She stared at me as one stares at an insect one has just pulled the wings from and then watches to see if it can still fly.

Father stood helplessly looking at me also, perhaps waiting for me to say something or to break down, but I could not.

"I will come again," he said finally.

Then he walked away in the direction he came.

That night I lay in my bed trying to squeeze the tears from my eyes, but they wouldn't come. I could only picture my mother, with my eyes wide open, doing those familiar things I had seen her do so many times. I watched her walk through the field before me, her skirts ruffling gently, and the wind blowing her long dark hair. I watched her kneading dough and blowing on the fire. I spoke to her and listened to her voice in singsong call my name, "Themía. My sweet Themía," but still I could not cry.

"Will you come for me?" I'd ask before I closed my eyes each night.

"Yes," she always answered, "I will come."

25

AND THEN THERE
WERE NONE

*B*_{*INT,*} " R U T H S A I D to me one day soon after. "You must have a real name. I can't pronounce that name you have now. I have decided to call you Sano. It's a good Kurdish name. I think it suits you."

"But I have a name," I said.

"Well no one can pronounce it, so what good is it? Huh? A name no one can say?"

She was the only one who said she couldn't pronounce my name.

"But I don't like that name," I said.

"Well I don't like your name," Ruth said. "Sano is a better name."

I just won't answer it, I thought.

"Sano! Don't you hear me calling you?" Ruth shouted.

No! But I turned to do her bidding anyway.

Mother's death released Ruth's anger. She knew her abuse would no longer bring my mother to take me away. She waited like a spider for me to fail so she could pounce on me, knowing I was more alone than ever before.

"Have you been throwing yourself at my brother again?" she shouted at me one day.

"What do you mean?" I said.

"I know you make eyes at him as if you are something to look at," she said.

"But I haven't even seen your brother since I first came here," I said. He had left the house soon after I had arrived and I had not seen him again.

"I don't believe you, you dirty girl," she said. "Maybe you are seeing him when I'm not around."

I looked at her dumbfounded, not understanding how she could accuse me or why. At the age of ten, the only man I wanted to see was my father. Each day, there were new accusations or reasons for her to attack me that I couldn't explain.

꒷   ꒷   ꒷

Sometime after Mother died, we heard a light tapping at the door.

"Go and see who's at the door," Ruth said.

I went to open the door and to my surprise, Cristodula was standing there. She looked almost haunted, with dark circles under eyes that darted back and forth, constantly searching, as if watching for an inevitable blow. She stood with a stooped posture and a frightened look on her wan face. Her hand clutched at her side. I put out my arms to embrace her but she pulled away when Ruth shouted from inside the house at me.

"Who is that girl?"

"Don't tell them I'm your sister," Cristodula said. Her eyes grew larger.

"But why?" I said.

"Just don't tell them," Cristodula said.

"What do you want?" Ruth said, coming to the door.

"Please. Something to eat," Cristodula said. "I am so hungry. Could you spare something please?"

"Is this your sister?" Ruth said.

It confused me that I should not tell. I would have thought it would help my sister if the woman knew, but the frightened look in Cristodula's eyes told me to keep her secret.

"No," I said. Ruth narrowed her eyes, looking first at me, and then at Cristodula.

"She looks like your sister," she said.

"I never saw her before," I said.

"Well we have nothing right now," Ruth said to Cristodula. "Maybe one of the other neighbors can help you." Then she turned and walked back into the house.

"You look sick," I whispered to Cristodula when I was sure Ruth was gone. "Are you all right?"

"I'm a little sick," she whispered also. "And I'm hungry."

"If you wait, maybe I can get you something when the woman isn't looking," I said.

"No!" Her eyes darted toward the door. "She will catch you and punish you."

"But what will you do?"

"I will go and ask the others if they have food. Yanni is living with some other people now. Papa looks for work but there is so little for him to do and he is always sad since Mama died. I miss you," she said. Then she turned and walked away.

"I miss you too," I said.

I lay in bed that night wondering why she hadn't wanted me to tell the woman she was my sister, but I could find no reason to comfort me. I thought it would have helped if she knew. But as I remembered Ruth's meanness, I wondered if it would have mattered to her at all. I could not think of one kindness the woman had ever shown me. It was true there were times she was not mean to me, that she allowed me to go about my business . . . or rather, her business, without interference, but an absence of meanness is not kindness. No! It would not have made a difference.

Two months later Yanni came. He was bigger than I had remembered him, but his cheeks were not so round and he walked with his head always down. I hadn't seen him for almost five months. I almost flew into his arms. He put his head on my shoulder and began to cry.

"Cristodula is dead," he said when he regained his ability to speak. "They buried her yesterday."

"But how?"

"She was sick. She was sick for a long time."

With our arms wrapped around each other's neck, we crumbled in a corner of the courtyard and cried. Tears I had not been able to shed for my mother came gushing out of me now, now that I had someone to cry with, someone who also felt my pain, someone who could remember with me and know what we had lost.

"Stay with me here," I said as if it were really up to me. "I'll ask the woman if you can stay. Maybe she'll say yes."

"Do you think she would?"

"I don't know. I'll ask, all right?"

He nervously brushed his thick black hair from his wet eyes. "All right," he said.

"Sano!" Ruth called from inside the house.

"She's calling me," I said. I wiped my eyes. "Wait here and I'll ask her."

"But she called Sano," Yanni said.

"That's what she calls me. She says she can't pronounce my name."

"Sano! Why don't you answer me?" Ruth shouted again.

"I'm coming," I said. "Wait here, Yanni. I'll come back soon."

"What are you doing? I want you to clean the cow stalls. Why don't you answer me when I call you?"

"My brother is here," I said. "Maybe he can help me clean the stalls. I could do it twice as fast if he helps me."

"If he wants to help, let him help," she said with her sharp, almost hysterical voice. "But do it before it gets dark."

We worked until almost dark sweeping and shoveling and filling up the bins with hay. It was the first time in so long that I had a companion, someone to talk to and feel close to. The love I had for him swept over me in a flood of nostalgia. The love I had for all of them with no outlet left, was now all wrapped up in Yanni.

Please say yes! Please say yes! I said to myself over and over again trying to hypnotize the air around me so the woman would let Yanni stay.

When we entered the living room she said, "Are you finally finished?"

"Yes," I said.

"Well, its late. You should go home," Ruth said to Yanni.

"It will be too dark for him to see. Can't he stay here tonight?" I pleaded.

"Where will he sleep?" she said.

"He can sleep with me," I said. Ruth shot a look at me filled with disgust.

"With you?" she said. "You will not be disgusting in my house. I won't allow it."

"But we always used to sleep together," I said, not guessing at her accusations.

"How old are you boy?" Ruth asked in Turkish.

"I am nine," Yanni said.

"You're big for your age. It's disgusting for you to sleep with your sister."

Yanni looked at me with confusion.

" But I . . . I . . . ," he stammered.

"He can wash himself before he comes to bed," I said, thinking perhaps that's what she meant.

Yanni smelled his arm unconsciously.

"Yes," he said. "I will wash."

"Ahk!" Ruth said. She squinted at us, trying to see into our souls. "All right. But be careful there is no business going on."

"No!" I said. "There won't be any business going on."

A big smile brightened Yanni's face.

"No!" he said. "There won't be any business going on."

I closed my eyes that night and pretended we were back in our home high on our lush, green mountain. I pretended the sound of the woman and her family sleeping beside us was the sound of my father and mother, Cristodula, and little Nastasía. Yanni held my hand and leaned his head on my shoulder.

"Do you remember the festival?" I whispered in Greek.

But he had fallen asleep the minute his head touched down. I leaned my head against his and forced myself to stay awake, listening to the sound of his breathing.

"Will you sleep all day then?" Ruth's shrill voice shattered my dream.

"Let them alone for once," her husband said.

"How are we to make breakfast and pick up the beds if they stay sleeping all day? I knew it was a mistake to let him stay."

"He's not hurting anyone. He's alone."

"He has people to stay with. Let him stay there. Let them feed him," she said.

Yanni sat up and rubbed his eyes, then almost jumped up off the mat. I got up too. I hadn't realized it was so late. In fact, I hadn't remembered falling asleep.

"It's late," Ruth said to Yanni. "Your people will wonder where you are."

He looked at her dumbfounded.

"Wait!" I said to him in Greek.

I took a handkerchief and ran into the supply room hoping no one would see me fill it full of grain. I held it behind my back and walked again into the other room where Yanni had been with the woman and her husband. Yanni was gone.

"Where is he?" I said.

"He's gone," she said.

She didn't bother to turn from the fireplace where she knelt preparing a meal. I ran outside to find him, clutching the handkerchief in my hand.

"Where are you going?" she called after me. "Come back here."

"I want to say good-bye," I said.

"I want you to help me feed the baby."

"I just want to say good-bye." I ran out the door to look for him.

"Sano!" she shouted.

The courtyard was empty. I ran out onto the road and looked up and down. It hadn't been that long since he left. But he was nowhere in sight.

"Sano!" she shouted.

I stared at the road, incredulous. I couldn't believe he was not there. I ran down toward the other houses a little way, but he wasn't there either.

"Sano!"

What could I do with the grain now?

"Sano! Where are you?"

As my heart pounded, I ran to a pile of hay and tucked the grain inside. Then I ran back to the house with an empty hole in the pit of my stomach.

"Devil! Don't you hear me calling you?" Ruth shouted.

In the months that followed, my relationship with the woman did not improve. I tried to stay out of her way and do as she said, but it was no use. I sat out in the courtyard on warm autumn afternoons watching the ox pull the plows to turn the earth while the children lay down for their nap. With a sad heart I'd remember my father walking behind the plow and Mother spreading the freshly washed clothes out on the grass to dry in the bright sunshine. How sweet my life had been in my beautiful land. How I had taken it all for granted as if it would never end. I tried to remember the smell of the forest, the moist, green air and the scent of pear blossoms. But the only trees here were the five dusty members of the wedding party standing in the field, and the arid grit of Tlaraz burned my nostrils if I breathed too deeply.

When the woman found the grain I hid in the hay she said nothing. The chickens had pecked and pecked until they pulled the handkerchief from its hiding place and spilled the grain on the ground at a moment when Ruth stood near. She knew I had taken it. I hung my head waiting for her black, raven's tongue to fly out at me and cut me with her words.

"Your father is gone," she said to me instead. "He has taken your brother and left Karabahçe."

"Where did he go?" I said. I hadn't even thought to doubt her.

She smiled smugly to herself.

"Who knows," she said.

"But he can't leave me behind," I said.

"Huh! He not only can, but did."

She turned and left me standing in the road with my jaw hanging open and my flesh burning cold. An agonizing fear gripped at my heart. I ran down the road not knowing where I was going. Tears streamed down my face.

"What's wrong, Sano?" the neighbor woman called after me.

But I ran and ran, out into the field and beyond until I could run no more, until I collapsed in a heap on the ground and cried myself to sleep.

"What are you doing here?" A man's voice woke me.

I looked around surprised to find myself so far from the village.

"Nothing," I said.

"You were crying,"

"No," I said.

I could feel a blush color my cheeks, embarrassed to have let a stranger see me cry.

"You are the Greek girl who lives with that nasty woman and her family. Do you like living with them?"

"No," I said. "But where else could I go?"

He looked around before answering. He was the man who had come to the village to build the pigeon houses.

"You're a pretty girl," he said. "Maybe if you're nice to me I will let you come home with me instead."

"I don't want to go home with you," I said.

I jumped to my feet and backed away from him. He had moved too close to me and the look on his face made me feel uncomfortable.

"Don't be afraid," he said. He smiled between two broken teeth. "Don't tell them what I said to you. I like you. Where are you going? I'm not going to hurt you," he called after me.

But I was already running back to the village. I wanted to have the woman put her arms around me and comfort me so I would feel protected. But at the courtyard I stopped, out of breath, knowing she would do no such thing.

"Who is that," the blind boy, who lived in the next house, called out.

"It's me, Sano," I said, wondering why he was sitting in the courtyard when I returned.

"Oh!" he said. "I heard your father went away. Will he come back for you?"

"I don't know," I said. Again I felt the same panic seize me.

"She isn't nice to you, is she?" he asked.

"Who?" I asked.

"The woman you live with."

"She's not so bad," I said and sat beside him on the low wall.

"Does she make you work too much? I'll help you if you like."

"It's not so bad."

"Well, I could do little things to help when you need me. I can chase the chickens out of the grain. Or help you carry water from the well. Or I can even do a dance to cheer you up," he said.

"All right. You can chase the chickens away from the grain," I said, glad for the distraction. "They're getting very close to it."

"Just tell me which direction to go in," he said.

He spread out his arms to scatter them even before I answered.

"Go straight," I said.

"Shoo! Shoo!" he shouted as he waved his arms about. "Shoo!"

"To the left," I called.

"Shoo!" he said. But this time he did it in a comic way. He jumped up and down and flailed his arms about his head to make me laugh.

"Shoo chickens! Shoo! Shoo!" he said over and over, encouraged by my laughter.

He ran first one way and then the other, back and forth, flailing his outstretched arms. I had not laughed in more than a year.

"Where have you been?" the woman called to me when she saw me sitting there. "I've been looking for you."

"There was a man in the field and . . ."

"And what?" she said.

"He said things to me," I said.

"What man?" Ruth said.

"The pigeon man," I said, using the term I had heard others use.

"What kind of things did he say?" she asked in an incredulous voice.

"He said . . . he said I was pretty and he would take me home with him if I was nice to him," I said.

"Ahk!" Ruth said with disgust. "You pretty? You used to be pretty when you were hungry, but now that you're well fed, ahk! Now look at you! You're not pretty now. Not anymore. And who told you to talk to strange men? No wonder he said things to you."

"I didn't," I said.

"I think you're pretty, Sano," the blind boy said. "You're the prettiest girl in the whole village."

Instinctively I looked at his eyes to see if they spoke the truth, but they stared at the horizon beyond me.

"Humph!" Ruth said. "Only a blind boy would think so. Go wash the children. And you," she said, turning to the blind boy. "You go home and let her do her work."

"You are," he insisted as he backed away. "I can tell. You're prettier than all of them. You're the prettiest girl in the whole village, and the nicest too."

I followed the woman into the house. The children sat patiently on the edge of the low wall, dangling their feet into a small tub of water. The little girl's tiny hands knitted themselves together as she stared up at me and her smile formed little dimples at the corners of her mouth.

"Come wash us, Sano," she called when she saw me walk into the house.

"Come wash us," the little boy echoed his sister. He touched his cheek with his shoulder in a shy gesture and laughed. It reminded me of Nastasía.

The evening sun streamed through the window and caught hold of the handle of the tub and turned it orange, then spilled down onto the clay floor at my feet. The light of the fire danced on the wall. Was it so long ago that I myself stood naked on a stool by the fire in front of my mother as she lathered a soft cloth and rubbed my body until I foamed in every crevice?

I rubbed the little feet of the boy with the rag I had soaped to a rich lather. He giggled as it squished between his toes. In his laugh I heard the same childish laughter I used to hear in Nastasía's voice.

"What's the matter?" the girl said.

"Nothing," I said, surprised by the question.

"Then why are you crying?" she said.

"I'm not crying," I began to say, but as I began to speak I realized the tears were falling from my eyes. "I don't know," I said instead. "Maybe I have something in my eye."

26

LITTLE LOAVES

THE CHILL OF winter had turned once more to the blazing heat of summer, and the lion-colored stalks of wheat swayed in the hot wind that blew across the flat, dusty plain. Although in the south there were those who slept outside in huge beds that fit four or five people crosswise, at night we slept under the stars on the roof on simple blankets we lay on the roof's hard clay. As the others slept in noisy contentment, I lay silently counting the stars, comforted by a cool, evening breeze, until I also dozed off to sleep.

"Sano! Get up and grind the wheat. It's already four o'clock."

I opened my eyes wearily to find a thick mass of stars above my head. With great effort I dragged myself from my blanket and walked to the back of the roof where the house attached to a mound of earth.

The bull waited in the courtyard in front of the house. I yoked it to the wooden harness, then brought him to the huge cone of wheat that sat waiting on the ground. Slowly I walked the bull around and around over the wheat in the dark.

Was anyone else in the world awake? Was there even a sound other than the sound of the bull's hooves clapping against the hard earth and the crunching of the wheat?

The bull mooed in deep protest to his early-morning chore as I stumbled along in the darkness. A rooster called out impatiently to a sun that still slept on the other side of the world.

For a time, there in the darkness, the sound of other roosters crowded my memory. The cool early-morning air, and the sound of the bull's hooves crunching the shafts returned me to my own village in autumn, our busiest time of year. Neighbors, and even Turks from nearby villages, worked from early morning until the sun went down, gathering the barley, wheat, and corn before the rains of autumn came to soak them. They stacked the wheat near the threshing floor in huge, inverted cone-like piles, just across the road from the barn.

The men made two long paddles, each two and one-half feet by four and one-half feet long. Under each paddle, small, sharp, white stones were inserted. The paddles were attached to the bulls gear so when they walked around and around on the hard clay surface of the threshing floor, pulling the paddles behind them, the paddles acted like knives to cut open the shafts of wheat and barley, to release their grain. They even chopped the stalks for winter feed for the animals.

On a windy day we set to work. Yanni and I sat on the paddles to give them weight while the men threw the wheat in the bulls' path. Someone was always ready with a handful of hay to catch a bull's droppings so it wouldn't foul the wheat. Around we went on our bumpy journey to nowhere, pulled as our parents were once pulled before us, and their parents before them, adding another link in the chain of ancestors who sowed and harvested and threshed on clear windy days like those, in the same manner, going back, who knows how many hundreds or thousands of years.

When they were finished with one of the huge piles of wheat, they would put the bulls aside and toss the grain in the wind with a shovel, to separate it from the shaft. Then the grain was swept up and put in burlap bags. Most was carried home to be stored in the huge bins in our supply room, but some was placed in a cart and drawn by donkey to the town to be paid in taxes. The chopped shafts were carried into the barn for feed.

I remembered the necklace of roasted chestnuts Grandfather used to hang around my neck in autumn. I'd prance around picking them off one by one with help from Yanni and my sisters, until they were all eaten up.

Now, as I walked alone behind the bull in the dark, I could feel the hot tears trickling down my cheeks.

When the sun peered over the horizon, Ruth and her husband came down from the roof and fussed about before setting out for Diyarbakir for supplies. I watched in horror as she fastened the belt my mother had given me into a knot around the cow's halter and fastened her to a post. The cow shook her head, and her bell rang out in the cool, crisp morning air.

"You don't need this. And anyway it's too big for you," Ruth had said soon after my mother died. And each time she picked up the belt to tie the docile beast, I cringed but said nothing.

I remembered Mother's hands as she wove the colored strands of wool into the long belt to wear around her waist. It was the only thing I had that belonged to my mother; the only thing I had that belonged to my past.

Almost the moment they left the courtyard and started down the road, dragging their long shadows behind them by their heels, I felt a weight lift from my soul, as if I had been holding my breath for 100 years.

At noon, when my chore of grinding the wheat was done, I decided to make bread to surprise them when they came home. For the first time since I had come to live in the woman's house, I felt the thrill of having the house to myself. There was no one there to cast a disapproving shadow on the things I did, to remind me I didn't belong. The squat shape of the room, with its clay floor and dull earth walls had become familiar to me, but I hadn't realized it until then. Every nook and crevice of the room was rounded off. Each step, each shelf built into the mud-brick walls, had soft, rounded edges. Nowhere was there a sharp corner or straight line. The heat outside the window pressed against the outer walls without penetrating, held at bay by an invisible barrier, even where the sun's rays streamed through the window and sent a soft, glowing light bouncing around the room. The sound of children playing further down the road and a dog barking in the distance became imbedded in the thick, still air.

I took out the large clay tub Ruth used to make bread and put it on the floor. Then I scooped flour from the barrels into it and sprinkled it with salt. I took the piece of dough left from the last time the woman had made bread, and soaked it in a bowl of water to soften it. Then I knelt on a mat before the large tub and made a well at the edge of the pile of flour like my mother used to do. I poured the water from the leftover dough slowly into the well, little by little, stopping after a few sprinkles to push down part of the wall of flour and work it in, until all the water was used up and the dough began to form.

All these things I had watched my mother do, and now I imitated her movements as I remembered them, diligently punching and pulling and pressing my fists against the dough with all my strength, as the woman's children played quietly beside me.

I pretended my mother was beside me also, making her own bread in our great wooden vat. I leaned my whole body into the dough as she had done until my arms ached with a gratifying ache. I smiled down at my creation before I lovingly covered the tub with a cloth and set it in a warm place in the supply room to rise as I had seen the woman do. Then I swept the floors and dusted all the shelves. I cleaned out the cow stalls and straightened the wheat and grain in the supply room. I even swept the courtyard, making the dust swirl with each swish of the broom and sparkle in the sunlight, as the chickens clucked around my bare feet.

Later that afternoon, when the dough had increased in size, I formed it into small, round, flat loaves, as big as an open hand; not the kind of loaves Mother used to make, which were round and plump and much larger, but the kind of bread common to the people in this area; the kind I saw the woman make. I set aside a chunk as big as my fist, which would be used for the next batch of dough, as I had used a piece from the last batch to help the new dough rise. Then I brought the loaves to the oven to bake. The women of the village laughed.

"What have you done, Sano?" one woman said. "Your dough is so lumpy."

"But I kneaded it for so long," I said.

"It will be all right," said another. "You will learn. This is a good start."

"Will they taste terrible?" I said.

"No. They will taste fine. But next time you must knead the dough until it is smooth."

The oven was called a *tanour*, and was already heated when I arrived. It was not made of stone like the ovens in my country. It was made of clay and shaped like half a barrel, which had been cut on an angle. It was about three and one-half feet high and two feet in diameter. In the center of the oven floor, dried manure burned as fuel.

"Let me show you how to put in your bread," a woman said when it was my turn to bake.

She took my tub and lifted each loaf out so it rested flat against her palm. Then she slipped her hand into the hot oven and slapped each loaf, one at a time, against the inner wall and ceiling all around, until she had managed to insert all of the loaves I had made.

I watched the oven with great impatience until the bread was finally baked. Then I brought the loaves home and set them on the shelf. I sat on a mat beside them and looked at them lovingly for a long time. I had made them with my own hands. Even though they were lumpy, they still looked like bread.

For the rest of the day, each time I passed them, I stopped to admire them as one might admire a great work of art, tilting my head this way and that to get the full impact of the wonderful thing I had made.

"What is this?" Ruth said when she returned from Diyarbakir. "Who made this bread?"

"I did," I said.

A vertical crease plagued her brow between her eyes, and her narrow lips pursed bitterly, but she said no more.

We ate dinner in silence that night, and although Ruth did not compliment me on my little loaves of bread, she and the others still ate them with their usual appetite. And although my arms ached for two days after from pounding and kneading so much dough, with each loaf we took from the bin to eat, my aching arms only made me feel more proud.

🕊   🕊   🕊

Again summer passed into fall, and winter brought a dusting of snow; a rare thing in that part of the land. The wheat had been harvested and ground and the grains stored in big sacks. I had formed the cow dung into patties using a wooden form, then lay them to dry in the field in the sun so we would have fuel for the fire.

"Sano," Ruth said one day. "Go look for henna leaves in the field to wash my hair."

With a pouch slung over my shoulder, I walked out of the house and up the road. The village girls were standing around talking as usual. They turned around to watch me only when I was quite close by.

"Where are you going?" one of them asked when she saw me with the big pouch.

"The woman wants me to collect henna leaves from the field," I said, hoping they would come with me.

"Maybe we will go and collect henna also," another said.

"You don't know how to find henna," the first girl said, addressing me.

"Yes I do. Ruth showed me," I said.

"Well, let's go then," she said.

The other girls slid off the low wall they had been sitting on and sauntered down the road. They paid no further attention to me, talking among themselves as if I were not there. Still it was good to have company to do a chore.

When we got to the field where the low shrubs stuck up roughly from the ground, I saw the patch of leaves they called henna.

"Look there!" I shouted. I ran to gather them up first.

"What do you think you're doing?" the tallest girl shouted. "You can't pick them without us."

They all chased after me trying to grab the pouch I had started to stuff some leaves into.

"You think you're so smart to run to them first. How dare you take them without asking us. These are ours."

"But I found them," I said.

"You found them?" she said, smacking me hard on the arm. "You found them?" She pushed me again and again, forcing me backward with each shove. "These are mine. I saw them first."

"But you couldn't have. You were talking," I said.

"I wasn't talking. I was looking for the leaves and I saw them first. Give them to me!"

"But they're for the woman. She'll be angry if I don't bring some back," I said.

"Then get your own," she shouted and pushed me to the ground.

In an instant they were on top of me, beating me. When they were through, they took the leaves from my pouch and threw the empty sack at me as I lay on the ground crying.

"I'm going to tell the woman you took her leaves," I said.

But all they did was laugh. I ran all the way back to the house with tears streaming down my face and the empty pouch, flapping against my side, reminding me of my humiliation.

"Did you bring the leaves?" Ruth asked first thing when I entered.

"No," I said. "The girls took them away from me and beat me."

"What do you mean they beat you? Is there nothing you can do right? Why must you be so stupid?"

"You have no right to talk to me like that," I said.

"No right?" she screeched. "This is my house and I have a right to do anything I wish."

"You have no right to call me stupid. I am not stupid."

"Don't talk back to me. You are very stupid. You can't even go to bring leaves from the field without making a problem. You can't do anything right. You eat my food and sleep in my house and what do I get for it. You're no help to me. I can talk to you any way I want."

"Leave her alone," her husband said. "Why do you pick on her all the time?"

"Me? Pick on her? She's lazy and stupid and you say that I pick on her?"

"No!" I shouted. "Then I won't eat your food or sleep in your house."

I ran out the door, and seeing my mother's belt, unfastened it from the cow.

"Come back here, you devil," Ruth shouted after me.

But I ran as fast as I could, clutching the belt to my chest. I had run before when her sharp tongue was too much for me, but I had only run up the road or to a neighbor until the pain subsided. But this time I ran until my heart pounded, and I kept on running until I felt my chest would explode. When I could run no more, I walked until I could run again, and finally I reached the river near Karabahçe.

By then my breath came in such explosions that it forced me to the ground. I looked at the water rapidly passing by. *Where was it going? And where was I to go?* I had no one. Not even girls my own age to talk to or play with. I stood always on the outside, watching them laugh and talk with one another, but they never included me. And all of a sudden I realized how alone I really was, and that I would never see my mother again.

A hollowness began to grow inside my chest, larger and larger, until all I could feel was a great emptiness filled with gravity that weighed me down; an emptiness like I had never known before.

"Mama!" I cried up to the heavens.

But the vastness of the dimming sky silently circled around me, stretching out in all directions before falling to the curved edge of the earth along the horizon.

I felt like a tiny speck alone in the universe, or a single bloom on the surface of the moon. I wished I could just turn back time as if nothing of the last two years had happened, as if it had all been a dream, a terrible dream that I could wake from and start all over. Maybe I had sinned and I could repent. I remembered the bishop coming to our home each year asking us to confess our sins. But we children could only giggle for we could find no sins we had committed at our age. But now. Maybe now I could repent. I could find a sin and repent it. I searched my mind and my heart for even one small sin. But no sin came to my mind. I wished again to make the years not so.

"Don't wish for things you cannot have," I heard Mother's voice speak to me. And for the first time since my mother died, the tears sprang to my eyes and I cried for her. I cried almost in a delirium. The tears just kept coming out from so deep inside me that I thought my heart had just split open and all my life was flowing out and spilling on the ground. I thought I would just keep on crying for the rest of my life without being able to stop; that I would sit there on that hard ground and cry and cry, until I became a flood of tears that found its way into the river and flowed to the ends of the earth, anonymous, unseen, licking the banks at every turn, but never to rise again to the shore.

"Mama," I cried again up to the heavens. But no one answered.

27

DON'T LOOK BACK

In KARABAHÇE, IN the ruined house where we had first taken shelter, I found the priest from our village sitting with a small group of people. I recognized his apple cheeks above his long, thick beard. He still wore the robe, now patched here and there. His shoulders stooped as if the robe itself weighed him down.

As I entered the dimly lit room, he looked up at me. His face was illuminated by a few candles that sat lighted on the floor.

"You've been crying," he said. "Come sit here with us and tell me what has happened."

Again I burst into tears and try as I might, I couldn't speak.

"Bring her some tea," he said to one of the women. "Come sit beside me and rest and when you are ready, you will tell me."

I sat beside him choking back my tears until finally my heaving chest became calm as I listened to his gentle voice in our own language.

"General Mustafa Kemal has pushed the Greeks out of Smyrna," he said to the group gathered around him, continuing where he had left off when I entered. "They are saying the Greeks burned the city before retreating, but others say it was not the Greeks, but the Turks themselves who deliberately set the fire. Only the Turkish quarter was left standing in Smyrna."

"Does it mean that we are lost forever in this place then, Father?" one man asked. "Will we never be able to go home?"

"I don't know, son," the priest said. "It's not a good sign. If the Greeks lose . . ." He broke off and shook his head. "They have moved many of the Greeks to Greece. At least those living on the western coast. But many more have died or were slaughtered. They say that many thousands of Armenians too have been slaughtered in the east. The Greek forces have been very strong until now. It's a major defeat. We can only wait and see."

"Are they getting rid of all the Christian population, Father?" another man asked.

"It looks like that is so. Perhaps it is only a matter of time before they chase the rest of these Assyrians out also, and any other Christians living here in the south. We will have to move on too."

I curled up beside him on the mat where he sat, wondering where I would go, and soon fell asleep, lulled by his voice. I didn't think to ask about my father and brother, or my mother. I was too overcome with grief to speak, and I assumed my father had left me, thinking I was safe.

A few days later, just when I began to think I was free of Ruth forever, her brother came to the door.

"I am looking for Sano," he said to the priest.

"There is no one here by that name," the priest said.

"She is the girl who lived in Tlaraz with my sister. She is a Greek girl," he said. He shifted his weight uncomfortably and peered around the room through the open door.

"He's looking for me," I said, coming to the door.

"My sister sent me to ask you to come back," he said.

"I don't want to go back," I said. "She's always mean to me."

"She's mean to me too," he said. "She's mean to everyone. I don't blame you for not wanting to come with me, but I promised I would try to bring you back."

I stood looking down at my bare feet not knowing what to say. I didn't want to go back but I didn't want to be a burden to the priest and the others either. They had so little to share.

"Maybe now that you ran away she will treat you better," her brother said, seeing my hesitation. "Maybe she has learned."

"Do you really think she will be better?" I asked, hoping it was so.

"I don't know. You can only see for yourself. She's a difficult woman," he said.

I wish I could say it was different the second time around, but it was the same.

"The children need tending to," Ruth said when we arrived back at

Tlaraz. It was as if nothing had happened; as if three days had not passed for her in that village; as if she had opened her mouth to speak three days before and had stood frozen in that spot with her thin-lipped jaw suspended open waiting for the words to come out, while in Karabahçe, the days had passed as usual.

The house looked smaller to me, and dingier, but the sour look on her face had not changed. Again I felt the same panic I always felt in her presence; the same tightness in the pit of my stomach and the same shallowness of breath. But I obeyed.

Except for the friendship of the blind boy who occasionally came to cheer me with his antics, I was alone. I looked neither forward nor backward but simply hung suspended like a star adrift in the universe.

"Sano! Come wash my feet," the woman's little girl called to me one day. I was in the back of the house cleaning out the stalls for the cows.

"I will do it," Ruth called to her child.

"No! I want Sano to do it." The children ran to me and playfully threw their arms around me and buried their faces in my dress.

"Go to your mother," I said. "She'll do it for you."

"How dare you tell me what to do," Ruth shrieked. "Who do you think you are?"

"I only meant . . ." I stammered.

"You only meant what? I will break your neck if you talk like that again. How dare you?"

"But I . . ."

"Don't talk back to me you ignorant devil! Do you want every bone in your body broken?" she screamed.

"What is she up to this time?" the neighbor woman said when she saw me standing in her doorway.

She shook her head. "Come, Sano. Come sit and rest for a while until she calms down. She is too nervous."

"She is always shouting at me for every little thing. I can't take it anymore. Why is she always so mean?" I said.

I could feel the tears welling up. The neighbor clucked her tongue.

"Yes. She is difficult. Even her own brother will not speak with her anymore. He has left the village for good he said. Come, calm yourself and soon she will be calm too."

But she was never calm. I could always feel her waiting like a panther in the dark, her hot, foul breath coming in short, steady spurts as she watched, ready to pounce on her prey.

At last winter again gave way to summer and the sun again beat down on the plain with searing intensity. Occasionally the village girls peeked into my thin cotton dress to see if my tiny buds had begun to blossom. I was twelve, but I was still as flat as the desert floor.

"Maybe they'll never grow," one girl said at a festival. "Do you have your period yet?"

"What's that?" I asked.

She rolled her eyes. "Do you bleed?"

"No. Why should I bleed? I didn't cut myself," I said.

"Leave her alone," a young woman from Diyarbakir said. "Why don't you go and mind your own business."

I looked at her gratefully, not so much for pushing the girls away, but for defending me. She was someone I had seen many times working the edges of the wheat fields in summer, cutting the corners where the farmers had not shorn, and gathering the fallen stalks of wheat from the ground that had been missed when harvested. She came every year and sold the wheat she gathered to buy fabric to make clothing. Her aunt had also come once. She had come to the house to visit, because Ruth was related to her husband.

The girls moved off giggling among themselves. I crawled into one of the tents that was set up to shield people from the sun, and lay down to rest. A light, hot breeze flapped the edges of the cloth and made it dance. I closed my eyes and listened to the people laughing and children playing tag.

"Come dance, Themía," I thought I heard a familiar, child's voice calling. I lifted my head to see who was there, but instead of a child, a larger figure blocked the sunlight seeping through the opening of the tent.

"What are you doing, you devil?" the woman's voice shrieked at me. "Can't you hear me calling you? I will teach you to ignore me when I call. I will break every bone in your body. Ungrateful slut!" she shouted and began to beat me with her fists.

"No!" I screamed. "No!"

I jumped up and ran out of the tent toward a building to get away from her, but she followed me and beat me as I ran. I climbed up on top of the roof to get away, but she climbed up also, beating me with her fists.

"No!" I cried. "No! Stop her! She's beating me. She's beating me. Stop her! Stop her!"

"What is it? Why are you screaming?" the young woman said, shaking me. "What's wrong?"

"Stop her! She's beating me," I cried.

"Who's beating you?" she said.

"The woman. She's beating me. Stop her."

"But there's no one here," she said. "There's no one here but you and me."

I sat up still sobbing unable to control myself, and looked around in disbelief. Even when I saw that I was still in the tent and the woman was not there, I couldn't believe it. The dream had been so real, and the blows struck me with such a sting, that it was a while before I could adjust my senses.

"What is it?" another woman shouted as she ran to the tent.

"It's nothing," said the first. "She was only having a dream."

My dream brought home to me just how frightened I really was inside. I sometimes wonder how I survived at all.

One afternoon, after I had walked the bulls across the wheat from before dawn until noon, Ruth called to me in her shrill voice.

"Clean out the stalls," she said. "But before you do, give the cows to the shepherd boy to mind them."

I went to the shepherd with the cows but he refused to care for them.

"But the woman told me to leave them with you," I said.

"Well, I don't want them," he said.

He shrugged his shoulders and turned away from me. I left them with him anyway and went back to clean out the stalls. But about an hour later, as I brought out a load of manure to spread in the sun to dry, I saw the cows in the field eating what they call corn.

"Oh! The cows are in the corn," I called out to Ruth.

She ran out to see.

"Stupid!" she shrieked. "Why did you let them go into the corn? I told you to give them to the shepherd. Why didn't you obey me?"

"But I did and he didn't want them," I said.

"You are a liar. I'm going to tear you to pieces. Do you see that beam up there?" she said and pointed to a place near the roof. "I'm going to take a rope and hang you from that beam until you are dead."

"Can't you ever stop this?" her husband shouted. "If you don't stop fighting I'm going to make each of you go in different directions so I can have peace. Enough of this. I'm tired of hearing you fight all the time."

"She let the cows into the corn," she squealed.

"I don't care. If it's not one thing it's another. If you don't stop, it's the end of both of you," he shouted.

I ran out of the courtyard to the neighbor's house. When her door opened to me, I burst into tears.

"I can't take it anymore," I cried. "She said she would tie me with a rope and hang me until I was dead. She would do it too. He said he would throw us both out if we don't stop fighting."

"You are not the trouble. She is," the woman said.

"But they are fighting because of me. I want to leave this place. What should I do?"

She shook her head thoughtfully. "I won't tell you to stay and I won't tell you to go," she said. "She is a miserable woman."

"Then I will go and this time I won't come back," I said. I stood staring at her for a moment to see if she would try to stop me. But she simply stared at me with sadness in her eyes.

"Good luck to you," she said finally. "And God be with you."

I went out and climbed up onto the roof to go around the back so Ruth wouldn't see me. Then I ran as fast as I could. The neighbor must have told her I was going, because soon I could hear Ruth's shrill voice calling me. But the more I heard her calling the faster I ran. "Sano! Sano!" she called. "Sano!" I knew this time she was chasing me down the road. I didn't look back. I just ran and ran. And when I could run no longer I still ran, driven by her awful raven's voice behind me. "Sano! Sano!" chasing me for what seemed like miles, the sound itself pushing me forward, until finally, I heard her no more.

28

DIYARBAKIR

Wₕₑₙ I wₐₛ very far away I saw a man on horseback coming down the road. I waved for him to stop.

"How do I go to Diyarbakir?" I said.

"Why are you going so far? Is someone waiting for you there?" he asked.

"Oh! Yes," I said. "My parents are waiting for me there. They're expecting me."

"Well just follow this road until you come to the river. On the other side of the river is Diyarbakir."

The road was empty. It was as if I was truly alone on the planet. But still I pushed on. Finally a man on a donkey headed toward me along the road.

"You are not too far from the river," he said to my request for directions. "Just keep going and you will come to it."

Four or five hours later I heard children playing. The river lay directly in front of me, and another man on horseback was crossing it with his bags of goods bulging out on either side of the horse's ribs.

That's where I'll cross too, I thought. *It can't be very deep there.*

I watched him until he crossed and was on his way. Then I went into the river. At first it was shallow. I stepped as carefully as I could, but as I went further toward the center, the current became strong. I lifted my foot to take another step and the water pulled me so quickly that my foot was dragged almost from under me. The water suddenly rose to my chest.

In a panic, I pushed back to the shore and ran up onto a mound above the river. There I sat and cried with my heart pounding uncontrollably.

"Did you see which way they went?" a young boy asked me out of the blue. I hadn't noticed the group of boys playing close by.

"No," I said. "I wasn't watching."

"Why are you crying?" he asked. He was no more than eight years old and came only to my shoulders; a thin boy with short cropped hair, dusty knees and hands from playing tag, and wearing a sweater that was too tight.

"I want to cross the river to go to Diyarbakir but the water almost pulled me under and I can't cross," I said. Again I began to cry.

"Why do you want to go to Diyarbakir?" he asked.

"I'm looking for a woman," I said.

"You're looking for a woman? Do you know where she lives?"

"No," I said.

"What's her name?"

"I don't know," I said.

The boy shook his head. "If you give me a penny, I'll take you across," he said.

"But I don't have a penny. I only have the clothes I'm wearing," I said, pulling on the soaked cotton dress I wore.

"Well, then," he said, "I'll take you across anyway."

"But how? The water is too deep and the current is too strong. We'll drown."

"Come with me," he said.

Before I could answer, he ran downstream. I chased after him. When we got to his spot he said, "I'll stand downstream and you stand upstream. And when the current pushes you this way, I'll push you the other way and we'll get across."

"All right," I said. He was so small, but somehow I trusted him.

"How will you find this woman when you get there?" he asked.

"I don't know, but I must find her somehow," I said.

"Diyarbakir is very big," he said. He stared at me a moment waiting for this to sink in. I could only stare back at him.

"All right, then," he said. "Come along."

We waded into the river, he on the downstream side and I on the upstream side, just as he had promised. But by the time we were halfway across, the water reached only to my knees.

"But it's not deep here," I said.

"I know," he said. "It's a good place to cross."

As I got closer to Diyarbakir, more and more people were on the road; some rode donkeys, some walked beside donkeys laden with goods. Soon I saw the giant walls of the city before me. I remembered it from when we passed through on our way south with the soldiers. The wall was dark and imposing, a sturdy barricade against invaders. I entered one of the four giant doors that allowed access to Diyarbakir. Each one was four stories high. Each sat on another side of the wall: south, north, east, and west.

When I walked through the giant gate, my heart sunk. Diyarbakir was enormous. I realized for the first time how impossible it would be to find the woman I searched for. I had only seen her once when she visited the house where I had lived with Ruth. I knew only that she was the aunt of the girl who came to pick the wheat from the fringes of the fields. The girl's parents had been killed by the Turks, and the woman had taken her brother's daughter in as her own.

I looked around in awe at the city that spread out before me. People scurried about. Merchants hawked their wares. Children played and shouted along the roadside. I wandered around not knowing where to begin to look for the woman. The sun was already low in the sky. My stomach was empty.

"Little girl," an old woman called, and beckoned me with her bony hand. "Will you help me draw water from the well?"

"Yes," I said. I dropped her bucket into the well and pulled up a pail of water.

"Are you hungry?" the old woman said, sensing I was lost or a refugee.

"Yes," I said.

"Come," she said. "I will give you a sandwich."

I followed her to her house not far away, carrying the pail of water for her. She went inside and soon brought out a sandwich.

I walked back and forth for hours. I didn't know which way to go or where to look for the woman. The sun was almost gone and lanterns were being lit in windows and in stores.

"Here! *Bint!*" a shopkeeper beckoned to me. I must have passed his shop for the tenth time. His outstretched hand held a thick slice of watermelon. "You look hungry."

I looked up in astonishment. "Thank you," I said.

I felt so shy that I took the piece of watermelon and went behind a house to eat it so no one would see me.

Soon, only a vague glow palely lit the city. For the first time I realized I had no place to go. I hadn't expected the city to be so big, or maybe I hadn't stopped to think at all when I ran away. Where would I go? What would I do? Again I sat on a stone and started to cry.

"What are you doing here?" a woman's voice demanded of me.

I looked up, surprised by her tone, and even more surprised to see who it was. I could only think that God, or an angel, or perhaps my mother in some form walked beside me, because there, standing before me, was the woman I searched for. In that vast, sprawling town, I had found her, or rather she had found me, against all odds, like finding a particular stone on the bottom of a raging sea. There she was. Had I crossed the river where I first tried, it is almost certain I would not have found her, because I would have entered the city through a different gate.

"I ran away," I blurted out.

"No!" she said with alarm. "You must go back. You can't stay here."

"I can't go back. I won't go back. I'll never go back," I said.

And the tears leapt from my eyes.

"My daughter is there," she said, referring to her brother's daughter. "She'll hurt my daughter. She's a miserable woman."

I looked at her in disbelief.

"All right," she said when I didn't stop crying and didn't budge. "You can come home with me now, but tomorrow you must go back."

She walked away swiftly and I ran behind her trying to keep up. "She's a miserable woman," she said again, talking to herself as she walked. "But no! You must go back tomorrow. How can I keep you? Where would you stay? No! It's not possible." She went on and on until we reached the house where she lived.

"Who is this?" her natural daughter said when we entered. "When did you come to Diyarbakir?"

"Today," I said.

"She must go back tomorrow," her mother insisted. "She can't stay here."

"She will do no such thing," her daughter said. "That woman is too cruel. You can't send her back." She sat me down and brought me a small glass of tea.

"Come." The woman said to me, jolting me awake. The morning light was streaming through the window. I hadn't realized I had fallen asleep.

"Here are a few pennies. You can buy yourself some bread. I must go to work. You can't stay inside the house while I'm gone. I'll be back later."

She handed me the pennies and locked me out of the house, and for the next three days she continued to lock me out when she went to work.

As soon as I arrived in Diyarbakir I began to have violent bouts of shivering. Each day when the woman locked me out I'd sit against the side of the building trying to keep warm in the sun. But even though the summer sun was scorching and the air still, my body could not feel warm. One day I also got a terrible headache.

"What's the matter with you?" a neighbor asked me as I sat against the wall shivering.

"My head hurts," I said, "and I'm cold."

"Wait. I will get a pail of cold water and pour it on your head. That will cure you," she said.

I allowed her to do it. My headache stopped, but I shivered all the more. That was when I met Zohra and her family.

"What are you going to do with that girl?" Zohra asked the woman I was staying with. "You can't keep locking her out of the house."

"What can I do? I can't care for her," the woman said with her usual nervous frenzy.

"Then give her to me. I'm going to have another baby. She can help me care for it."

"Yes! Yes! Take her. Please! It will be better for everyone. I can't care for her, you see."

"Would you like to come live with me?" Zohra said.

"All right," I said. I followed her into her house and stood awkwardly waiting. My belongings were still just the thin cotton dress I wore. I had even lost the belt Mother had given me.

Zohra's old, bent mother, whom Zohra's child called Nana, called to Zohra from the other room. "Who is it?"

"What is your name?" Zohra asked.

"Sano," I said, thinking they might also laugh at my real name.

"Who is it?" Nana asked again with her thin, sharp voice.

"This is Sano," Zohra said. "She is coming to live with us."

"Mmm," Nana remarked, but said no more.

"There is someone here to see you," Zohra said from the doorway a few days after I moved into her house. I looked up to find the husband of Ruth standing in the doorway. I went to him.

"Are you all right?" he said.

"Yes," I said. "But I'm not going back! I'm never going back!" I could feel the tears spring to my eyes.

"I didn't come to take you back," he said gently.

I studied his kind face, not fully understanding why he was there.

"Are they good to you?" he said.

"Yes," I said.

"Good," he said and walked away.

We lived in a two-story house with an enclosed courtyard, which was common there. It was a nice house. It's funny the things one remembers. I remember the color of Zohra's bedroom. It was downstairs and it was yellow.

Part of the downstairs was rented out to another family. In the courtyard there was a well, but the water was not fit to drink. It was only used for washing clothing. I once dropped a slipper down the well by accident.

"What is it?" Zohra asked her husband. "Could it be a cat that has fallen in?"

But he didn't know either, and I could only watch them with my heart beating wildly as they leaned over the wall of the well. Even though they were kind to me, I was afraid to tell them. I had already lived too long as an orphan and the meanness of the woman of Tlaraz made me afraid.

Sonya was born a few months after I arrived. She was a sweet child with jet-black eyes and black curly hair. Her face was as round as a turnip and she laughed easily. Her sister Arexine was about two, and like Sonya, was rosy-cheeked and lively.

My strange bouts of shivering in the afternoons continued for almost a year. It was only after Zohra visited an American doctor for herself, that she spoke to him of my condition. He told her to first rub my back with red pepper, then keep me in the hottest part of a Turkish bath for as long as I could stand it, which she did. The heat was suffocating. I stuck my head out now and then for air. But when I left the bathhouse I felt better, and the attacks never came again.

Diyarbakir was a city of merchants and it churned with life. Beautiful colored rugs hung everywhere in the marketplace and huge sacks of grain and dried fruit lined the road in front of shops. Fresh figs and watermelons, piled high on carts drawn by mules or oxen, were hawked by their vendors while children yelled and raced about playing along the great wall that surrounded the city. Oxen-pulled carts, and sheep with painted marks on their backs to identify the flock, ran bleating through the streets on their way to market in front of their shepherds. The tea shops were always full of men wearing fezzes and baggy pants that tapered along the calf to the ankle, and bound by colorful sashes below their waist-length vests. They sat on low stools drinking their tiny glasses of tea, or a thimbleful of coffee, as they discussed the events of their day. Women, dressed in black, gauzelike veils that covered their faces, and black habits that reached to the ground, walked the streets like black holes cut from the dazzling, sun-drenched scene. They lugged baskets of wash or groceries, or just strolled together, arm in arm.

Even Zohra, who was a Christian, wore the black habit that covered her face when she left the house, and Hagop wore the fez, so they wouldn't be identified as Christians. There were still quite a few Armenians and Assyrians left in the south, like Zohra and her family and those living in small villages like Tlaraz. Being in Turkey at that time was not safe, and Christians were extra careful. I already had learned to speak Arabic, Kurdish, and Turkish, and now, living with Zohra and her family, I learned to speak Armenian too. Those languages came to me quickly, and later were forgotten just as quickly. Even my own Greek language was later forgotten because I had no one to speak with in Greek. Only Arabic remained.

"Where is the money?" Nana asked me one day out of the blue.

"What money?" I said.

"There was a *medici* under the pillow of Zohra's bed and now it's gone," she said. "Did you take it?"

"No," I said. "I never saw the money." It was a coin as big as a half-dollar and worth about twenty cents.

"Well it couldn't have walked away," she said.

"But I didn't take it."

I could feel that same panic that had often seized me when I lived in Tlaraz and was accused unjustly.

"If you took it we will not punish you," Zohra said. "Just tell us so we know where it is."

"But I promise I didn't take it," I said.

"Agh!" Nana said with disgust and waved me away.

I went outside and slowly walked up the road wondering where I was to go now.

"Where are you going?" Nana shouted at me.

"Nowhere," I said. "Where can I go?"

"Come back here," she said, hobbling after me. She grabbed my hand and led me back to the wall surrounding the house. "Wait here," she said.

She went back into the house. I waited obediently. I could feel the tears coming to the surface.

"What's the matter? Why are you crying?"

I looked up to find Hagop looking down at me with concern.

"They said I took the money under Zohra's pillow," I blurted out through my tears. "But I didn't. I didn't even know there was money there," I cried.

"Ahk!" he said. "I took the money," and he went into the house. I never knew whether he really took it or whether it simply rolled onto the floor and was lost. It was never mentioned again, but the incident was a bitter reminder that I was still an outsider.

29.

ON THE ROAD TO ALEPPO

Wʜᴀᴛ's ᴡʀᴏɴɢ ᴡɪᴛʜ your nose?" Nana shouted at me one day.

"I don't know," I said. I had developed a sore on the bridge of my nose that bled easily if I touched it.

"Come here to me," Nana demanded in her usual sharp tone.

I went to stand before her. She examined me with her shrewd eyes, then waved her arms frantically.

"Did you see that man whose nose has fallen off?" she shouted at me.

I nodded my head. We had seen him in the neighborhood begging from door to door. The end of his nose was missing all the way to the bridge where the reddened stump oozed.

"Leprosy! That's what he has. That's what you have too!"

I could feel my eyes bulging in disbelief and my mouth sprung open. "No," I said. "I can't have leprosy. I can't."

"Then what do you think that is on your nose? It's leprosy I tell you."

"No!" I shouted and turned to run away.

"Come back here!" Nana shouted. "Where do you think you are going? Do you think you can run from disease? No! You cannot."

The tears sprang to my eyes at the thought of becoming a beggar with no nose, who went from door to door in rags. I was sure Zohra and Hagop would now ask me to leave their house and that Nana would insist on it.

"This disease will devour you," Nana said. "Come with me."

She took me by the wrist and dragged me to the chimney as my heart pounded in my breast.

"Wait here!" Nana demanded.

She took a small pan and hobbled around collecting various ingredients. Then she came back to the chimney where I stood crying. She reached into the chimney with a spoon and scraped a small quantity of soot from its walls into the pan. My mouth again sprung open in disbelief. I thought she would cover me with soot from the chimney before she threw me out the door, so that people would know I was diseased and would stay away. This new thought made me cry all the more. I again turned to run, but Nana grabbed my wrist and held me tightly in her bony, but iron grip.

"You cannot run from it I tell you! It will devour you if you do."

She mixed the soot with the other ingredients she had collected to make a salve. Except for the soot of the chimney, I don't remember what she used. When she was finished making the salve, she spread it on a small square of the extremely thin paper that Hagop used to roll cigarettes. Then she placed the cigarette paper with the salve across the bridge of my nose to cover the sore.

Twice a day Nana beckoned to me with her bony hand to stand before her. Then she reapplied the salve to my wound, once in the morning and once at night, making a new batch every so often. She still found fault with me every chance she got, so it surprised me how patiently she attended to this task that she had taken upon herself.

Time passed slowly and uneventfully for the next six months. My nose was finally beginning to heal, but it was still tender to the touch and still bled easily. Hagop made string cheese in the courtyard and a dish called *kibbeh* from raw meat he chopped with a knife as finely as if it had been ground in a machine. Then he mixed it with bulgar and green onions and salt. He made brandy for friends and family, from raisins I think, which he fermented in huge ceramic jars that were about five feet tall. Incense was burned around the house and yard to disguise the smell as it cooked, because it was illegal to make alcohol.

It was during a small gathering at a friend's house that we heard the news. Everyone was sitting around eating, drinking, and talking. Even women drank the brandy. A young girl sat at the table drinking so much, I thought she would surely fall to the ground, but she held her own, smiling sweetly.

"This is fine brandy, Hagop," one man said. "It warms every inch of me."

"It's your finest batch yet," another man shouted. "Let's make a toast to Hagop."

"To Hagop!" they all shouted in unison.

"Thank you," Hagop said. "But it's the same recipe I use year after year. If it's better, then it must be the raisins that are better this year. They should get the praise."

"It is not only the fruit but the hand that is to be honored here," the second man said. He raised his glass to Hagop. "You are too modest my friend."

"Modesty is a virtue not only in women," said the first man. "We accept your modesty and praise you all the more."

All laughed. Zohra sat beside me with little Sonya on her lap. She gently pulled the edge of the child's diaper aside to look inside and then continued rocking Sonya on her knee.

"Sano," Zohra said. "Go to the house and get me another diaper for the baby. Sonya is soaked and I forgot to put the diapers in my bag."

"All right," I almost moaned.

I raced out the door and ran down the road to the house as fast as I could so I could return quickly and not miss too much of the festivities. I ran in the door and into Zohra's bedroom, then dug through the chest where the baby's things were kept.

"Who's there?" Nana called from the other room.

"It's me. Sano," I shouted. "I've come to get diapers for Sonya."

"Oh!" she said, hobbling into the room. "I have no water. You must go and get me water after you go back with the diapers."

"But . . ."

"Don't forget!" she said.

"All right," I said.

I raced out the door again. When I arrived back at the house where the group was assembled, the mood had changed. No one laughed now, and a new man was there. He sat at the side of the host and stared somberly into his glass of brandy.

"Mustafa Kemal has seized power from the sultan and has set up a government in Ankara. All Christians have been warned to be out of the country as quickly as possible."

He emptied his glass in one gulp and again fixed his gaze, this time on the empty glass.

"What are we to do with our homes, our businesses?"

"Leave them. Or sell them if we can. But we must go. They have already slaughtered thousands of Armenians. What's stopping them from doing it again? Each person is ordered to be photographed, maybe so they can identify us if we don't leave."

"How long do we have?"

"Only a matter of days, or a week at most."

In the excitement and confusion of the news of Kemal's orders, I had forgotten Nana's water. I thought now for sure she would ask them to leave me behind.

During the next few days we packed up the whole house. With each thing I folded and tucked into a bundle, I wondered what would become of me, where I could go.

"Hagop!" a neighbor said as they loaded the wagon. "What do you intend to do with that young girl?"

"What do you mean?" Hagop said.

"The Greek girl. What will you do with her? She is also in danger."

A look of amazement came across Hagop's face.

"I don't understand you," he said. "What do you think I am to do with her? She will come with us, of course. How could you think I would leave her behind? She is my daughter now."

"Well, I thought . . . no, of course. You would never leave her behind."

"When she is ready to marry, I will ask her betrothed only what I have spent on her. But until then, she will go where we go, eat what we eat, and rest when we rest."

I looked at Nana to see if she heard and what she would say, but she only nodded in agreement and continued to hobble about loading the wagon.

🕊   🕊   🕊

Each day a new group of Christians rolled past our house in creaky wagons, or walked alongside donkeys piled high with bundles.

On the fifth day, we started on our own journey south to Aleppo. The trip was long and tedious, but could not compare to the forced march south with my own family. At least there were no corpses on the road, and we had enough food and money to keep us, even if it was not in great abundance.

Our wagon bumped along the dry, pitted road as we crossed the border that marked the end of Turkey and the beginning of Aleppo. A monotonous rumble accompanied the wagon's every move, and a thick veil of dust danced in our wake in the last rays of sunlight.

In all the world, of which I knew so little, I could not imagine a more desolate place as that area through which we drove our horse and wagon on our way to Syria. It was even more desolate than the empty plains of southern Turkey, where the wind blew hot as if from Hell itself, and the blinding sun found its way into every crevice of one's being; where the wheat grew high and strong and rippled in a mirage of yellow waves against the yellow earth.

Perhaps it was only my own loneliness that made our journey seem so barren. A profound sadness settled within me. It was the first time since I left my own home, a million years ago, it seemed, that I had time to think about what had happened and to realize my loss. I looked back one last time toward the country that had been a great joy to me in my first years of life; the country that had become the cause of all my sorrows. All that I had loved was receding further and further behind us, wheel length by wheel length. I knew in my heart the chance of seeing my father and brother again was now lost forever. They had vanished from my life without a trace, except for the memory of them that I clung to like a thin, invisible thread that connected us as surely as if it were bound around my heart.

I pictured my father and my brother as I had last seen them walking along in the distance, as if they would wander like that till the end of time, never stopping, never finding rest, while the perfect bodies of my mother and sisters lay serenely, as if in sleep, beneath the thick blanket of earth that covered them, unchanging for all eternity, like jewels embraced in sand.

30

SAY I DO

I N A L E P P O , S Y R I A , Hagop found an apartment for us. It was in a two-story building with a courtyard. Our apartment was on the second floor with only one room for all of us. Almost immediately I came down with the measles. The four children on the floor below ours got it also. An epidemic had already killed so many children, that when I came down with the disease, Zohra was beside herself. She burned charcoal in a pan and, after all the smoke had burned off, she put the pan with the hot charcoal under the table.

"Get under the table with the charcoal," she said to me. "Wrap this blanket around you and sit there."

Then she put a blanket over the table that reached to the floor.

"It's so hot under here," I said. "I'm sweating."

"That's good," Zohra said. "That's good. Stay there and sweat out the disease."

By the next day my fever broke, but all four children of the family in the apartment below ours died.

We had been in Aleppo for about a year when I married Abraham. It was 1925 and I was fifteen years old, I think. My nose had long since healed. The sore had left only the tiniest scar, which was not noticeable at all. On the day Hagop told me about Abraham, Zohra had asked me to take care of the children and to keep a fire under the stew she was making for dinner until she, Hagop, and Nana returned from market.

"We'll be back in about an hour, Sano," she said before the whole family trooped out the door.

I kept piling the wood on the fire to keep the stew cooking. I was afraid it would go out and I would disappoint them, so I put on more and more wood until the fire blazed. That's the way I kept it until they came home.

Nana was the first to look into the pot on their return.

"Sano! What have you done?" she shouted in her shrill voice.

"What?" I said. "I kept the fire going as Zohra said. I didn't let it go out for a minute. I promise."

Zohra looked into the pot also and her mouth fell open.

"Sano," Zohra said more gently. "You burned the stew. Even the bones are burned to a crisp."

"But . . ." I began, ashamed of my blunder.

"Don't you know anything? You can't do a simple thing like that?" Nana shouted.

"All right!" Hagop said. "We'll cook something else. It's not important."

"But . . ." Nana began again.

"I said it's all right. We will cook something else. She's never been taught to cook. Why should she know? Anyway," he went on. "There is something we must talk to you about."

I looked from one to the other to fathom what was about to happen. My heart raced. Except for Nana's sharp tongue, they were kind to me, but they were not my parents, and I was always inwardly afraid that one day they would say I must leave. Then where would I go? I looked over at the blackened pot of stew. The pot had melted into a lopsided shell of zinc and soot, and the smoke from the wood stove had streaked the rough whitewashed wall above the fire from years of cooking.

"There's a man named Abraham," Hagop said. "He comes from America."

I stared up at him. There was a man. He had accosted me on the stairs the day before. "Maybe you will be my wife," he said to me, but I didn't take him seriously. He was tall and strong-looking, with stern eyes. He had grabbed for my hand, but I pulled it away and ran into the apartment.

"He came to ask his relatives to help him find a wife," Hagop said. "They live in the apartment beneath ours. One of his cousins was interested in marrying him, but she's crippled. He doesn't want to marry a woman who may not be allowed to go to America with him."

I just stood there looking up at him dumbly. I didn't guess what he was talking about. I didn't think he was telling me to marry him.

Hagop stared at me as I stood fidgeting before him. Zohra and Nana stared at me also. I didn't know what to say. I didn't know what he was driving at.

"They told him about you," Hagop said, referring to Abraham's relatives. "I have spoken to him. He wants to marry you and I have given my consent."

"He wants to marry me?" I said.

"He's an Assyrian from near Diyarbakir. From Mardin. He's a Christian like us."

Hagop waited, watching my face. Then he continued.

"He has been living in America for twenty years. He will take you with him when he returns. He has a house there."

He stopped again to study me. He didn't ask if I accepted. He had accepted for me. I sometimes thought, if I could get married I could be free. I could have my own home. I wouldn't have to listen to Nana's angry words anymore. I'd have a place on earth where I would really belong; where someone would again belong to me. Of course, the intimate details of marriage were still a mystery.

"I'm sorry about the stew," I said, not knowing what else to say.

"Ah. Ah. Ah," Nana pouted. She twisted the pot this way and that to see if she could salvage something as a sliver of late afternoon sun struck the dull black of the pot and sliced Nana's bent figure in two.

🕊 🕊 🕊

Ten days after Hagop spoke to me about Abraham, they both took me to the eye doctor to get my eyes examined. It was a necessary step for a passport to America. The three of us walked in silence. I stole glances at the man who would soon be my husband. He walked with his shoulders back and his chest out. His hair was dark and thinning. His stern eyes roamed in my direction from time to time as if guarding his prize. He was tall and straight, with a strong voice and the manner of a man who knew his own mind, a mind not easily changed.

I felt shy with him, even shyer than I usually felt with strangers. Occasionally the two men spoke to each other as we walked. For the most part they ignored me and I was secretly grateful. I was too busy trying to control my bladder and too shy to tell them I had to relieve myself. I could feel the wet traveling down my leg. I glanced behind me to see if the dust of the road had been stained darker in my trail. Finally I could contain myself no longer and ran behind a building to relieve myself.

"Where are you going?" Hagop yelled after me.

"Don't come!" was all I could answer.

The doctor said my eyes were fine, so on our return home Abraham paid Hagop $100.00 in gold, and the day of the wedding was set.

I had no hope chest for my wedding. I had only the clothes on my back and maybe one or two other things of no value. If it weren't for Merlina, the girl who ran away with Dmitri, I wouldn't know about such things as hope chests.

Abraham and I were married in a church on March 24, 1925. I guess it was a Protestant church because that's what Abraham was. I don't remember too much about the wedding, except there were candles everywhere. I was so shy I just couldn't take it all in. I remember standing before the minister as he spoke. Abraham stood beside me. The wedding dress Zohra borrowed for me had belonged to her sister's daughter, who had died. The bodice in front sagged unused where breasts should have filled it out.

I think I wanted to be any place but there, and I guess I was any place but there, because so much of the wedding and the things that happened that day are a mystery to me. Standing there with all those strangers staring at me, and a man old enough to be my father standing beside me, was enough to make me want to disappear. All I could think of was running down the hillside with my little calf Mata running by my side. And when they began to sing, I could only think of my father singing before the fire. I wasn't shy like that in my country. I used to go into the church even by myself all the time, but it took me years to get over the shyness I developed when I lost my mother; when I lost them all and found myself an orphan, a nobody's child, a servant girl I guess you could call me. Maybe I never did get over it.

I could feel the shoes Abraham bought me for the wedding squeezing my feet uncomfortably, but I loved them all the same. They were the first high-heeled shoes I had ever owned. They were made of strong black leather, and they had buttons and little straps that crossed from one side to the other. They reminded me of the dolls we used to make at home with high-heeled shoes.

It was only when Zohra poked me and I looked up to find the minister staring down at me, that I realized I hadn't heard a word they said.

"Say I do," Zohra said.

So I said "I do."

After the wedding, Abraham's relatives gave a big party. Someone brought a lamb, which was to be used for the feast, into the courtyard where we lived. They called me outside. Then they killed the lamb in front of the door while I watched. I had never watched an animal being killed before. They just slit its throat right in front of me. I'm sure it was meant to honor me, but instead it distressed me more. I don't remember if I ate any of it when they roasted it.

"You're my wife now, eh?" Abraham said.

He stood towering over me with a look that said I own you.

"I know," I said.

"Don't be shy," he said, changing his tone. He touched my cheek with the back of his strong fingers. "It's all right."

"I know," I said again, but I looked around for someone to save me.

"You must leave her to me Abraham," Zohra said.

She put her arm around my shoulder and guided me to a corner of the courtyard, away from the crowd of people who were enjoying the wedding celebration.

"Tonight you will stay here with us, but tomorrow you will be with your husband." She took my hand and led me into the house. "I am going to give you this little blanket," she said. She took a small white cloth from a chest and handed it to me. "Tomorrow, when you have sex with your husband, you must wipe yourself with this blanket."

"I don't understand," I said.

"Your private parts. Down there," she finally said and thrust the little blanket toward me to indicate the place when I stared at her in confusion.

"Why?" I asked.

"So they can all see that . . . ," she faltered. "Just do it please, and then bring it back."

That night I spent with Zohra and her family alone in my own bed as usual. Or rather, alone on my mat with the whole family crowded into that one room the way all the other poor people and refugees lived.

Each time I closed my eyes, I saw Abraham standing before me, looking down at me with his stern eyes.

You're my wife now, eh? he said over and over again. I looked at the small white blanket sitting on a stool near the window. With an importance all its own it waited, bound in the moon's radiance, while I wondered at the secret of its mission.

31

THE MYSTERIOUS LITTLE

BLANKET

WE WERE ALL up and dressed when Abraham arrived the next morning.

"Is she ready?" he said.

He stood in the doorway blocking the light. I held baby Sonya in my arms and stared at him. My little bundle of belongings sat neatly tied and waiting by the door.

Hagop nodded his head reluctantly. "You must take good care of her. She is like a daughter to me."

"It will be all right," Zohra said to me.

She stretched out her arms to take the baby without taking her eyes from my new husband. "You will be happy in America. You will be free."

I walked slowly to the door and stood beside him. My feet already felt swollen and pinched from being crammed into my new shoes. Nana came to watch from the doorway of the other room, bent and frail, still holding the handkerchief she was crocheting. Little Arexine, who was five years old by then, sat on a cushion on the floor playing. But as if realizing she would not see me again, she jumped up and ran to me and threw her arms around my neck when I bent to embrace her. She clung to me tightly before finally letting go. I hadn't realized until then how pale the yellow of the walls were, or how bare. I picked up my bundle.

"Good-bye," I said.

"Good-bye," they said in a disjointed chorus.

I turned away and walked down the single flight of stairs to the courtyard below. Abraham descended heavily before me.

"Where are we going?" I asked when we were on the street.

"We're going to a hotel. In a few days we'll go to Zahlé in Lebanon. I have family there. We can arrange for your passport from Zahlé at the American Consulate."

I ran slightly to keep up with him, trying to ignore my burning feet.

"Have you ever been to a hotel?" he asked.

"No," I said.

He smiled to himself and called out to a passing horse and buggy. "Do you want to ride in a carriage?"

"All right," I said.

The horse snorted and threw back his head as he was pulled to a stop before us. His brown coat was damp and he pawed the ground impatiently as Abraham helped me into the cab.

The air inside the small compartment smelled of warm wood and leather. I breathed in deeply to fill my lungs and ran my hand along the cracks and crevices etched in the black leather seats. The cracks had worked themselves into an intricate pattern, like a road map drawn in chalk on a blackboard and then lightly smudged. The carriage jerked to a start, then rattled down the narrow, familiar streets of Aleppo, past the rows of courtyards hugging their small houses, past the marketplace where I had shopped with little Sonya and Arexine. Many-colored carpets lay stacked against the walls or hung brightly around the stalls. Sacks of grain and dried fruit seemed to float past the creaking carriage as did the men in baggy pants and fezzes. All the little stools in the coffee shops were filled with men sipping tea or coffee from tiny glasses, and women with long dresses also floated past as they walked along carrying huge bundles.

Abraham called out the name of the hotel to the driver, and suddenly the carriage turned onto a tree-lined street that was wider than the rest. Until then I had thought Aleppo was simply a small town with narrow streets and small buildings; wash hanging in courtyards to dry; the smell of stew and charred kebobs; and smoke from outdoor fires curling toward a pale sky. Suddenly it was grand.

It was difficult to imagine what Abraham was thinking. He sat silently beside me in the carriage. He looked out of the small square window on his side of the carriage and occasionally glanced over at me. The *clop-clop* of the horse's hooves struck the ground like hammers striking stone.

"We're almost there," he said as the carriage rounded another corner.

The coachman pulled up the horse in front of a beautiful white building. An ornately carved stone arch waited above a small stairway. The windows too were surrounded by carved stone, and dainty curtains of lace hung on the other side of the glass. The door was a rich, brown wood with a large pane of glass. Beside it, a man in white stood waiting. His loose pants and white shirt gently fluttered in the soft breeze.

"*Salaamu alaykum,*" he said as he reached for the brass handle and pulled the door open wide for us to enter.

"*Wa alaykum salaam,*" Abraham said automatically.

The walls inside were painted pale green with white on the fancy borders. A staircase, such as I had never seen before, curled up and around with a banister of wood and brass. The ceiling was high, and a lantern of many drops of clear glass sparkled from its center.

"All right." Abraham's voice startled me. "We can go to our room now."

A porter carried my small bundle to a room on the second floor and swung the door wide for us to enter before him. Long wine-colored curtains hung to the floor in front of three tall windows. The porter went to the curtains and pulled them back to let the dazzling light pour in. Outside, a small stone balcony clung to the side of the building.

"That's all right," Abraham said to the porter. "I'll do that."

Abraham handed him a coin and we stood waiting quietly for the porter to leave the room. The porter stopped to turn back the covers on the bed. He glanced at me sheepishly and then left. As soon as the door closed behind the porter, Abraham smiled.

"Do you like it?" he asked as he moved closer to me.

"It's beautiful," I began, but almost before the words left my lips, he threw me down on the bed and was on top of me. I lay pinned beneath him, half on and half off the bed, unable to even stretch out my legs.

"Stop! What are you doing?" I said in astonishment.

"Shhh!" he said and reached his hand up under my dress and ripped off my underwear.

"But . . ."

"You're my wife now!" he said.

I could find nothing else to say. I lay there staring up at the ceiling with the edge of the bed pressing hard against the small of my back and my shoes pinching my feet.

I'm his wife now, I thought as he worked himself into a frenzy.

I tried to straighten my legs but there wasn't enough room. I could only close my eyes and bite my lip to disguise the pain. When he was finished he stood up and straightened his clothes.

"Wipe yourself," he said handing me Zohra's mysterious little blanket.

"I'm bleeding! I'm bleeding!"

"It's all right," Abraham said. "That's natural."

"But I'm bleeding!"

"Come on. It's all right. Fix your clothes and wash yourself."

I stood staring at the bloody little blanket still not comprehending that its mystery had just been solved.

"Look, Sano!" Abraham said.

He led me to the bathroom like a father coddling an irritable child. A huge brass tub with claws for feet and brass faucets gleamed in the sun streaming through the window. He gloated like a small boy about to show his favorite toy.

"And look at this!"

In the corner stood a toilet. I had never seen anything like it before.

"It's a toilet," he said. "And look!"

He pulled on a brass chain coming from a wooden box above, and a loud gush of water splashed into the bowl. I gave a start.

"Who puts the water in there?" I asked.

"It comes in by itself," he said and laughed, delighted at my surprise.

He leaned over the tub and turned on the faucets. Water came tumbling out so fast I again jumped back in surprise.

"Come! Wash yourself. The water is warm. You will like it. Come! And afterward I will show you a magic light."

He put a stopper in the drain hole, then left the bathroom. I stood numbly watching the water fill the tub.

"Are you bathing?" He shouted at me through the door.

I slipped off my thin dress and climbed into the tub. The warm water felt soothing as I sunk down. Soon only my head remained above. Would it always be like this, quick and brutal, without affection? Had it been like this for my mother? No! My father had loved my mother dearly. You could see it in his eyes when he looked at her. You could feel it in the air when she stood near. You could hear it in his voice when he spoke her name. I had never thought of that before. I had always taken it for granted. No! It was not like this for them.

I closed my eyes to better feel the water's warmth. It enveloped me. It washed me. It took away the sting, and I again drifted off to my own land.

"Are you almost finished?" Abraham called from the next room.

"Yes," I called, trying to keep my voice steady.

"Hurry! I want to show you something."

I stood and wrapped the plush white towel around me and sunk into its warmth and luxury. So this is what my grandmother's towels felt like. No wonder she had treasured them.

"Look here!" Abraham said when I came out of the bathroom. "Watch me make a magic light."

He pulled a cord hanging from the ceiling and a light went on. Then he pulled it again and the light went out. I stood staring at it dumbly. He laughed nervously, trying to infect me with his enthusiasm.

"It's called electricity. Come on! You try it."

I reached up obediently and pulled on the cord. The light came on again.

32

THE BIG BET

THE NEXT DAY Abraham took me to Zahlé, a town in central Lebanon, to stay with some distant cousins of his.

"Oh, how pretty she is, Abraham! How lucky you are!" his cousins fussed over me when we arrived in Zahlé. They had been driven out of Turkey around 1915 when the Turks were again slaughtering Assyrians.

"Come sit down next to me and tell me all about your trip," his young cousin said grabbing my hand. "Are you excited about going to America? You must learn to speak English, you know," she rambled on, not giving me a chance to answer. "You will live here with us while you wait for your papers. I'm glad of that. We are also from Turkey, you know. Abraham's father owned seven houses in Mardin, but the Turks took them away and he and his eldest sons were forced to leave Turkey with nothing but their lives.

"We were forced to leave too. Our family is now spread around the world," she went on, after a pause.

The sound of her voice was comforting and friendly. No one had talked to me so sweetly since my mother so long ago.

"Oh! I'm so glad you're part of our family now. You must think of us as your family you know."

I could feel the tears well up in my eyes.

In the morning they brought me to church. When the collection plate came around I put in a coin worth about ten cents, which was quite a lot in those days. The others put in the equivalent of a penny or even half a penny.

"Oh!" they whispered. "Who is she? Who is she? She put in so much money."

"She is married to an American fellow," someone whispered. "She's going to America."

"Oh," they said.

"Come," Abraham's cousin said to me when the service was over. "Come and confess to the priest."

"What will I confess?" I said.

"Your sins, of course," she said.

"But I don't have any sins."

"You must have some," she insisted. "Everyone has some sins."

"Well I don't have any. What would I tell the priest?"

"The bad things you've done."

"I've done nothing bad," I said. "How can I confess something I didn't do?"

When Grandfather had tried to get us to confess to the priest we could only giggle. Our priest would pat our heads gently and smile. But now I felt my face grow red with shame. How could she think I had done something bad that I must confess to? She rose impatiently. Her pale skin and gray eyes were so like those of my husband. She put her firm, strong hand on mine.

"Don't you even have bad thoughts?" she demanded in a whisper.

"What kind of bad thoughts?" I asked.

She sat down beside me again and studied my face.

"All right," she said, realizing my innocence for the first time. "All right. Maybe you don't need to confess. You are so young. How old are you?"

I calculated quickly back from Tlaraz. Two years there, two years in Diyarbakir, and one year in Aleppo. "Fifteen, I think."

"Oh, yes. You are young," she said. She took me by the hand and led me out of the church. "Well, never mind. Everything will be all right. Abraham will take good care of you. He is very strong you know. Oh," she laughed suddenly, remembering something from the past.

"My father told me that many years ago there was trouble with the Turks. A war perhaps. I don't remember the details exactly. I guess there has always been trouble with the Turks for our people, on and off. Abraham was still living in Mardin then. He was young and strong. Our people needed someone to take a message to another village. It was very dangerous because, besides the war, there were also many Turkish bandits on the roads. Abraham volunteered. He set out on foot. He ran all the way and got the message to its destination. On his return with an answer, he was set upon by bandits. There were many of them and they would have killed him if they caught him. He was alone, so he hid behind a great rock and gathered small stones into a pile. Each time one of the bandits tried to advance to get him, he picked up a stone and threw it so hard and straight that it hit the bandit on the head. That bandit would turn and run for shelter. Then another would try, and another. But each time Abraham would throw stones that hit his mark.

"He is an expert you know. He was a stone mason when he was young. In Mardin where he comes from, all the streets and buildings are made of stone with stone archways around the doors and windows. He could look up at a space above a door that needed to be filled by a stone and cut a perfect fit without bothering to measure it. He has the eye of an eagle."

"What happened?" I asked, anxious to hear the rest of the story.

"What do you mean?"

"With the bandits?"

"Oh." She chuckled to herself. "Yes, the bandits. It seems they were very impressed with Abraham. He had held them off that way for hours. 'Brother!' they finally shouted to him. 'You are a brave man. Go on your way.' They stood aside then and let Abraham pass unharmed."

She was a wonderful storyteller, and, as I was later to find out, so was my husband.

🕊 🕊 🕊

Each day we were in Zahlé, Abraham attempted to teach me to speak English and to read and write. I constantly stumbled over the words, repeating them one minute and forgetting them the next.

"Look!" he shouted in frustration. "It's not hard. You're not paying attention."

"Let me try again," I said.

"The boy went to the store," he read.

"The boy went to the store," I imitated.

"OK," he said. "Now you read it alone."

I looked down in embarrassment. "I don't remember," I said.

The words looked like nothing I had ever seen before. The alphabet was not what I had learned in my little schoolhouse . . . the alphabet Grandfather had burned into a board. Neither were they the scrawl of Arabic, which I could not read either. The little boy with short pants in the picture walked along with his little dog running by his side. It was prettily drawn but that didn't help me read.

"You're not supposed to copy me. You must learn to read the words," he said. "Try again. The boy . . ."

"The boy . . ."

"Went to the store!" he shouted. "Why can't you learn that? Went to the store!" With that he gave me a slap.

"I don't want to read," I cried, angry and hurt. "You have no right to hit me."

"You will never get into America if you can't read," he shouted.

"Then I don't want to go to America."

My face burned more from shame than the sting of his hand. No one had ever hit me before, except perhaps my father once when I wouldn't behave, or Grandfather. But that was rare and always just a tap on my bottom; never a slap in the face.

"How could I have married such a stupid girl?" he said.

"I'm not stupid," I said. "I can speak five languages."

"Then why can't you read? Those languages are not important. You must learn English. That's what they speak in America."

He paced back and forth in the small room with his hands on his hips. "All right!" he said. "Let's go out."

We went out into the street. I had to run to keep up with him as usual.

"Where are we going?" I said.

"We're going to see a woman. She's a relative of Hagop. She will tell us whether you will be able to go to America."

"How can she tell?" I said. I was surprised he even knew relatives of Hagop.

"You will see," he said.

We turned down a small street. The sun was blinding. A few houses from the corner we entered a courtyard. Vines had grown over the top of the wall and a fig tree stood shading a niche near the house.

"Wait here," he said.

I stood obediently near the entrance to the house as he knocked and was admitted. In the shade of the fig tree, a frail old man sat on a stool. I hadn't noticed him when we entered the courtyard and I gave a start. He sat so still. His back rested against the wall and his left hand rested on a cane. He stared at me with his crinkled, gray, red-rimmed eyes as if he looked right through me to the other side.

"So this is your wife," a woman said, approaching me from behind with Abraham.

I spun around to face her. She was a short woman with large dark eyes and black hair streaked with gray. Her skin was dark and yellowish like Zohra's. In her hands she carried a tray with tea and four glasses. She smiled at me sweetly and nodded toward the little table beside the tree for me to go and sit down.

"Abraham tells me he wants to take you to America with him. How exciting for you," she said. "America is such a big place. They don't let just anyone go there, you know."

I sat quietly not knowing what to say. She poured tea into a glass and put it in front of me. Then she poured tea for Abraham and for the old man leaning against the wall on his stool.

"Some tea," she said to him in an extra-loud voice. She leaned over to hand him the tea. His hand came toward hers in slow motion. He wrapped his fingers around the glass and they paused, each holding the glass suspended, until the woman finally let go and the old man slowly brought the glass to his lips.

"So!" she said turning back to me. "Have you learned to read yet?"

"No," I said. I lowered my eyes in embarrassment.

"I told her she must learn to read English if she wants to go to America," Abraham said.

"Well. Come. Finish your tea and I will read the leaves. They will tell us everything," the woman said.

I brought the tea to my lips. My hand shook slightly from the strain of her sympathetic stare. Abraham sipped his hot tea noisily to cool it as it passed his lips. I had heard of people reading tea leaves and also the grinds on the bottom of a cup of Greek coffee, but I didn't really believe in such things. I looked at her warily.

"It's a gift from God to read the signs in the leaves," she said "Now come. Are you finished? Turn your glass upside down on your saucer."

I took a long gulp and drained the glass leaving only the leaves behind. Then I turned the glass over in my saucer.

"Now give me your glass," she said.

She stretched out her hand to me. I handed her the glass and she peered inside.

"Tch, tch, tch," she clucked, shaking her head. "How sad your glass is. Look, Abraham!" she said, showing him the glass. "You see here? This means she will not be going with you. You must take this trip to America alone. If she can't read, it says, she will not be admitted. Oh! I'm so sorry for you," she said. She put down the glass and looked at me mournfully. "I'm afraid it's hopeless if you can't read."

I could feel the blood rushing to my face and all the anger in me seemed to boil up inside. My earlier resolution not to go to America vanished as quickly as it had come.

"You are wrong! I will get in. I bet you a hundred lire I get in," I said. I stood and walked over to the door of the courtyard. I couldn't remember when I had spoken so strongly. *Besides,* I thought to myself. *I am his wife. He can't leave me behind.*

Abraham clucked his tongue also, but rose and followed me to the door. "Good-bye," he said.

"I will send you a letter from America," I said as we were leaving. "Then you'll see."

In the street the sun was again blinding. There were no trees to shade us, and the grit from the road had lodged between my toes and filled the sides of the shoes, until I could feel the blisters beginning to form.

"Abraham," I said. "Let's take a horse and buggy home. My feet hurt so much."

"No!" he said. "We'll walk."

"Then I'll walk barefoot," I said. I knelt down and unfastened the buttons on my shoes and took the shoes off. Abraham stared down at me.

"Tch, tch," he clucked again, then turned and walked on for me to follow.

Back in our room Abraham paced the floor. He had said nothing all the way home. I went into the bathroom and washed the dust of the road from my feet and hands. Then I came to sit on the bed to dry them off.

From the courtyard, a Turkish song drifted up through the open window from a phonograph player in someone's apartment. I think.

"Listen Saniti," Abraham said, calling me "my little Sano." "They're singing about your people. 'You think you're coming back, but you'll never come back. You'll fly like a bird on the wing up to the blue sky, and never again drink the cool water.'"

He stood silently for a while, perhaps remembering his own exile. Then he lowered his eyes and sat beside me.

"Come," he said more gently. "Let's try to read again."

33.

THE KIDNAPPING

We SPENT THREE months in Zahlé waiting for my papers. Abraham's cousins were good to me. "You are family now," his young cousin said to me often as she squeezed my hand. She told me many stories about my new husband. *Husband.* The word itself made me feel less alone in the world; less of a spectator to life and more of a participant.

My husband. I said the words over in my mind. Even the word *my* gave me satisfaction. Someone belonged to me again. I belonged to someone. Someone had chosen me.

I listened intently to the stories about my husband. They were now my stories too, in a way. I was part of him and therefore all that he was, was in some way part of me.

Abraham was born on Christmas Day in 1879. His life was filled with adventure, bravery, treachery, and danger.

"When the Turks kidnapped his sister, Hartoon," his cousin told me, "she was alone with her mother at the time. Abraham was one of the youngest sons. He and his younger brother, Elias, and two sisters were the only ones still living at home with Abraham's mother. His father and older brothers had fled from the Turks when Abraham was only a boy. One brother was murdered by soldiers. Stabbed, more because he was a Christian than for any other reason.

"Abraham's mother was a weaver. She sat at her loom day and night after Abraham's father and brothers were exiled, weaving to put food on the table for her family. The sound of the shuttle gliding through the *shed* to the left, the shifting of the harness, and the gliding of the shuttle to the right, filled the house with its music from sunup to sundown, day after day. Abraham's mother taught Abraham to weave also, telling him he must have more than one trade to fall back on. So Abraham also learned to weave. He wove himself a very fine, strong cloth, then made himself a jacket of many beautiful colors that he wore wherever he went.

"Abraham was out of the house when two strong young Turks came and called to his sister Hartoon. She was a beautiful young woman, tall and pale with dark hair and green, limpid eyes; the younger of two daughters. Abraham loved her dearly.

"It was legal to kidnap a woman there as long as she was not in her home at the time. So the Turks called to Hartoon to come outside. But Abraham's mother would not let Hartoon go to the door. Instead, Abraham's mother left her loom and went herself to see who called her daughter. The commotion at the door soon brought Hartoon to protect her mother and, once she was near the door, the young Turks knocked her mother down, then grabbed Hartoon and carried her away struggling.

"When Abraham came home and found his mother in tears and wounded, he went straight to the local pasha, the town official whom he knew, to ask him to intervene and get his sister back. But the pasha refused, saying there was nothing he could or would do. Abraham left disheartened but determined to free his sister.

"He devised a plan with the help of two friends. One evening he went to the house where the parents of the young Turks lived with their daughter Warde, a name which meant Rose. Abraham introduced himself as the brother of their son's new wife and they invited him in for supper. About halfway through the meal, a knock came at the door.

"'Warde,' Abraham said. 'Someone is at the door. Why don't you go and see who it is?'

"But Warde's mother was very shrewd.

"'No!' she said. 'You stay here and I will see who is at the door.'

"When the mother left the table, Abraham again encouraged Warde to go to the door. He walked close behind her and nudged her on. At the door, two men waited. Warde's mother opened the door and when she did, Abraham pushed Warde out into the courtyard.

"'No!' the mother screamed. But Abraham threw Warde over his shoulder and ran with her as fast as he could. The mother continued screaming, and Warde's father ran for his rifle. Soon shots were whizzing by Abraham's head.

"'Throw that bitch down,' his friends shouted at him as they made their getaway.

"'No!' Abraham shouted back. 'She's mine.' And he ran with her slung over his shoulder like a sack of potatoes to the horses he and his friends had hidden for their escape. Then Abraham rode with her across his lap all the way to his own village.

"He hid in a small building and told his friends to go and get the preacher. When they returned, he asked the preacher to marry him, but Warde refused. She said she would never consent, and the preacher, feeling sorry for her, told Abraham to bring Warde home.

"They spent the night innocently together. In the morning Abraham sent word to the family, that if they gave him back his sister, he would return their daughter. Their answer was a swift 'No!' Realizing they would not bargain for her, Abraham brought Warde home anyway.

"For his troubles, a warrant was sent out for his arrest. He kissed his mother and his other sister, Nejmy, goodbye, put on his fine jacket, and fled the country. It took him almost a year to reach Beirut, Lebanon, the port town where he could take a ship to America. He worked as a stone mason along the way to make enough money for his passage. He sometimes lived among the Kurds whose language he learned easily, and whose customs he watched and carefully copied to fit in, and they took him in as one of their own.

"The people he worked for paid Abraham in gold coins. When he finally arrived in Beirut, he was just about to board the ship, safe at last, when he told a man about his escape from Mardin. The man turned out to be in the secret police. He arrested Abraham and he was put into a dungeon; down forty steps as it was called. It was filthy, dark, and damp. Each day the guards demanded Abraham give them his fine jacket, and each day Abraham refused. They whipped him for it, but the cloth of the jacket was woven so tightly, that Abraham hardly felt the whip. But finally he gave his jailers his jacket. He was there for many months before they sent him back to Mardin where he was sent to the pasha.

"'He is a Christian,' his enemies whispered to the pasha. 'Kill him.'

"'Abraham,' the pasha said. 'You are lucky I like you or I would have you put to death. Go from this place and don't return.'

"Abraham went to see his mother one last time. His reverence for her was very touching. The villagers called his mother a saint because she was such a good woman. His kidnapped sister, Hartoon, had died in childbirth while he was in prison. Abraham was heartbroken. He kissed his mother and sister Nejmy good-bye again, and this time left Turkey forever, never to see them again."

Abraham's cousin left off then and bowed her head as if remembering some secret pain of her own.

"You know?" she said. "Our family was almost entirely destroyed once. But that was long ago. Six hundred years ago, in fact. The Turks were killing Christians then too. The people of one whole town ran away and hid themselves in a deep cave. Our people were with them. But as they hid, one of the children began to cry. The mother took the child out of the cave so the Turks would not hear it and find the others. But the Turks saw her leave and let her go. Then they poured fuel down into the cave where the others were hiding and set them on fire. They were all killed. All except that one woman with her child. They were our ancestors. The only ones left."

I looked over at my husband sitting with the men at the table. For the first time I felt close to him.

"Yes," I thought. "For better or worse, Abraham is my family now."

34.

CROSSING THE

GREAT WATERS

My PAPERS FINALLY arrived. We had only to wait now for passage to America.

"Maybe you should stay here," Abraham told me one day. "You can stay with my family until I send for you. Maybe they won't let you into America now."

"No!" I said. "I'm your wife. I won't wait here. I'll go with you. They will let me in. I know they will."

I found my voice with Abraham, the voice I had lost when I found myself alone in a strange land, surrounded by strangers. It was not a strong voice at first, but at least I could speak my mind. I belonged some-where, or at least to someone. And someone belonged to me.

As he paced back and forth, I sat silently watching him, determined not to budge from my resolve.

"All right," he said finally. "You'll come with me. Maybe they'll let you in."

We went to Beirut, Lebanon and stayed in a hotel to wait for the ship to take us to America. It arrived two months later. We boarded the S. S. *Braga* of the Fabre Line in the late afternoon. Abraham brought our bags down into the barracks below. Row after row of beds lay side by side and stacked one above the other. I thought nothing of it at first. No one else was there before us. The magic of climbing on board such a huge vessel and floating on the water was all I could think of at the time. I had never seen so much water before in my life. I searched the horizon, but as far as I could see, no land existed on the other side. I stayed on the ship's deck watching the water until they hoisted up the gangplanks and blew the deep horn.

"What's that?" I said, almost jumping out of my skin.

"We're off," Abraham said. "Take a last look. They're telling all the visitors to leave the ship and then we are on our way."

As the ship let go its hold of the dock and slowly moved away, rising and falling with the heaving waters, my heart raced and my legs wobbled beneath me. I felt like a child letting go of her mother's skirts to finally walk alone. I stood staring first at the horizon where the sea met the sky and then back again to the shore we left behind. It grew smaller and smaller as the light from the summer sky faded into night, revealing a billion stars. Phosphorescent lights crashed against the sides of the ship as it cut through the black waters, and sparkled frantically in the churning waves.

"Come Saniti," Abraham said, breaking the magic of my trance. "It's getting late. We should find our beds."

"All right," I said. I tore myself away from the railing and followed him down the long deck to a door, then down the stairway that led into the belly of the ship.

The room was full of men lying around on the cots and bunks, or sitting in groups playing checkers and talking over low boxes used as tables for the game. Smoke from cigarettes mingled with the smell of sweat and old shoes.

"What are we doing here?" I said, shocked that he would bring me to such a place.

"This is where we sleep," he said.

"Oh, no!" I almost shouted. "I won't sleep here with all these men."

"But it's the only passage I could afford. We spent so much time waiting for your papers."

"I don't care," I said. "I won't sleep here. I'll sleep outside. I'll sleep under the stars if I have to."

"But . . ." he started.

"No!" I said and ran out of the room and up the stairs to the deck.

"But you can't sleep outside. It will take twenty-eight days to get to America," he shouted after me. But I was already long gone. He raced up the stairs after me.

"I don't care if it takes forever. I won't sleep there."

I threw myself into a chair on deck and curled up with my legs drawn beneath me. I wrapped my arms around my knees to make myself as small as possible to keep my warmth from escaping. Abraham paced back and forth on the deck, mumbling under his breath. He took his hat off and scratched the back of his balding head, then looked around, hoping a miracle would save him, I guess.

"All right," he said. He put his hat back on his head and straightened his shoulders. "All right. Come with me."

"Where are we going?"

"To the captain," he said.

"What's a captain?" I said, running behind him to keep up.

We came to a stairway and climbed to the upper level and went straight to a door with a sign on it. Abraham stood outside staring at it for a long time. Then he raised his hand to knock. But before his knuckles hit the door, he lowered his hand again.

"What's the matter?" I said.

"Nothing!" he said. He straightened his back and squared his shoulders again. He raised his hand to knock again, and this time knocked loudly.

"Who is it?" a voice boomed from the other side of the door.

"Excuse me, sir," Abraham said. The door opened and the captain stood staring at us. "We are having a little problem."

"What can I do for you?" he said.

"Well, you see . . ." Abraham began. He looked at me for help, but realizing there was none to be had, "you see," he began again. "I'm taking my new wife to America, sir, and I bought passage for the lower deck. But my wife says she won't sleep there with all those men. Now I don't know what to do."

The captain looked at me and then looked at Abraham. "I see," he said.

Abraham fidgeted. I could only stand with bowed head, too shy to look too long at the captain's face.

"Well," he said after a moment that seemed an hour. I could feel him look at me again with those two patches of sky set in his round, pink face. His yellow mustache drooped down to his chin before curling up again to his ears. Without answering, he turned and went into his cabin and pulled on a cord hanging near the wall.

Scene after scene ran through my mind. Would he tell us we must leave the ship? Would he force us to sleep in that hole with all those men? Would he lock us up somewhere or simply throw us into the ocean? Just when my mind was beginning to think up the most fantastic disasters, a young boy came running.

"Find these people an empty cabin," the captain said. "And make sure they are comfortable. Congratulations," he said turning back to us. "I hope your trip to America is a pleasant one."

"Thank you, sir," Abraham said. I looked from one to the other not understanding what had taken place. "Thank him," Abraham told me.

"Thank you," I said and lowered my head again.

He smiled at me, and the boy led us to a cabin on the main deck. It was beautiful and private with two little beds, one on top of the other. And so my trip to America was made in luxury.

ꙮ   ꙮ   ꙮ

Our first stop was Istanbul but we only saw it from the port until the cargo was loaded. Then we were on our way again. On board I saw two young women crocheting little baskets with colored thread. I watched them from a short distance too shy to ask them how it was done.

I bet I could do that, I thought. It's the thing that has carried me through life, this feeling that I could do what I set out to do. I can tell just by looking at something if I could master it or not, and once I determine that I can, there is no way to stop me. A little gift from God perhaps, this resolve of my will.

When we stopped at Algiers they let us go ashore. Women wore a kind of balloon pants I had never seen before. The men also wore balloon pants, and over them they wore tunics that came down to their knees with a slit up the sides.

I asked Abraham if he would buy me a crocheting needle and some thread. He said yes. I think he felt proud that I could do something I had never done before.

"Look, Sano!" he said.

He pointed to a strand of amber beads that sat in a shop window.

They had almost a translucent quality to them and I thought them the most beautiful beads I had ever seen, except perhaps the ones Grandfather had brought me from Fatsa when I was a child.

"They're beautiful," I said.

"Let's go ask how much they are."

He went into the shop and spoke to the man behind the counter. A few minutes later the man was handing the beads to Abraham wrapped in paper.

"You bought them?" I asked as I ran along beside him back toward the ship.

"They're yours," he said. "I bought them for you."

He handed me the wrapped beads. I couldn't believe he had really given them to me. I stared up at him waiting. But he didn't take them back.

"They're really mine?"

I pressed them close to my chest as if they were the most precious things I had ever owned. I guess they were. In fact, they were my only real possession outside of my clothing. They were the only thing I could call mine since I left my own home so long ago.

I never wore them. Instead, I tucked them into our trunk so they wouldn't get damaged, and each day I dug them up, unwrapped them, stared at them for a long, loving moment, and then wrapped them up again.

On board I tried to fathom how to make the little crocheted basket. I began with a knot; a master knot I guess you could call it; the same knot for any weave or design one wishes to make; the first knot from which all else begins.

I worked day and night in every spare moment, looping the colored thread around the needle and slipping it through the knots already formed. I looped each loop to the other. I curled it 'round and 'round. It grew bigger and bigger and soon it began to take shape. I was proud of it. It curved up and became a sort of bowl shape. With each new row I stopped over and over again to admire my handiwork, proud of my ability to create a shape from a simple thread. But in the end, I had not made a basket at all.

"It's a good hat, " Abraham said when I was finished.

"But it was meant to be a basket," I said.

"Next time you'll make a basket. This time you made a hat," he said. "It's a good hat, and if you let me, I'll wear it."

"All right," I said, feeling proud of it after all. And he did wear it for the whole trip to America.

We next stopped in Greece but didn't go ashore. Then we set off across the Mediterranean Sea, and then the Atlantic Ocean. As far as the eye could see there was only ocean and sky. Flying fish leaped from the water, and dolphins followed by our side, curving their sleek bodies in and out of the rippling ocean like needles stitching cloth.

☙ ☙ ☙

On the twenty-fifth day of August, 1925, we arrived at Ellis Island, twenty-eight days after we had set out.

"We're here," Abraham said with some anxiety in his voice. He stood at the railing and stared off across the river as we pulled into port.

"Is this New York?" I asked.

"No," he said. "This is a place we have to stop first to see if they'll let you in. New York is over there."

He pointed his finger to a mass of land. Manhattan lay like a beached ship in the sun, its barnacled surface jagged against a clear sky. It sat there in the August heat with the sun shimmering off the peaks of buildings.

"Come on," Abraham said. "We've got to go through customs."

He picked up our baggage and headed toward the gangplank. Other passengers had already lined up to disembark. They shoved and jockeyed for position almost knocking me off my feet.

"Hold on to me so you don't get lost," Abraham said.

I grabbed his coat sleeve and squeezed my way through the crowd behind him. We stood in line waiting to go through the authorities with nervous expectation. At least Abraham was nervous. I had long ago given up on the idea of wishing for anything, and along with that decision went all the excitement of expectation.

I was sent into a room and asked to sit on a table in front of a doctor. Abraham came with me.

"*Buono!*" the doctor said after listening to my chest and examining my eyes. "Now I must see your legs. I'm not going to hurt you. Don't be afraid," he said to me through Abraham.

He pushed my dress above my knees and felt my calves.

"What are these scars?" he asked.

"All that's left," I said.

He looked up at me. "How old are you?"

"Fifteen, I think."

"Okay! *Buono!*" he said. "You can go."

We went through customs fairly quickly. A man asked me to sign my name, but I couldn't, so he pressed my thumb on an ink pad and told me to make a thumb print on the paper. I did. Then Abraham pressed a few of our bundles into my arms, grabbed my hand and pulled me toward the exit. With his other hand he struggled to half carry, half drag our luggage.

"Hurry," Abraham said, "before they change their minds."

A ferry was waiting to take passengers across the river to Manhattan.

"Quick!" he said with the same anxious look on his face.

We ran aboard just as a bell rang and the ferry gates were drawing closed. I could feel the water churning under my feet as the ferry slowly moved away from the dock with a rumble.

"Wahoo!" Abraham half shouted. "Wahoo! They let you in. We're safe. Wahoo! Look, Saniti! That's New York. Your new home. Wahoo! We're free!"

I stared again at the great line of jagged buildings stretching out in front of me. I had never seen anything like them in my life, yet I felt nothing stir inside me. I felt neither pangs nor flutters nor twinges of hope; nothing at all. Nothing, that is, until we reached the shore and disembarked. Out on the pavement, on that beautiful, sunny August afternoon, the streets of New York were alive.

"What's that?" I asked in amazement.

"What?" Abraham said, looking around to see what I saw that made me so excited.

"There!" I said, pointing to a group of boys and girls in the distance who were gliding along as if on a magic carpet.

"They're children," Abraham said and laughed. "Children on roller skates."

"Children on roller skates," I repeated, not understanding what roller skates were.

"But they're flying!" I said.

Abraham laughed that elated laugh that comes from holding one's fears of failure in check for so long, that when the danger is abruptly removed, the flood gates of emotion burst open and it's difficult to reign in one's joy.

"Yes. They're flying," he said.

I felt a kind of exhilaration at last, watching them fly by so effortlessly. My own childhood had been so short. My heart leapt with them as if I too sailed above the pavement without a care in the world, like a low-flying bird, or a butterfly flitting from bud to bud, released from the burden of my unhappy life.

"Abraham," I said, not taking my eyes from the children gliding down the street. The smile was still stuck to his face.

"Tell that woman who read my tea leaves to give the hundred lire she owes me to Zohra's children."

"Hundred lire?" he said.

"The hundred lire she bet me they wouldn't let me into America."

Abraham laughed again. "Wahoo!" he shouted.

I looked around at my new land, and once again at the flying children.

"Yes!" I whispered to myself. "Maybe this is freedom."

Book Four

AMERICA, AMERICA

Like a child without the comfort
of my mother's hem to guide me
I stepped across that great divide
between the old world and the new
leaving my grief on the banks
of that other shore

35.

AMERICA, AMERICA

COMING TO AMERICA was like stepping from one century into the next. Everything was new to me and I was once again a stranger in a strange land. But it was not my new land that made me wonder about the mysterious twists and turns of fate. It was fate's cunning on my wedding day that had made me both a wife to a man old enough to be my father and a mother to a boy who was almost as old as I. What did I know about being the mother of a ten-year-old boy? I knew practically nothing about practically everything there was to know in the world. What good was it to know how to paint my fingernails red with the dye I made from leaves I found in the forest? There were no forests in New York City. There were no gamish to prod to separate the wheat from the chaff. I didn't need mushroom matches and I had no cows to take to pasture. Neither was there a mill to grind the flour.

And what did I know about being a wife?

When we disembarked the ferry from Ellis Island, Abraham piled our things into one of the horse-drawn carriages waiting near the pier. As I settled myself into the carriage, Abraham gave the driver the address of the boardinghouse he had lived in before going to Syria and marrying me: West Nineteenth Street. Then he climbed in the carriage and sat beside me.

The sun was bouncing off the windows of skyscrapers as we started uptown from the pier. The smell of the old, cracked leather of the seats and the oiled wooden walls of the carriage brought back memories of my first carriage ride on the day after our wedding in Aleppo. But instead of men in red fez hats and baggy pants sipping coffee in cafes, and beautiful colored rugs hanging in a bazaar, what floated by outside the carriage window now were huge ships gracefully moving down the river, or docked at a pier. Dock workers also floated by, and immigrants in long black dresses or suits, with their mismatched suitcases and weary bundles gathered at their feet. Weary too, were the expressions they wore. A man on his knees with his hands clasped in front of him, his eyes locked on the blue August sky, and his lips moving as in prayer, also floated by. And then a row of small red-brick buildings gathered themselves up, as did the huge skyscrapers behind them, to float past the carriage window, all to the tune of *clop-clop, clop-clop, clop-clop.*

When we arrived at the boardinghouse, we had barely stepped out of the carriage and climbed the few steps to the ornate wooden door, when we could see the Irish widow who ran it, Mrs. Keneally, waving to us from behind the door's engraved glass.

"Oh, Mr. Halo," the widow said when Abraham walked through the door. "Is it yourself then? We've missed you. And this must be your new wife. Come in. Come in. Ah, but she's a pretty young thing, she is."

Mrs. Keneally was a small, round woman with tightly curled hair the color of wheat at sunset. She was wearing a dress full of flowers when we arrived, and when she smiled at me, her thin pink lips spread across her face like a ribbon.

"I'm Mrs. Keneally," she said, directing herself to me. "Why don't you put your bags down and come take some tea. I'll have the housekeeper make a fresh pot right away." Then turning again to Abraham, "Oh, yes. It's good to have you home again, Mr. Halo. Farage will be so glad to see you."

Before we married, Abraham told me he had been married once before to an American woman from Ohio and that he had a child. He had left his son in New York with Mrs. Keneally until his return from Aleppo.

As she entered her parlor, Mrs. Keneally called to Abraham's son in the next room.

"Farage, my boy. 'Tis your father home at last, and he's brought with him a fine young woman to be your mother. Come and meet her."

Abraham put down his bags in the hall and I let go of mine. Then we followed the widow into her parlor. The room was as plump and comfortable as Mrs. Keneally. The overstuffed sofa and armchairs were also full of flowers, almost the same style as Mrs. Keneally's dress. There were little shaded lamps on tiny tables. A multicolored braided rug lay near the potbellied stove, and lace curtains, white and frilly, hung from every window. I had never seen such a home before.

"This is your new mother," Abraham said as Farage approached.

I had been so busy taking in the pleasantness of the room and the music of Mrs. Keneally's voice, that I hadn't heard Farage come into the room. His presence startled me and I jumped at the sound of Abraham's voice. Farage looked at me shyly and I looked at him just as shyly. I was to be his mother. He was ten years old. I was fifteen. Abraham was forty-five.

"Well then," Mrs. Keneally said as she came back into the room followed by the housekeeper. "Make yourselves comfortable."

We still stood awkwardly as the housekeeper set the tea tray on a low table in front of the sofa. Mrs. Keneally sat her flowered self down there, mingling the bouquet of her dress with the flowers of the sofa.

"Come," Mrs. Keneally said. "Come sit down here and take some tea."

She patted the seat of the sofa for me to sit beside her and I did.

"I'm sure your trip was very long and tiring but you're home now, lass. You'll be comfortable in no time, won't she, Mr. Halo?"

I couldn't understand a word Mrs. Keneally was saying. Abraham later told me what she had said. But the words themselves were not important. There was kindness in her voice. It was comforting and motherly and I sank into the sofa and let the music of her voice dance around me in its field of flowers.

"Here you are," Mrs. Keneally said as she poured the tea through a strainer into a cup.

She handed me my cup and I peered inside, grateful to find no tea leaves on the bottom for her to read.

🕊 🕊 🕊

We had just one large room to ourselves on the second floor. It's furnishings were simpler than Mrs. Keneally's, but like her rooms it had no heat except for the potbellied stove that now stood cold near the wall. But at least there was hot water.

Farage came to live with us on the day of our arrival. He was a beautiful boy; a storybook boy, like the boy in the illustrated children's book Abraham had used when he tried to teach me to read English. His gray eyes, so like his father's, kept stealing glances at me from across the room as I stole glances at him. I kept trying to imagine what I should do to be his mother.

Also on the day of our arrival, we had barely made ourselves comfortable when a man came to visit. He brought with him a cloth shopping bag full of bananas as a gift. It was a fruit I had seen only in Lebanon, but one that I loved. The man sat himself down in one of the chairs and did not budge again until late in the evening. He was a handsome man, shorter than Abraham, and younger, with a groove at the tip of his prominent nose that seemed to divide it into two halves.

He and Abraham talked together the entire day without paying attention to me. Abraham even forgot to introduce us.

When is this man going home, I thought. But he sat and sat.

"Who was that man?" I said to Abraham when the man finally left.

"That was my brother, Elias," Abraham said.

🕊   🕊   🕊

Abraham's father, Amos, and Abraham's two eldest brothers, Amos and Abdulahad, had been the first in his family to emigrate to America sometime in the late 1800s. Abraham's father was a Protestant missionary. It was because of his work as a missionary that he had been forced to leave Turkey. His family had once been quite wealthy there, but the local pasha had confiscated all of his lands and houses and threatened to have his father put to death for spreading the word of Christianity.

It was Abraham's father who helped arrange Abraham's passage to America when he left Turkey the second time. Abraham's father contacted a parish and they raised the money.

I'm not sure what his father and brothers did to make a living in America when they first arrived, but in 1905, when Abraham emigrated to join them after his own exile, they were selling doilies door to door. Abraham was twenty-five years old then. On his arrival he worked as a traveling salesman like his father and brothers for about six years. Then he enrolled in college in Ohio. He studied dentistry and chemistry. One day in a chemistry class his professor told him to analyze some substance to see what was in it. Abraham said his analysis showed there was a lot of lead in the substance that shouldn't be there. He told his professor, but his professor insisted Abraham was wrong. Abraham was sure he was right, and as it turned out, he was right. He would have liked being a chemist, I think. He used to collect different herbs and roots and use them as medicines or tonics, until he almost killed himself one day by drinking a brew he had concocted. After that he relied on doses of castor oil as a remedy for practically everything.

Abraham also played baseball in college for a while, but that was short-lived. Once when they hit the ball to him, instead of throwing it to first base he threw it home, so they threw him off the team. But his real intention was to become a dentist.

One day, Abraham saw a notice in the newspaper for a mail-order bride. In those days people sometimes advertised in the newspaper to find a husband or wife. Abraham had been in America for about seven years by then. He answered the ad by writing to the girl's parents and when they replied, he went to meet them. But when Abraham met the girl, he told her father—who was a judge, I think—that he didn't want to marry his daughter. The girl's father told him he had to marry her, so Abraham did. They married in 1912.

While he went to school, he worked at the metalworks making tools to help support himself and his wife. But between school and work, he found the hours too long, and the pay too short; just ten cents an hour. It wasn't easy. Finally, he dropped out of school.

When Abraham quit college, he moved with his wife to South Carolina and again became a traveling salesman, selling doilies door to door. He bought land and built a house for them to live in. A year later they had a son. But his wife was not the mothering kind. She refused to nurse the child. She said it hurt her nipples to nurse. There were no baby bottles in those days. At least I don't think there were. Anyway, the baby died while Abraham was on the road selling doilies. He said his wife had starved his poor son to death.

Soon after Abraham married, his father and brothers decided to return to the Middle East. They went to Baghdad—which was still part of the Ottoman Empire in those days—since they couldn't go back to Mardin. In Baghdad, Abraham's brother, Abdulahad, met a woman and wanted to marry her. He needed money to marry, so he wrote to Abraham and asked him to send the money he had left in a bank in New York. But when Abraham went to the bank they told him there was no money.

It wasn't the first time Abdulahad wanted to marry. He had met another woman on the way to America whom he had wanted to marry, but his father had forbidden it, reminding his son that their goal was to reach America. This second disappointment was too much for Abdulahad. He never forgave Abraham. He thought Abraham had stolen the money, but I know he didn't. He wouldn't do such a thing. I don't know what happened to the money. Maybe his father had taken it. Or maybe the bank stole it. They knew he was too far away to do anything about it. Or maybe Abdulahad was just mistaken about how much he had in the account. Angry because he thought his father and brother had destroyed both his attempts to marry, Abdulahad moved to Borneo and married a woman there, severing all ties with his family.

In Baghdad, Abraham's father never recovered the fortune he once had in Turkey. Years later, we heard he had died in poverty.

Around 1914, Abraham decided to help his younger brother Elias emigrate to America, so he mortgaged his house and sent his brother the money. When Elias arrived he lived with Abraham and his wife. About a year after Elias arrived, Abraham's wife gave birth again, again to a son. Abraham named him Farage. And again his wife didn't want to take care of their child. It was then that Abraham realized his wife was running around with other men. He began divorce proceedings, intending to take Farage and leave. It was 1917 and the First World War was raging.

To stop him perhaps, or just to make trouble for him, his wife accused Abraham of being a foreign spy, which resulted in a full investigation of him by the U.S. government. Of course they found nothing. When Abraham finally went before the judge for his divorce, the judge gave him full custody of Farage.

Abraham packed up his few belongings and brought Farage, who was just two years old then, to New York to live. But on his way through Washington D.C. the police stopped him, suspicious because he was traveling with such a young child. They questioned him about Farage, then locked him up and forced him to spend the night in jail. They thought he had kidnapped Farage. Only when Abraham showed the judge Farage's papers the next morning did they let him go.

That's when Abraham found his way to Mrs. Keneally's boarding-house on West Nineteenth Street. After school, Mrs. Keneally, or her housekeeper, looked after Farage while Abraham worked. In the evening, Abraham took over the care of Farage himself. But Abraham's problems were still not over.

Before his trip to Syria in 1925, Abraham sent a letter to a lawyer in South Carolina telling him he wanted to sell his house there. He received no answer. When he returned from his trip with me in August of '25, Abraham again wrote to the lawyer to sell his house. The lawyer wrote back that Abraham no longer owned the house. He said the bank had taken it because Abraham was behind in paying the mortgage he had taken out to help his brother Elias emigrate to America. In fact, the lawyer said, the town had already torn the house down and had run a highway right through the property. All of the equity Abraham had built up in America over the last twenty years was gone.

36

THE OLD AND THE NEW

Mrs. Keneally's housekeeper prepared dinner each evening for all the boardinghouse guests. Abraham, Farage, and I joined the others at the long mahogany table in Mrs. Keneally's dining room. Brass wall sconces with small glass globes sent out a warm glow to light the room. I wasn't used to eating with so many strangers. It took all of my willpower to eat at all. I just wanted to hang my head and hide, or better still, go to our room and eat in private.

The table was set as I had never seen a table set before. At each seat a china bowl for soup had been placed on top of a large flat china plate. A knife, soup spoon, and teaspoon sat to the right of each plate, and at the left, two forks sat on a neatly folded napkin. Goblets sparkled above each setting.

The Greeks also used knives and forks in my country, and we each ate from our own plate. Sometimes mother made fresh pasta by slicing the flattened dough into thin strips, and when it was cooked, she poured melted butter over it. We ate things like pasta with a fork. But we had mostly eaten soups and stews, which we ate with a spoon. In the south of Turkey, other than soup, which they also ate with a spoon, but from the same pot, they ate with their hands or used a piece of bread to scoop up the food from a single large dish. Of course, on the ship we had place settings similar to Mrs. Keneally's, but not as pretty.

I watched Mrs. Keneally and did what she did. I unfolded my napkin and placed it on my lap when she did, then picked up my soup spoon and ate the soup that the housekeeper ladled into my bowl. When the bowl was cleared away, I was surprised to watch the housekeeper place other thing on my plate: a slab of roast, a portion of mashed potatoes with a little well of gravy in the center, and a portion of greens. I used the knife and fork the way Mrs. Keneally used them, cutting my piece of roast a piece at a time. I even drank when she drank and lay my knife and fork across my plate when she was done.

Over dinner one evening Mrs. Keneally said to Abraham, "Mr. Halo, your young wife is obviously well educated. She has such fine manners."

She was a kind woman. It was the first feeling of home in my new land. But the one room for the three of us was cramped, so a few months later we moved to a three-room apartment on West Seventeenth Street. Abraham went out and bought secondhand furniture. He bought a big round oak table with claws for feet. He bought a sofa and chairs, lamps, beds, and little lace curtains like those of Mrs. Keneally's; all the things we needed. Then he set about painting and decorating the apartment. I knew nothing about those things.

For most of each day I was alone. Abraham worked at odd jobs paving sidewalks or fixing a roof, even carpentry, and Farage went to school. Soon after our arrival, Abraham took me to the 5 & 10 Cent Store. When he opened the door to the store my eyes also opened wide. There were rows of tables, each containing things I had never seen before.

"Look, Sano," he said. "They sell things here for five or ten cents."

On one of those days when I sat alone with no one to talk with, I decided to try my own hand at shopping at the 5 & 10 Cent Store. I went in and strolled around not knowing what to look at and touch first. In America I saw women who were all made up with lipstick and rouge and I looked for the counter that had such things. I didn't know then that Abraham's first wife had been the kind of woman who ran around with other men.

"May I help you?" a young woman said from behind me.

I whirled around and stared at her, not understanding what she said. I could only look at her and then in shyness look away to the counter in front of me where cosmetics were neatly arranged, each kind in its own bin. The saleswoman said something else and pointed to a photograph of a beautiful woman whose face was painted in warm, rich colors. I picked up a compact of powder nervously. The saleswoman said a few more words to me, then held the compact up to my cheek and examined me. She put that one down and selected another and another, holding each close to my face until she found just the right shade. Then she picked out rouge, followed by lipstick, and did the same. She smiled at me a sweet smile that said she was pleased with her selection. I smiled also and followed her to the cashier to pay for my new face. I was happy with my purchase. The woman in the photo looked so wonderful; so unlike anyone I had ever seen. I wanted to be glamorous too.

I brought the cosmetics home and put them on. God only knows what I looked like. I don't even know if I did it right.

Abraham was working repairing a roof in the neighborhood, so I went to surprise him. I walked onto the roof and stood before him with a great red smile on my new face. Abraham looked up and his face fell.

"What are you doing with that shit on your face?" he said. "Take it off. I never want to see you wearing that again."

I went straight home and threw the cosmetics on the floor and stepped on them again and again to smash them. Then I threw them into the garbage. That ended my glamorous period.

🕊 🕊 🕊

Since I had always been good with languages, it didn't take me long to learn to speak English. Farage spoke only English, so I learned it more quickly speaking with him.

"I can't call you Mother," Farage said to me one day when Abraham was out. "You're just a kid."

"I know," I said. "You don't have to call me Mother."

"Then what should I call you?" he said.

"Just call me Sano," I said.

I was not only still a child, I still looked like a child. I still had no breasts. I was as flat as a flapjack. I was a child in all ways except the most dramatic ways. I was already married, and for too long Death had been my constant companion.

It was around Christmas of that first year, about four months after my arrival in America, that I finally began to menstruate for the first time. I don't know why it took so long to start. Maybe it was because of the hardships, or maybe I was even younger than I thought. Abraham had gone out to buy a Christmas tree, the first I ever saw. He bought little candles and candle holders, little colored balls, and lead tinsel. He made a stand for the tree with two pieces of wood he nailed together into a cross. Then he stood the tree near the wall and covered the base with cotton to look like snow, and told Farage and me to help decorate it. When we were finished hanging the colored balls and tinsel, he put candles in the holders we had clipped to the branches. Then he lit them one by one. It was one of the most beautiful things I ever saw.

When Farage went to bed, Abraham put a few pieces of candy as a gift in Farage's shoe to find on waking.

I sat staring at the flickering lights of the candles and the reflections on the colored balls and tinsel until I could barely keep my eyes open.

"I'm bleeding," I told Abraham when we finally went to bed. I still didn't know what that was. In the little village where my mother had left me, the women and girls of the village never told me anything because they thought I was just hiding what I knew.

"That's all right," was all Abraham answered.

I used a cloth to catch the blood, probably like my mother before me. When it was soaked I washed it out and hung it up to dry and used another.

On Christmas morning Abraham handed me a small package.

"Here," Abraham said. "Merry Christmas."

I looked up at him with gratitude that he had given me a gift. I opened the package and found a small purse inside.

"What's this?" I said.

"It's a purse for you to carry money in. You see, it even has a little chain to carry it."

I had never seen a purse before. Women in Turkey and Syria didn't use such things in those days.

"Oh, Mr. Halo," Mrs. Keneally said and laughed when we went to visit one day. "That purse is for a child."

"That's all right," Abraham said.

I was so embarrassed that when we went out I hid the purse in the palm of my hand.

"Let's go see the old man go out and the new man come in," Abraham said to me one evening soon after Christmas.

We bundled up and walked to a place, probably Forty-second Street, and stood around for a while. The streets were full of people blowing horns and wearing funny hats. They were shouting and laughing and kissing each other. People were even hanging out of the windows banging on pots and pans.

In Aleppo they also banged on pots and pans and shouted, but then it was to scare the evil spirits away when the moon eclipsed the sun. The whole town banged and shouted until the sun finally slipped from behind the moon's barrier.

But now it was late in the evening and there was no sun for the moon to hide. I looked all around to see if I could find the old man and the new man but I couldn't figure out which was which.

"All right," Abraham said after a short time. "Let's go home now. The old man went out and the new man came in."

"Where is he?" I said. "I don't see a new man. And I never saw the old man."

Abraham didn't bother to explain it was New Year's Eve, a holiday I had never celebrated before. That was so like him. He didn't seem comfortable with conversation, except perhaps with his brother, Elias.

But in the beginning Abraham did try to show me some things. He even brought me to the movies. We sat way up front and I had to crane my neck to see the giant people on the screen. The screen was so big that the actors' heads were at least a story high. The first movie I saw in America was a silent movie. I'll never forget Marion Davies. She looked like a mountain. I couldn't read at that time, but it wasn't hard to tell it was a love story. In my country we didn't have such things as moving pictures, but I don't think there's one place on earth where they don't know about troubles of the heart.

꙳   ꙳   ꙳

We lived on the ground floor in an apartment that faced the street. I had no friends to talk with. In the daytime, while Abraham worked and Farage went to school, sometimes after doing my chores I'd sit at the window for hours watching the people go by. One day I watched a man sweep the streets with a large push broom. Every so often he stopped to scoop up the trash and dumped it into the large garbage can on wheels that he pushed from place to place. The man must have seen me watching him. Maybe he thought I was flirting, because he finally put down his broom and came to the door. He knocked and knocked, but I didn't open it. I just sat there staring at the door very quietly waiting for him to go away and finally he did. I never told Abraham, and I never again sat at the window watching.

I became pregnant with our first child a few months after Christmas. About a month before the baby was due, Abraham said, "Come on. We have to go shopping to buy clothes for the baby." So we went. I knew nothing about those things either. I barely knew what was happening to me. Once Abraham brought home a big fish to cook and when I cut it open there was a small fish inside its stomach. I began to gag uncontrollably at the sight of that little fish.

"What's the matter with you?" Abraham shouted at me when he saw me trying to control my urge to vomit.

"It's dead!" I said, and again began to gag.

"Of course it's dead," he said. "Do you want to cook a live fish?"

"But it's pregnant," I said, "and now it's dead and its baby is dead too."

I thought the poor little fish inside the big fish's stomach was in there waiting to be born. Abraham came to see what I was talking about and when he saw, he began to laugh.

Abraham picked out only pink things for the baby. It wasn't until much later that I learned pink is for girls and blue is for boys. I don't know if he knew, but sure enough, it was a girl. Mariam was born in October, 1926.

I was washing the dishes when I felt the first pains of childbirth. My knees buckled beneath me and I grabbed the edge of the sink for support. Abraham looked up at my cry and rushed to me, but by the time he reached me, the pain had already subsided.

"I'm all right," I said. But a short time later the pains came again, and again I gripped the counter for support.

Abraham led me to our bed and made me lie down. Then he put a blanket over me to keep me warm.

"I'm going to get the doctor," he said, and raced out the door.

I lay there staring at the huge mound of blanket that was my stomach. The pains had again subsided and were only mild when they did come. I remembered the day Cristodula and I stood outside the door of our home listening to my mother give birth without knowing what we were listening to at the time.

"Where did the babies come from?" I had asked my mother when she presented us with our new sisters.

"They came from my knees," Mother said, and my eyes had opened wide in amazement. I had gone back to our room then and lifted the hem of my dress to examine my own knees, but had lowered the hem again without a clue as to how it was possible.

Now as I lay in my bed waiting for Abraham and the doctor, I could feel a smile spread across my face remembering my mother's smile as she told me. Then with a great involuntary sob my tears began to flow at the memory of her beautiful face.

"She's not ready yet," the doctor said when he examined me. "The baby hasn't dropped yet. It will probably be a few more days."

It was Wednesday morning when the pains came again, this time like the kick of a mule. Abraham rushed me to my bed and raced out the door, again to get the doctor. This time the pains came too quickly, one after the other, to give me time to reflect. I could only scream in agony, sure I was going to die.

"He's coming," Abraham said as he came through the door again. "The doctor's coming. We should tell the neighbors."

He ran out the door again and I could hear him pounding on the door across the hall and then on the door on the floor above. "It's coming," he shouted. "Our baby is coming. Come and watch. Our baby is coming." I had never heard of such a thing, but Abraham was so excited about having a child.

We had just moved to that apartment. It was on West Twenty-sixth Street between Sixth and Seventh Avenues. I knew no one in the building and no one knew me. But two women actually came to watch just as the doctor came through the door with his black bag. All I could do was scream in agony at the pains.

"Push!" the doctor said over and over again. "Push!"

And I pushed and pushed until finally I felt our child spring into the world.

"What are you going to name her?" the doctor asked as he cut the cord and wiped our new baby down.

Abraham seemed beside himself with joy. He straightened his shoulders and puffed out his chest. "Mariam Elizabeth Halo," he said.

I knew Mariam was his mother's name and it also had the same meaning as Maria like my sister, so I was glad, but I didn't know where he got the name Elizabeth.

"Saniti," he said to me when everyone was gone. "Look at her. She's beautiful; as beautiful as a queen." And he clucked his tongue in amazement.

Abraham had always kept up with the news. I didn't know it then, but Queen Elizabeth II of Great Britain had also been born that year.

Abraham hired a nurse to come and care for me and to cook and clean after the baby was born. Abraham said I couldn't get out of bed for fifteen days, so that's where I stayed, except to go to the bathroom, of course. I had never been in bed for so long in my life except when I was bitten by the snake and almost died.

I guess I'm going to die, I thought, and for fifteen days I lay there wondering when it would happen.

"Why don't you make something to eat?" Abraham said to the nurse.

"Oh," the nurse said. "I already made myself some tea and toast. I'm not hungry now."

"Not for yourself," Abraham said. "You were hired to cook and clean for me and my wife."

"Well, I'm sorry," said the nurse. "I don't cook and clean for anyone."

Abraham clucked his tongue in disgust. The next day he fired her and hired another woman. This time he made sure she understood she was to cook and clean.

It was wonderful having a baby, but when Mariam's eyes became sore I didn't know what to do for her. She cried and cried, and I cried with her. I was so worried and so inexperienced, all I could do was cry. Abraham took us to the doctor who delivered Mariam and the doctor made her better. It was on one of my trips to the hospital to see him that I discovered sanitary pads for the first time. That was always how I learned something, by seeing it somewhere. No one ever told me a blessed thing.

"Where did you get the baby?" Farage wanted to know.

Farage was eleven years old at the time and so ashamed to walk down the street with us because we had a baby in a carriage. In those days, people didn't tell children how babies were born or where they really came from. They never even talked about being pregnant, at least not where I came from. As my mother had done, they wore clothes to hide it as best as they could.

"Well," Abraham told Farage, "the doctor goes to the mountain and brings back a baby and gives it to the one who wants it most."

Years later, when my children began to ask where babies came from, I told them the mother carries her baby inside her for nine months, tucked just under her heart, as I had carried them. And after they're born, she carries them inside her heart for the rest of their lives, where I carry them.

🕊   🕊   🕊

"Do you know how to swim?" Abraham asked me one sweltering day the summer after Mariam was born.

"I guess so," I said.

"You have no bathing suit," Abraham said. He rummaged through his drawer and pulled out one of his black wool bathing suits. Even men's suits had tops in those days. "Here. You can wear this one."

"It's too big," I said.

"That's all right," he said.

We put our bathing suits on under our clothing, packed a picnic lunch and some towels, and took the subway to the beach; Coney Island, I think. I had never set foot in so much water. The Tigris River of Diyarbakir that I had crossed was less than a trickle compared to the Atlantic Ocean.

While I took care of the baby, Abraham and Farage went into one of the little bathing stalls set up on the beach to undress. Then, while they spread the towels out on the sand, I reluctantly went into a bathing stall and also undressed. As soon as I left the bathing stall, a man looked at me and started to laugh. My breasts had grown quite large when I became pregnant, and one of them had popped out on the side of the suit. In Aleppo, Syria, it was natural for a woman to take her breast out right in the street to nurse her child. No one even bothered to look at her.

I was so embarrassed by his laugh that I just stood still. I looked at Abraham sitting on our towels but he was too far away and was facing the ocean. I looked at the man again and he sniggered. I made up my mind that I wasn't going to give him the satisfaction of knowing I was embarrassed, so I took my breast as if it was nothing and stuffed it back in again. But when I stuffed one breast in on one side, the other breast popped out on the other side. While I took care of Mariam, Abraham went into the ocean for a swim. From the shore, I could see a sliver of his black bathing suit in the shimmering peaks of silver and blue; his arms slashed waves that swallowed and released him with each stroke. I was surprised to see how good a swimmer he was. It looked so easy that when Abraham came back looking refreshed, dripping ocean with the sun shimmering on his bare shoulders, I jumped up to take my turn.

"Mind the baby," I said before racing to the edge of the water.

I put my foot in tentatively, then waded in deeper and deeper. The ocean was wonderful at first. At least it was wonderful after the shock of the first chill. It splashed at my ankles, my knees, my waist. It lifted me gently off my feet and set me down again. Then a wave came that lifted me up so swiftly and forcefully that I found myself sailing toward the shore, where it threw me down with a great crash of foam. I barely had time to catch my breath when the wave went out to sea again, sucking me in and under with it. I could feel the sand sink away beneath my hands as I clawed at it to get a grip.

Oh, God, I thought. *I'm finished. I'm going to die.*

Each time I tried to stand, a new wave swept over me before I was fully on my feet, as if the ocean had a mind and a will and it had concentrated its energies on me. Again I tried to stand and again I was swept up and then sucked away. Abraham and all those people were standing around, or sitting on the sand, going about their business while I was struggling for my life, and no one knew. I was invisible; separate from the rest of the world; as separate and invisible as my people had been as we dragged our wasted bodies across the desert lands of Turkey. I felt as insignificant as a jelly fish floating about in the waves. I couldn't even shout for help because the water would have filled my lungs if I had opened my mouth. I tried to lift my head above the waves, but each time I struggled, the undercurrent sucked me in deeper and deeper. Then suddenly the ocean released me. I scrambled to my feet and ran to the shore, and never went swimming again.

🕊 🕊 🕊

Two years after Mariam was born I gave birth again, again to a girl. Abraham named her Helyn after his grandmother.

"This one is even more beautiful than the first," he said when Helyn was born.

This time I gave birth in the hospital, and when I came home there was no nurse to care for me. Motherhood was no longer new to me, but I was just eighteen years old and already the mother of two.

In 1929, we moved to Harlem. We took a two-bedroom apartment on One hundred twenty-ninth Street and Lenox Avenue. That was the year the talking pictures began. I asked Abraham if I could go to see *Dracula*, starring Bela Lagosi, with a woman I met. Abraham said no, but I went anyway. When they showed the dead man with blood and tiny holes on his neck I whispered to the woman, "I know what happened there." I guess I thought I was very clever to have figured out that Dracula had sucked the man's blood. Of course, everyone else in the theater had figured it out too.

Abraham had taken me to a movie in Syria once, but I had slept through it. In America, I loved the movies. As the children came, the movies became my only relief from the growing pressures of motherhood. I was usually so tired after working all day in the house, and caring for Farage and the babies, that I'd take the babies to the park and fall asleep on the grass with them beside me.

On one day in midsummer of that year, I had just finished cleaning the whole apartment. I had mopped the floors and done the dishes. I had washed the clothes by hand as usual in the bathtub using a scrub board. I had hung the clothes out to dry on a line stretched across the backyard to another building on the farthest side. And of course, in between all the housework, I had cooked and fed the babies and Farage, who was fourteen years old by then. As usual, I was exhausted and my head was pounding by the time I was done.

I had just pulled the clean sheets tight on the last bed and tucked in the blankets, when Farage took a newspaper and spread it out in sheets over his bed. Then he lay down on the papers. I suppose in his young mind he was trying to keep the bed clean by spreading the newspapers over it, but in my exhaustion, I could only focus on the work I had just done to make the apartment look neat and clean.

"What are you doing?" I shouted at him. "I worked so hard to make everything nice and now you're spoiling it. Get off that bed!"

Farage jumped off the bed and ran to me. "You can't tell me what to do," he said. "You're not my mother." And with that he punched me in the face and knocked me down.

By the time Abraham came home I had already stopped crying but there was a welt on my cheekbone where Farage had hit me.

"What's the matter with your face?" Abraham said when he saw the red mark and the swelling.

"Farage hit me," I said, and the minute I said it I was sorry.

Abraham grabbed Farage by the hair and smacked him across the face.

"How dare you hit your mother," Abraham shouted at him.

"She's not my mother," Farage said.

Again Abraham slapped him. I grabbed Abraham's arm, ashamed that I had caused him to hit his son.

"Wait," I cried. "It's all right. It was just a misunderstanding. He didn't mean it. He won't do it again."

I struggled with Abraham, shouting at him to stop and finally managed to get between them. Farage ran out the door.

That evening we waited for Farage to come home. Eleven o'clock came and went, then twelve, one and two, but Farage didn't come. The next day Farage didn't come home either, nor the day after that.

I had just finished baking a coffee cake and had set it on the table to cool when Farage opened the door. Three days had passed since he ran away. He stood in the doorway and waited. I looked up from what I was doing and our eyes met. We stood there looking at each without saying anything.

"Are you hungry?" I finally said.

Farage nodded his head and lowered his eyes.

"Come and have some cake and a glass of milk," I said.

Without answering, Farage came to the table and sat down. I brought him a plate and a knife to cut himself a piece of the cake, and a fork to eat it. Then I brought him a glass of milk. He cut himself a piece of cake and began to eat it in great big chunks.

"Where did you stay?" I said.

"In the park," Farage said.

"Did you have anything to eat?"

"Sometimes I begged for money," Farage said. "Sometimes someone gave me a few pennies to buy something. But most of the time I had nothing."

"I'm sorry," I said.

Farage nodded and took another huge bite of cake, then picked up the glass of milk and drank without stopping until all the milk was gone. I poured him another glass of milk and he drank that too. He cut himself another piece of cake and gobbled that piece also. Then he cut another piece until he had eaten the whole cake.

It was right that Abraham should punish Farage for hitting me, but I hadn't been prepared for the kind of punishment he received. Farage was still embarrassed to walk with me when I had the babies, but he was a good boy. After the beating I promised myself I would never tell on him again no matter what he did, but Farage never hit me again and we had no more incidents. In time, even his embarrassment about the babies seemed to disappear.

37

BUTCHER, BAKER,
CANDLESTICK MAKER

As ABRAHAM ADJUSTED the lid on the potbellied stove, I reached my arms around him and leaned my head on his shoulder. We had been married a few years and had two children together, but it was the first time I had done such a thing. I was beginning to feel more comfortable with him and wanted to be affectionate.

"Now what do you want?" he said and pushed me away. "You want sex?"

I could feel my face color from shame. "No," I said, "I . . ." But I couldn't think of how to tell him I just wanted him to put his arms around me and hold me. That wasn't something you saw much in the old country; husbands and wives being affectionate and hugging each other. At least not the people I ever saw. They were too old-fashioned for that. Abraham was old-fashioned too.

I tried to be affectionate with him at other times over the years, but he always pushed me away and embarrassed me. Finally I stopped trying. Maybe he thought I learned such things from the movies. Maybe I did. I didn't know how much it embarrassed him.

Harton was born two years after Helyn, and then Nejmy. I had a difficult time with Harty's birth. The doctor's had left the afterbirth inside me and I became delirious in the hospital. A patient in the next bed gave a scream when she saw me tossing and turning, and rolling toward the edge of the bed about to fall off. The nurses came running and pulled up the guard rails on the bed, but they didn't discover what was wrong with me.

As I lay in my hospital bed, I had a strange dream, or maybe my heart had stopped beating. I saw a long tunnel, very narrow like a pipe, and white inside. I had to crawl on my hands and knees to go through it. When I came to the other side, my mother and father were standing there waiting for me. I was so happy to see them after all those years that I stood up and started to run to them to throw my arms around them. But they put up their hands to ward me off.

"You mustn't touch," they said. "You must go back. You don't belong here."

It was almost a week before the doctors discovered what was making me ill.

With each birth Abraham said, "Sano. This one is even more beautiful than the last." He named them after his sisters. Nejmy means morning star. It was a beautiful name, but it sounded so foreign, so I called her Mitzi after a famous movie star at the time.

It wasn't an easy life. With four children there was so much to do and so little time to do it. Everything was done by hand, and with no central heating, stoking the fire in the potbellied stove and feeding it fuel, beginning at four in the morning, became one of my many chores. Like my mother before me, my hands were busy from before the first blush of morning, until long after the last hush of night.

I began to get terrible headaches in those years. I would get so sick I could barely get out of bed or even lift my head from the pillow. My head would ache so, and my stomach would churn.

During the Great Depression, Abraham tried to work on his own as a mason, building sidewalks or whatever needed to be done, but more often than not, the people who hired him refused to pay. He took them to court, but still rarely got his money. But somehow we survived.

Once when Abraham couldn't find work, he saw men digging a trench in the street. He asked the foreman for a job, but the foreman said there were no openings. Abraham just jumped down into the trench anyway and picked up a shovel and started to dig. The foreman was so impressed he gave Abraham a job. But because of the Depression, none of these jobs lasted. He even worked driving a trolley car for a while, but the hours were so long and the job so monotonous, that he fell asleep at the wheel and almost ran someone over, so he quit.

"God will send us the money," I said to him one morning when he went out to collect money that was owed to him and came home empty-handed.

"There was once a man walking down the street," Abraham said, and his whole face lit up as it usually did when he told one of his old country jokes or stories. It was as if he was transported to that other land and I was transported with him. I could feel my eyes open wide as they once did when my grandfather told tales by the fire.

"And as the man walked, he prayed," Abraham said. "'Oh, Lord. Please send me $500.00. I won't accept a penny more, and I won't accept a penny less.' He walked for many blocks praying the same thing over and over. He walked past a high fence, and kept on praying, 'Oh, Lord. Please send me $500.00. I won't accept a penny more, and I won't accept a penny less.' A man on the other side of the fence heard him and said to himself, 'Let's see how honest this man is when he speaks to God. He says he won't accept one penny more or one penny less than $500.00.' So the man tied up $499.99 in a handkerchief and threw it over the fence in the path of the man praying. The man ran to it and picked it up. He opened the handkerchief and counted the money. 'Oh, thank you Lord,' the man shouted to the sky. 'And I don't even mind that you charged me one penny for the handkerchief.'"

Money was always a problem in those Depression years, but even in the worst of times our children never went to bed hungry. We never let them do without. Abraham went to a charitable organization, I never knew where, perhaps a church, and brought home a few pennies to buy food when he couldn't collect what was owed him. They gave just enough to keep people alive, but that was all we needed. We made wonderful stews and soups as my mother had done in the old country. Potatoes were cheap and beans were plentiful and cheap also. A few chunks of meat when we could afford it, or even soup bones, a few tomatoes, and we ate well. I learned to bake cakes and pies and I made bread. Apples were also in great abundance.

Abraham bought me a sewing machine and I taught myself to sew, again by once seeing someone sewing. I sewed badly at first. I didn't know there was such a thing as a dress pattern, so I made my own patterns. Sometimes the things I made were pretty lopsided, but with time I learned, and I became good at sewing. And I crocheted little sweaters and hats and booties for the children. Those too at first were not well made but they kept the children dressed and warm, and soon even in that I excelled. God blessed my hands, which were never still.

"Do you want to go to school?" Abraham said to me one day.

I did want to go, but he didn't explain to me that I would go in the evening with other adults. Maybe he thought I knew. But I thought I would be put in a classroom with little children since I had never attended school in America. I would be too embarrassed to do that.

"No," I said. But when Farage brought books home from school I turned the pages one after the other, over and over. I couldn't read, but I loved those books so much. I loved the look of them, the smell of them, the feel of them. I made time to study, and little by little, the things Abraham had tried to teach me in Lebanon came back to me and, with that as a base, I taught myself to read. Farage showed me how to do long division. As he did one example, he told me what he was doing and why, and then I knew also and did them too. Later, as my children grew, I read to them. When they began school, I taught them tricks with long division that Farage had taught me. I helped them read, and they taught me words I didn't know.

৩৮   ৩৮   ৩৮

Maybe one of my greatest thrills was when I went to vote for the first time. Calvin Coolidge was president when I arrived in America. He did nothing to help the people. Then in 1928, Herbert Hoover was elected, and with him came the Great Crash. They were desperate times.

One day I heard some noise outside the window. It was bitter cold out, with an icy wind that cut through to the bone. I went to the window to see about the noise and saw a woman going through the garbage cans. Farage came to look also.

"Oh," Farage groaned. "I know that woman. Her son is in my class. That's how she gets their food."

Each night she went from garbage can to garbage can to find food for her children, Farage said. It was not an unusual sight. Abraham read in the newspaper that a man had died from eating spoiled garbage. But still no one reached out to help the masses of hungry people, good people, people willing to work if there was only work to be had.

Then came the Great Hope. In 1931, Franklin Delano Roosevelt ran for president. There was a man one could hang one's hopes on; a man who gave Americans back their dream. We'd listen to his speeches on the radio and even I was swept away.

"I'm going to vote," I told Abraham.

"Go ahead," he said.

I went to the polling place by myself and filled out the forms. Then they gave me a test. "Where does butter come from?" one question read. *Any fool knows that,* I thought. But when I saw my test score was 98 percent, I could not have been more proud.

"I got a 98 percent on the test," I shouted when I got home.

Abraham laughed. "Wahoo!" he said, and his smile told me he was also proud.

And so, at the age of twenty-one, for the first time in my life, I cast my ballot in my new land, and I have cast my ballot ever since.

Newsboys shouted on every corner. "Extra! Extra! Read all about it! Franklin Delano Roosevelt elected president!" Men set bonfires in the streets when FDR won. Kids cleared out basements of anything they could find that burned and set it ablaze. It was exciting, and I had helped make it happen in my tiny way.

When Farage graduated from high school, he left home for a job in the Civilian Conservation Corps. There he met a girl.

"Dear Dad and Sano," he wrote. "I met a girl from Alabama. Her name is Sula and she's the most beautiful girl in the world."

"Oh," Abraham said to me. "Every man thinks that." But soon after, Farage and Sula got married. Farage worked at various jobs for a while, then enlisted in the army and made it his career.

Abraham went to work for the WPA building stone walls in Central Park and at the piers. When he proved his talents with stone archways, he was assigned to that task around the city. Both the WPA and the Civilian Conservation Corps were programs started by FDR. Each worker was given just three days of work to allow enough work for others who might also be in need. The New Deal had begun, but life for me was still very hard.

38

ANOTHER PLACE
CALLED HOME

B ETWEEN 1925 AND 1934, our lives were never settled. We moved seven times, uptown, downtown, and back again, usually to find a bigger place for our growing family. But in 1935, a year after our first son Amos was born, we moved to West One hundred second Street and stayed there for the next twenty years. With five children it was no longer easy to find a home. That's where all the rest of our children were born.

Today our old neighborhood is unrecognizable. City housing projects stand where all the old buildings once stood. Even the separation of streets for four or five blocks at a time were removed to make room for the projects. Only the fire hydrant in the middle of the block between Amsterdam and Columbus Avenues gives any indication where our building once stood.

But in the '30s, five- and six-story buildings lined the streets. Most of the people who lived on our street and the surrounding streets were immigrants like us. At least the parents were. Almost all were Irish on our street, but there was a Dutch family who lived a few doors down, and a German family too. The man who owned the small grocery store around the corner where we shopped for meat, milk, and other necessities was Jewish. We had a tab there that we paid once a week. I could just send my children to buy something and Morris, the owner, would mark it down in his book. Each time I went in he'd say "Look what I can do Mrs. Halo." I'd look at him and he'd wiggle his ears. It was the darndest thing. I couldn't understand how he did it.

We lived in a five-room railroad apartment. It was on the top floor of a five-story walk-up. The sun used to slip through the back window early in the morning and rest on my cheek and arm as I stood at the stove. I remember the patterns the fire escapes made on the sun-drenched brick across the backyard; the white wash flapping on a line. And on Sunday mornings, the sound of church bells; the smell of roast and my special rolls; *Let's Pretend* playing on the radio.

Even as late as the 1950s, men, and sometimes the teenage boys from the neighborhood, came through our streets on horse-drawn wagons to sell their fruit and vegetables or to pick up old junk. The whole neighborhood gave them their old rags and newspapers and shopped from those horse-drawn carts because it was a little cheaper than going to the store.

"Rags. Old rags. Any old rags today?" "Get your bananas. Fresh, ripe bananas." "Knives sharpened. Come and get your knives sharpened." They'd sing out their wares, and the ice man and coal man came to deliver when you called.

On Sunday afternoons in summer, the older boys played stick-ball games in the middle of the street. I used to love those games. In some small way they reminded me of the game we used to play in Turkey when we used a twig for a ball and a branch for a bat.

It was a good neighborhood with good people. Even though we didn't have too much time to sit and share a cup of coffee together, the neighbors looked out for each other and for each other's children. The church was only three blocks away and the elementary school, P.S. 179, was on our street. There was a firehouse on our street too: Engine 76. Even the firemen looked out for our children. West One hundred second Street had become my home.

My girls never cried when I walked them to school in the morning and left them there. But when my third daughter Harty started school, her teacher confronted me one day.

"Why won't Harton take her hat off?" Mrs. Fletcher said.

"Oh," I said. "Her father cut her hair and she doesn't like it."

"Oh," was all Mrs. Fletcher answered and Harty went through an entire grade with her hat on. Abraham would line them up and put a bowl on their heads and cut their hair around it. After that, I learned to cut their hair myself.

My girls did well in school, but for the boys, it was different. When

I think back, it was as if they didn't want the boys to succeed in those neighborhoods. When Amos was in the third grade, he came home crying. He flung his books on a chair and sat down heavily. I had just put a cake in the oven and was washing the bowl I had used to stir the batter.

"Shhh," I said. "Don't make so much noise or the cake will fall."

"I don't want to go to school anymore," Amos said.

"What do you mean you don't want to go to school? There's no such thing as you don't want to go to school." I wiped my hands on my apron and came to stand in front of him. "You must go to school," I said.

Amos looked down at the floor so I couldn't see his eyes fill with tears.

"What is it?" I said and sat beside him.

"The teacher said I was stupid," he said.

"What do you mean?" I said, not sure I understood.

"A teacher came to our classroom and asked who wanted to be a monitor. I raised my hand and my teacher said, 'Not you, Amos. You're too stupid to be a monitor.' I don't want to go back there."

I pressed his head against my breast and held him, but my heart was pounding. I was so angry I could have strangled his teacher. The next morning, I marched right over to the school and went to her class.

"I want to speak with you," I said.

"What do you want? I can't talk to you. Come out into the hall. I'm going to get the principal," she said.

She left the room and I followed her. Then she practically ran down the hall and I knew she knew why I was there. I waited in the hall but my heart was beating quickly and I was already on the verge of tears.

"What seems to be the problem?" the principal said when he came to me.

"How dare this woman tell my eight-year-old son he's too stupid to be a monitor? There's no such thing as a stupid child. There're only stupid teachers who don't know how to teach. Children are never stupid," I said. "And my son is not stupid. How dare you destroy his confidence?" And with that I broke down and cried thinking of my sweet Amos.

After that, try as I might, Amos was never interested in school again, even though I forced him to go.

"I can't," he'd say, and I'd say, "there's no such thing as can't. You can do anything you set your mind to."

"Mom," Amos said to me a few years later. "When I grow up, I'm going to buy you a mink coat."

"Just study," I said. "That's the best gift you can give me." But years later, for my sixty-fifth birthday, he and a few of my other children bought me a mink coat.

It wasn't until many years had passed that I realized Amos had never lost interest in learning, even though he had lost interest in school. He taught himself everything. He read the Bible from beginning to end, he said. He read books on philosophy, and he was one of those people who could just look at something to figure out how to make it work, like the fireplace he helped Abraham build. When our other children were teenagers and young adults, I'd wake early in the morning and sometimes find Amos and a few others around the dining room table where they had been for half the night reciting Shakespeare. That was Amos's doing. He became a sort of surrogate father to the younger ones. But that incident in the third grade took its toll. The damage was already done.

My terrible headaches came almost every day from the strain and anxiety in those years. It was difficult for boys in those neighborhoods. It was difficult for girls too, but for different reasons. As long as I could keep them tucked under my wing they were safe, at least from dangers in the outside world. But they were growing up. I couldn't protect them forever.

🕊 🕊 🕊

Abraham's brother, Elias, married an Armenian woman, named Agnes, and became very successful as an insurance agent. In 1937, during his travels for business, Elias saw a piece of land for sale in Spotswood, New Jersey and bought it. Abraham helped him clear a home site in the middle of the forest and they built Elias a house. Abraham then bought a piece of land from his brother and built a house for us too. It was a simple house, built with limited means; a house that was not meant for anything but vacations at first. We'd ready the children, six by that time and, except in the dead of winter, we'd head for the country by train every weekend and for long stretches in summer. It was good to get away. Even though it meant more work for me, I loved it there. Abraham loved it too.

It was such beautiful, untouched wilderness, probably the way it had been when Native Americans were the only people to roam the forests. The land was flat and the trees were not too tall. Little streams wiggled their way out of the forest, and at night the sky seemed to hang so close above our heads, you could almost reach up and pluck a star. There were blueberry bushes everywhere, and wildflowers, and one day I discovered small red berries growing in the swamp behind our house. I waded into the water almost to my waist and picked some.

"Look what I found," I said to Agnes.

"Oh!" she said. "Don't eat those! They're poison!"

"No," I said. "I think I saw them in the store." And I had seen them in the store. They were cranberries, millions of them bobbing like little red jewels against the green leaves and murky water of the bog.

Abraham dug a well with his own hands, and each year he tilled the soil and planted a huge garden. We had so many tomatoes by the end of summer, I'd can 200 to 300 quart jars, enough to last us the entire year. We had cucumbers so big and tender they were like small watermelons, and watermelons so big they must have weighed 35 to 40 pounds. He planted string beans, which I also canned, and peas, and corn, and so many other things, it's hard to name them all. He planted apple and peach trees too, and purple and white mulberry trees. He even planted a vineyard, all of it with his own two hands.

It was very different from our land in Turkey when I was a child, but the vegetable garden Abraham made every year, and the smell of the moist air, sometimes carried me back there. When all my children were finally fed and washed and put to bed, when the kerosene lanterns were put out, and all in the house were sleeping, I'd lie in bed and listen to the spring frogs and the whippoorwills, and smell the fresh, sweet air, and I'd think of my home long ago. I'd think of my mother and father, my grandfather, my sisters, and brother. I made it a point to think of them to keep them alive in my heart. But with all my children depending on me, even at night when they were all asleep, I couldn't afford to stay away too long. I was too afraid of being lost there. But the sound of the train whistle would drift through the open window and its lonely wail would tug at my heart. It was as if all the sorrow in the world was moving through town and wailing down the tracks.

It seemed the older I got the faster time flew by. David, and then Timothy, were born to us next. I got David's name from the bible. I thought it was such a beautiful name. Timothy was born on Columbus Day, and before I could stop him, Abraham went and registered his name as Columbus. Abraham was a riot. How could I call my son Columbus? So I named him Timothy, after Tiny Tim in *A Christmas Carol,* and that's how everyone knew him. It wasn't until he joined the navy years later that he found out his real name. By then, even I had forgotten his name wasn't legally Timothy.

By the time Thea was born, Abraham was in his sixties. With so many children, holidays were an extra special time of year, even for Abraham. The Christmas tree and presents usually took up half of our parlor in the city. One Christmas Abraham went out too late to get a Christmas tree. When he came home empty-handed the children cried so much that he went out again and came back with an armload of Christmas tree branches. Then he cut the broom handle off the broom and drilled holes in it and made a tree with the branches. It was beautiful in its way, but when he was finished, the children cried all the more.

On Easter, I colored eggs the way my mother had with onion skins, but I also used the dyes and little tattoos they sold in the store. After church we had egg-breaking contests just like in the old country. Abraham knew how to choose the strongest egg. He'd tap it on his front teeth, and from the sound it made he could tell if it was strong or weak. Then he'd challenge me or the kids to a contest, and we all challenged each other.

One Easter Abraham brought home two baby ducks for the children. He made a place for them on our back fire escape. Sometimes I'd fix a bed out on the front fire escape for the children to sleep on those summer days when it was too hot to sleep indoors. They liked sleeping under the sky as we had slept under the sky in Tlaraz.

By the summer, the ducks weren't babies anymore. They were full-grown white ducks, and they were beautiful. I'd pack a picnic lunch and a blanket to spread on the grass and we'd march the children and the ducks to Central Park.

"Mrs. Halo," a neighbor would say as we passed. "You're taking the ducks to the park, are ya? Let them have a nice swim for us too."

My boys took turns carrying the ducks the two and a half blocks to Central Park, but once we were off the streets, they put them down and the ducks followed us to the lake. While we had our picnic, the ducks went swimming.

There were Easters when Abraham brought home a baby chic. They were hard to resist. But one grew up to be a fine red rooster and at four o'-clock every morning it did what all roosters do. He'd fly up onto the fire escape railing and crow his heart out. You'd think the neighbors would have complained about a rooster waking them up so early every morning in the middle of New York City, but no one ever did. In fact, when we finally ate the poor thing, people would call to me across the backyard when I hung out the wash.

"Mrs. Halo," they'd say. "Where is the rooster? We miss him."

I think the sound of him crowing reminded us all of the homes we left behind.

🕊 🕊 🕊

Lena Horne was singing "Stormy Weather" on the radio and I was singing with her as I mopped the dining room floor. "Don't know why there's no sun up in the sky, stormy weather." I loved to sing. I sometimes wondered what it would have been like to stand on a stage in an evening gown, sparkling under a spotlight as I sang to the world. "Since my man and I ain't together . . ."

My daughter, Thea, was two years old and playing quietly in her crib with her doll. Tim and David, five and seven, were already in kindergarten and the second grade, and our other children were also in school. The front door opened and Abraham came in limping from an injury he got on the job a month before. He limped across the wet floor to the dining room table and sat down heavily in a chair.

"What did the doctor say?" I said.

Abraham clucked his tongue once and gave a small jerk of his head.

"Ahk!" Abraham said. "The doctor said, if I let him operate on my knee I could get more compensation."

"What did you say?" I said.

He shook his head again. "I said, no."

When Abraham hurt himself the company gave him $50.00 a month compensation because he couldn't work. We also got public assistance, but I hated it.

"I'm going to look for a job," I said, but I worried that I wouldn't be able to perform because of the migraines.

"Don't work, Sano," Abraham said. "I can work again and make enough to take care of us."

But he couldn't and I knew that. He was already in his sixties and his wounded knee made it twice as hard to find work.

"If you can work in the daytime, I'll work at night," I said. "Then we won't need public assistance."

Abraham leaned his cane against the side of the table and thought about it for a few moments. Then he nodded his head. "All right," he said.

The first company I went to, Uneeda Biscuit, hired me. My first day on the job my headaches stopped and never came again with such force.

I worked from four o'clock in the morning until eleven in the morning. Abraham sent the children off to school in the mornings. I worked at Uneeda Biscuit until I became pregnant again. I thought I was supposed to quit when I got pregnant, so I did. When I tried to go back to Uneeda Biscuit in 1946, a year after our daughter Adrian was born, they told me I was too old to work. I was thirty-six years old then. While the war effort was going on, they hired everyone between the ages of seventeen and fifty-five. But afterward that changed. I got a job in a box company for a short time, but the boss transferred me to a very dangerous machine. I told him I couldn't work on it because it scared me too much. When he insisted, I quit and went to work for the Pez company. I couldn't afford to get hurt. Who would care for my children? All I ever did in my life I did for them.

39

DOCTOR, LAWYER,
INDIAN CHIEF

ONE MORNING in the early spring of 1948, my son David came to me as he usually did in the morning.

"Do you want me to get something from the store before I go to school, Mom?" David said.

He was about twelve years old then and always dressed before the rest of the children so he could go to the store for crumb buns, or for milk, or some other thing we might need for breakfast.

I looked up from the blouse I was ironing for one of the other children. David stood before me with his freshly scrubbed face, made brighter still by the sliver of sunlight that slipped through the back window. His dark brown hair was still wet, and the grooves from the comb were still visible where he had slicked back his hair, leaving a small curl to dangle over his forehead. His checkered shirt, to which I had given extra starch at the collar and front to make it last the day without wilting, was neatly tucked into jeans that were cinched tight at the waist with a Western-style buckle, and rolled twice at the hem, where two shiny new pennies peered out from the mock eyelids on his shiny, brown penny loafers.

I usually sent him to Morris's store for what we needed in the morning, or to the bakery on One hundred third and Columbus Avenue, but that morning I sent him to the Safeway Supermarket three blocks away. The other children dressed and, when David didn't come home, I fed them and sent them to school. Then I put on my coat and rushed out the door and down the five flights of stairs to look for David. It wasn't like him to just disappear.

"Oh, Mrs. Halo," a boy in the street said to me. "The police took Dave to the police station."

I rushed to the One hundredth Street police station and burst through the door.

"Where is my son?" I said to the man at the desk. "They tell me the police brought him here."

The policeman peered down at me from his high perch behind the long wooden counter. His thick, tightly collared neck bulged slightly around the stiff blue of his starched shirt.

"What's his name?" the policeman said.

"His name is David Halo," I said, still panting from racing down the street.

He looked down at the records in front of him on his desk.

"Your son set a fire in the street on West One hundred Street with some other boys" he said. "Then he threw a bag of bullets into the fire. One shot out and hit a man in the neck."

"That's not possible," I said when he told me what time they had picked David up. "It couldn't have been my son who set the fire, because he wasn't out of the house long enough to have done such a thing."

"You're gonna have to bring your son to the courthouse tomorrow morning at 9:30 A.M.," he said.

He wrote on a card and reached down to hand me the address of the courthouse, then picked up the telephone and dialed a number.

"Bring Halo down. His mother is here to get him," he said into the receiver.

I paced back and forth, unable to stand still. Finally I saw David and a policeman coming down the hall. David's shirt was hanging out of his jeans and his hair was tussled. I looked at the policeman and he shrugged as David walked toward me.

"Are you all right?" I said.

David nodded his head but looked at the floor.

"Did you set the fire?" I said.

David looked into my eyes. "No, Mom," he said. "I was just walking by when they grabbed me."

The next morning I brought David to court and waited to be called as the policeman had instructed me. But by three o'clock, David had still not been called, so I took him home. Around five o'clock the phone rang.

"You were supposed to be in court today," the policeman said.

"I was in court," I said, "but you didn't show up and no one called us so I brought my son home."

"Well you have to bring your son back again tomorrow," the policeman said in a sharp tone.

"No, I don't!" I said in just as sharp a tone. "I'm not coming back, and neither is my son. I was in court when you told me to be there and you didn't show up and that's that." Then I hung up the phone.

They didn't bother us again. But after it was all over, David told me that when the police grabbed him and took him to the police station, they held him out of the third floor window by his ankles and told him they would drop him if he didn't confess. It was only when they were told I was there to get him that they pulled David in. I was so angry I wanted to sue the policemen. I even went to court and filled out the papers to sue, but the judge told me not to go through with it.

"You'll never win," the judge said. "Save yourself the aggravation. You'll never win."

There was always something in those days that kept me running. And of course there were also all the usual illnesses that children get that kept me on my feet, such as measles and mumps. Sometimes three children got sick at once.

Somehow, over time, I had developed an instinct about illness when my children began to grow. Maybe I had also picked it up from my grandfather and even my mother, or maybe it is simply born into all mothers and develops along with her children. Sometimes little things came back to me that I had learned from my mother, like her remedy for the sharp pains of gas. She'd put a plate on the floor face down and make us lie on it with the plate under our stomachs. The gas would expel almost instantly.

When my daughter Thea was about two years old, she developed a fever and cried each time I fed her. I took her to our family doctor at the clinic, Dr. Needles, but after he examined her, he couldn't figure out what was wrong.

"Take her to the hospital," Dr. Needles told me.

At the hospital the doctor squeezed her arm a little and then told me to give her salt water to drink. I took her home and did as the doctor told me. Thea became almost hysterical. So I looked into her mouth as the doctor should have done, and sure enough her gums were inflamed.

I put boric acid on a piece of cotton and rubbed her gums with it. Then I rinsed her mouth. Almost instantly her fevered dropped and within a day or two, the inflammation was gone.

When my son Tim wounded his hand, it blew up like a balloon. The doctor wanted to amputate his thumb.

"How can he go through life without a thumb?" I said to the doctor.

"The thumb has to come off," the doctor said and turned away from me.

"But he can't work without a thumb. Just lance it for me so it will drain the poison. He won't let me do it," I said.

"You're not listening to me," the doctor said. "The thumb has to come off!"

"Please," I said. "I can't let you amputate my son's thumb. Just numb it and lance it for me. I'll do the rest."

Maybe to get rid of me, the doctor finally agreed to do as I asked. I took Tim home and bathed his hand in a boric acid solution I made with boiled water to purify it. The infection drained away and the swelling went down in only a day.

Each time I discovered the cure of an illness in my children that had baffled the doctors, I went back to the doctor and told him what I had discovered and my cure so he would know for the other children he treated. I had come a long way since my first child when I sat crying with her because I didn't know how to cure her sore eyes.

Perhaps it's true that no two children have the same mother and father. We are always growing, always changing. Like me, Abraham was changing too.

40

ABRAHAM, ABRAHAM

As the children grew, Abraham became more and more strict. He worried about them. I worried about them too. They wanted to date and stay out with their friends. Abraham wanted them to stay home and study. One night we sat up until two in the morning waiting for our second daughter, Helyn, to come home. She walked in the door with her girlfriend and two boys. She was only fifteen at the time. Abraham was so angry he gave Helyn a slap and told the boys to get out. Helyn was so embarrassed she never brought a boy home again. He gave Mariam a beating once because she stayed out late, and that time I had to pull him away from her. I guess he felt them slipping out of his hands. He didn't know how to control them. They were good kids, but he was used to the way it was in the old country, and our children were not old-country kids. They were Americans. They had minds of their own. They wanted to do what they wanted to do. Our girls were growing up.

Abraham was strict with the boys too. He wanted them to stay home and study. They wanted to go out with their friends. Many fathers hit their children with a belt in those days, but I didn't like it when he did it. He usually threatened to beat them more than he actually beat them. He'd throw the strap over his shoulder and say a few angry words to get a reaction. But one time when he took a strap to my Tim, I grabbed hold of it so he wouldn't hit him. Abraham slapped me and knocked me down and my mouth began to bleed. David called the police and they came and took Abraham away. Later that night, the policeman came and knocked on my door.

"Mrs. Halo," the policeman said. "Your husband is real sorry he hit you. He's at the police station crying. He says he doesn't know what happened. He says he loves you and the children. Should I lock him up?"

"No," I said. "Let him come home."

With a house full of children it was pretty hectic at times. Sometimes everyone wanted something at once. One time Abraham told Tim to sit on the floor to eat because Tim wasn't behaving. He was about seven at the time. He wasn't doing anything wrong. He was just behaving like a child because he was a child. I always tried to reason with Abraham, but it never did any good. I finally got so angry, I took the plate of spaghetti I had just made and threw it against the wall.

"Enough is enough!" I shouted when Abraham insisted Tim sit on the floor. "No child of mine is going to sit on the floor to eat like a dog."

Abraham didn't say a word. When he tried to clean the spaghetti off the wall I told him "Don't you dare!" I wouldn't let anyone clean that spaghetti off the wall. When we painted the walls some time later, I painted right over it. I wanted it there as a reminder to Abraham, that enough is enough.

I was so upset about Abraham's behavior that I complained to the church people. I didn't mean for them to do anything about it. I only needed someone to talk with. I had no one else.

A few days later, Abraham went out on some errands in the early morning. One was for a doctor's appointment the church had set up for him. He left the house in the morning dressed in his suit and tie and fedora hat, the way he usually dressed when left the apartment. I went about my housework as usual, fixing all the beds, grocery shopping, feeding the children lunch. We usually ate supper late, about eight or nine o'clock in the evening. I gave it no attention that Abraham had not come home. But when supper time rolled around and Abraham was still not home, I began to worry. He wasn't a man who ran around at night. He didn't drink, so he never went to bars. He didn't even smoke cigarettes.

By midnight, he was still not home. I called the police and the hospital, but neither one knew of any accidents. For half the night I was up and down trying to figure out where he could be. I finally called the church the next morning.

"This is Mrs. Halo," I said. "My husband left to go to the doctor yesterday and he's still not home. Do you know where he is?"

"Why, yes," the church woman said. "I believe he's at Bellevue Psychiatric Hospital. We made an appointment for him there. That's probably where you'll find him."

I raced to the hospital and, after fifteen minutes of pacing in the waiting room, they showed me into a small room. Abraham sat there in a straight-backed chair waiting. When I walked through the door, he looked up and clucked his tongue at me once and shook his head.

"Where were you? Why didn't you come to get me out of this place," he said.

"What are you doing here?" I said.

"The church said I had an appointment to see a doctor here. I tried to kill two birds with one stone," Abraham said, "so first I went to the social security office to pick up my check and then I came here. I didn't know the appointment was with a psychiatrist."

Abraham said they were giving him ice cold baths and doing other things to him, all of which scared me.

"Can I speak with you for a moment outside," the doctor said to me.

I went out with the doctor to the hall and he looked at me gravely.

"Does your husband beat the children?" the doctor said to me.

"Didn't your father hit you when you didn't behave?" I asked him. His eyes fluttered, but he didn't answer. I could see by his expression that the answer was yes.

"We asked him some questions and he doesn't seem to be thinking in a rational way," the doctor said. "I think you should let us keep him here."

"What did he say?" I said.

"Well, he kept staring around the room and up at the ceiling, so I asked him what he saw. He told me the ceiling needed repair. Then I showed him some pictures to get his reactions. I showed him a picture of a ship and asked him what was missing. He said the American Flag."

I had to laugh in spite of myself. Abraham could be a very funny man sometimes and I knew he was playing with them. I looked at the ceiling and walls. They were dingy and almost everywhere I looked they needed repair. I asked the doctor to release him.

"We think you should let us keep him here," the doctor said. "We'd like you to sign these papers."

I knew if I signed the papers they would never let him go again. It would be out of my hands. I couldn't do that to him. There was nothing wrong with Abraham. He just wanted to make his children behave. I didn't always agree with his behavior, but that didn't make him crazy. His father had beaten him when he had misbehaved. That's the way he knew. That's the way most fathers behaved in those days.

"I won't do that," I said. "There's nothing wrong with him. I want to take him home."

"I'm sorry. We can't let you do that. You have to see the judge first."

I went back into the room to see Abraham.

"Sano," Abraham said. "They won't let me go home."

"It serves you right," I said. "You have to stop being so hard on the kids." But I was angry that the church had put him there. I was angry that they had betrayed my confidence, and I was angry that the doctors were treating him as they were.

A few days later, I went to court to get him released. The judge rested his elbows on the desk and leaned forward so that his chin rested on his clasped hands.

"Mrs. Halo," the judge said, looking me in the eyes. "Does you husband hit your children?"

"I'll answer that if you first tell me if your father ever hit you," I said.

The judge sat back and laughed. "Do you want to take him home?" he said.

"Yes," I said.

The judge laughed again. "Then take him home," he said.

Abraham was very quiet on the subway ride home. He sat on the train deep in thought. Every once in a while he shook his head and clucked his tongue.

"What is it?" I said. "You know they think you're crazy. Why can't you behave yourself?"

"They asked me so many stupid questions," he said, "and no matter what I said it didn't make any difference. The doctor kept asking me how I was born. I told him I was born the way everyone was born. But he kept saying, 'No, Mr. Halo. Tell me how *you* were born.' So I told him from my mother's womb. But he kept saying, 'No. Tell me how you were born.' I didn't know what he wanted. No matter what I said, he kept asking me that same stupid question. So I told him I remember the doctor pulling me out and holding me up by my feet. I told him the doctor slapped me on my bottom and I said, 'Wah! Wah!' Then I passed out and don't remember anymore."

With a straight face Abraham shook his head and clucked his tongue again. I burst out laughing. Then he started laughing too. Abraham said the doctor was so disgusted he left the room, and we started laughing all over again. Every time we thought about it we laughed some more.

The church people were angry with me for taking Abraham out of Bellevue. I was very angry with them for going behind my back. Abraham wasn't crazy. When our children were young he was very tender with them. But as they got older he seemed to be afraid he wouldn't be respected if he showed his tender side. That was the problem with a lot of men in those days. They just didn't know how to be firm and tender at the same time.

🕊   🕊   🕊

Soon after this incident, in November of 1949, I went for a checkup to the doctor. I again had all the signs of pregnancy. Abraham came with me to the doctor's office and sat beside me in the waiting room.

"Mrs. Halo?" the nurse said. "Come with me please."

I stood up and walked behind her. Abraham got up and walked with me.

"The doctor wants you to take off all your cloths and put on this gown so he can give you a full checkup," the nurse said. "You can use this room. The doctor will be with you shortly. Mr. Halo," she then said, turning to Abraham. "I'm afraid you'll have to wait outside. It's better if the doctor examines your wife alone."

Abraham cleared his throat and just stood there as the nurse led me into the room and closed the door. I took off my cloths and slipped on the gown, then sat on the edge of the examining table and waited. As I had expected, I was pregnant again. I was almost forty years old.

In January of 1950, as we sat at the dinner table, Abraham looked up at me and stared at me for a long time. The wind was howling through the cracks at the edge of the windows and a few flakes of snow were sticking along the ledge. By then I was a few months pregnant with Jonathan, our last child.

"I'm going to Syria," Abraham said.

He got up from the table and went into our bedroom. When he came out again he was holding some papers in his hands.

"Here are my tickets. I'm sailing in two weeks."

Abraham was seventy years old. He had taken the trip once before and had come back after three months. He had tried to take the trip another time but had made it only as far as the ship when he discovered someone had picked his pocket. They had stolen his tickets and all of his money, so he had returned home.

I thought nothing of it when he told me he was leaving. I was already so used to taking care of everything myself. I had become doctor, lawyer, and Indian chief.

"All right," was all that I said.

The night before he left, everything was as usual. I prepared dinner: roast chicken, mashed potatoes with gravy, and vegetables. That night we went to sleep as usual. We hadn't had an argument. But in the morning when he awakened, he sat on the edge of the bed with his back to me and he didn't say a word. He just sat there staring at nothing in particular.

"What is it, Abraham?" I said. "What's wrong?"

Abraham just got up and went to bathe. When he came back I watched him put on a clean shirt and the pants to his tan wool suit. He slipped a leather belt through the loops at the waist of his trousers and buckled it. He took out a tie and slipped it under the collar of his white shirt and knotted it as he stood before the mirror. Then he put on his jacket. I made breakfast for the family and he ate quietly. Then he got up, put on his hat and overcoat, picked up his bags, and walked out the door.

Our daughter Mitzi, who was eighteen then, took him to the ship with his bags. He never even said good-bye to me. And he didn't tell me "Sano, take care of the children while I'm gone," the way he usually did when he left the house. Abraham even said that when he went out of the house for a short time. It was almost a ritual, as if he remembered his first child who died while he was away.

I couldn't think of anything I had done wrong that would make him act so cold.

I went about my business as usual while he was gone. I even took the children to Spotswood when the weather warmed enough to spend the weekend in comfort with a small fire in the evening.

On one of those weekends in spring, Mariam's husband drove me and my younger children to our home. The sky was a pale blue and a soft wind was rustling through the forest when we arrived. Along its fringe the tiny white blooms of the blueberry bushes sparkled against the frail green, and the apple, peach, and mulberry trees were dressed in so many blossoms, pink and white, it seemed that the air around them had crystallized in the midst of an explosion.

I unlocked the front door to our house and the sweet, familiar, musty scent of country also bloomed. The chessboard and box of chessmen were on the small table in the living room where Abraham had left them, and the two chairs were still facing off in the spot where we had last sat together to play the game. The antique wooden arm chairs and sofa, with the heads and shoulders of women carved into the arms, were facing the fireplace Abraham and our sons had built. The ashes were cold. I went into the kitchen and put down the bags of groceries on the counter. I opened the windows to air the house, then I set about putting the groceries away and washing things down. I swept the cobwebs from the corners of the rooms. I wiped the countertops of the dust that had settled since the last time we had been there the previous year, and I put clean sheets on the beds. I could hear the children laughing somewhere behind the house where the tiny stream crept out of the forest. They had already hung the hammock between the two trees on the edge of the swamp and were now running around looking for frogs. I called to them to bring twigs and small branches that had fallen from the trees for the fire. Then I picked up the broom again and swept the floors.

When the children brought the firewood, I placed two cinder blocks a few feet apart at the side of the house. Between the cinder blocks I built a fire with crumbled newspapers and broken twigs. Over that I placed a large grill like one from the oven. I lifted the cover of the well and sent down a small bucket on a rope to get enough water to prime the hand pump, and when I had water, I filled the large pot, blackened from years on the fire, to boil spaghetti on the open fire. How many times had I knelt in that spot before a fire to jar tomatoes and string beans fresh from the garden; to roast fresh corn on an open flame and watch the children use the spent cobs as a brush to clean their teeth as we had done in my country.

With Abraham gone, I wondered who would till the soil for the garden that year. The withered skeletons of old tomato stalks were still sticking out of the ground and stretching their petrified branches this way and that. And the skeletons of corn stalks were also still grasping the soil with their many strands of roots like long bony toes. I was seven months pregnant and getting quite large. It was not possible for me to do all the digging that Abraham usually did with only a shovel and his bare hands.

I bent to blow on the fire and a stream of blue smoke scattered in my breeze, then rose to curl in loops as the flames began to leap.

"Sano," a man's voice called from across the garden.

I looked up from the flames to find Abraham's brother, Elias, standing at the edge of the garden.

"Hello, Mr. Halo," I said. I had called him Mr. Halo since I was fifteen years old. "I didn't know you were here. I didn't see your car."

Elias strolled over to me with a smile on his face.

"I just got here," he said. "When did you come?"

"Only today," I said. "I'm making spaghetti if you'd like to join us. Is Agnes with you?"

"No," Elias said. "I have a few tomatoes and some salad greens I could bring over."

I went into the house and chopped garlic for the pasta and opened a quart jar of the tomatoes I had put up the year before. I chopped onions also and the mint and oregano that were already sprouting on the edge of the garden. Then I brought everything, including the olive oil and a pan, out to the fire. Elias was already sitting there on one of the two chairs he had brought out from the house.

I placed the pan on the grill and poured in some olive oil. When the oil was hot I scraped the onion, garlic, and herbs into the hot oil and stirred gently until they were lightly cooked, before pouring in the tomatoes. Then I sat on one of the chairs beside Abraham's brother and watched the tomatoes begin to bubble.

"Have you heard from your brother, Mr. Halo?" I said.

Elias clucked his tongue on the roof of his mouth like his brother. "Why do you ask about him?" he said. "He's far away looking for a new woman."

I ignored his remark and leaned forward to stir the sauce, then settled myself again in my seat.

"Maybe he will find a new wife," Elias said.

"Look here, Mr. Halo," I said. "Once is a joke, but twice is no longer funny."

Elias put his hand on my knee. "Why don't you give me a kiss?" he said.

I was so shocked that I grabbed his hand and pushed it off my leg. Then I ran into the house and locked the doors and all the windows. I didn't know what he would do. He waited for a while, then realizing I wouldn't come out again while he was there, he strolled back to his own house and didn't bother me again.

🕊️ 🕊️ 🕊️

In the city, as I left the apartment house one morning, three months after Abraham had left for Syria, Mrs. Price, the superintendent, stopped me in the hall.

"Mrs. Halo," she said, "did you have a fight with your husband then?"

"No," I said. "Why would you ask such a thing?"

"Well," she said, "why didn't he go home to your apartment last night?"

"I don't know what you mean," I said.

In fact, I didn't even know Abraham was home. He had come back from Syria the night before and had knocked on the door of the man on the ground floor.

"Can I sleep here tonight?" Abraham said. "Tomorrow I will look for an apartment."

"No," said the man. "Why don't you go home to your family?"

Abraham told the man he couldn't do that.

I don't know where he slept that night but he didn't come home to me, and when Mrs. Price asked me about him, I didn't know what to say.

On my return from shopping, I had just put the meat, milk, and butter into the icebox along with a few vegetables, and stored the cereal and other canned and dry goods in the cabinet, when a knock came at the door. I opened it to find Abraham standing there.

"Can I come in, Sano?" he said.

His behavior was a mystery to me. I didn't know why he was so cold to me before he left and why he didn't come straight home when he returned. It was even a mystery why he thought he had to ask my permission to come into his own apartment. But it upset me that he had gone to a neighbor to sleep as if we had had a fight.

"No," I said. "You can't come in."

"Please, Sano. I just want to see the children," Abraham said.

"They're not home right now. They're still in school," I said.

"Can I come in and wait?"

"If I let you in to wait, you have to leave after you see them."

"All right," Abraham said.

We had been married for twenty-five years, and yet Abraham came in and sat patiently in a straight-backed chair as if he were a guest. I went about my work without giving him any mind. I didn't tell him about his brother. I didn't want to make trouble between them, and Elias had not bothered me again.

"Can I have a glass of water, Sano?" Abraham said.

"You know where it is," I said. But I felt sorry for him. He looked so strained sitting there like a stranger in his slightly rumpled tan suit.

"Are you hungry?" I said.

He made a face and shook his head in a way that said neither yes nor no. I knew that meant yes.

"Maybe you'd like some tea and a sandwich," I said.

"Maybe," Abraham said.

I gave him something to eat and he waited patiently for the kids to come home, but when they did, Abraham didn't leave. In fact, Abraham never left again, and I didn't ask him to leave. It would be twenty more years before he told me what was wrong.

ツ゚   ツ゚   ツ゚

A few months later, Jonathan was born. I had a difficult birth with Jonathan too. When I went home from the hospital I became very ill. Abraham was frantic with worry. He called the doctor and asked him to come right away, but after the doctor examined me, he didn't know what was wrong. He told Abraham to rush me back to the hospital. Abraham became even more frantic. I again almost died. Somehow the doctors had again left the afterbirth inside me as they had when Harty was born, and I was again in the hospital for a week before they discovered it. In fact, they may never have discovered it had I not finally demanded they examine me thoroughly.

As I lay in my hospital bed, Abraham walked through the door to my room. He stood at the entrance for a moment looking at me as I held Jonathan to my breast. It was a few moments before I noticed Abraham was holding a single red rose.

"I brought this for you," he said awkwardly.

He walked toward my bed holding the rose out to me. He had never brought me flowers before. I tried to imagined him going to a flower shop and picking out a single perfect rose with its petals just beginning to unfurl, but the image was foreign to me. Abraham had never been comfortable showing his feelings, maybe because of the place and time in which he had been born. Love and sentiment were a woman's domain. But it was clear that Abraham was a very sentimental man. You could tell by the concern he had for our children, even when he was hard on them, and the way he spoke of his mother and sisters.

Before his exile from Turkey, when Abraham was only about twenty years old, he had built his mother and sisters a home. When his sister was kidnapped by a Turk, it was Abraham who had tried to rescue her even though he knew it would place him in danger. When his sister died in childbirth, Abraham was heartbroken. After his exile, he had kept up family ties through letters for all those years. He had placed himself in debt to help his younger brother, Elias, get to America. He had even kept writing to his brother in Borneo, who never answered. And it was Abraham who always made sure there were photos of our children as they grew.

As he stood there holding the rose out to me, I couldn't help wondering how he might have been had his life been different. He had also lost everything he had ever loved, even his first child. And, like mine, his life had been filled with hardship and treachery. Knowing Turkey's record of brutality, I could only imagine the conditions of his imprisonment in those filthy dungeons.

There was so much cruelty in the world. The story of the genocide of the Assyrians by the Turks and Kurds through the ages was a tragedy still untold.

At Sairt in June 1915, the massacres of Assyrians by "The Butchers' Battalion," a term the military Turkish governor of Van, Djeudet Bey, chose for himself and his 8,000 soldiers, left at least 17,000 Assyrians dead. Sairt was only one of forty-one villages attacked that year where the

Assyrian inhabitants were slaughtered. Abraham's town, Mardin, was among them. There were even reports that the corpses of Assyrian women were burned to salvage the gold that the Turks and Kurds thought they had swallowed. As Christians, they had also been sent on long death marches to exile, or ran for their lives. On one such flight in 1918, 15,000 Assyrians lay dead on the road. By morning, 5,000 more had died of starvation and disease. At the French Mission 6,000 were slaughtered. Children were held off the ground by their hair and their heads were cut off in one stroke. In one village 750 headless Assyrian corpses were found in the wells and cisterns. The gruesome accounts went on and on.

In 1895, the year Abraham was sixteen years old, Kurdish soldiers slaughtered 13,000 Assyrian men, women, and children in and around Urfa, a city not far from Mardin. It was during this period that Abraham had volunteered to run with a message from his town to another.

There seemed a never-ending chain of violence and tyranny in the world that leaves behind a never-ending chain of wounded souls.

"Wahoo," Abrahm said as he peered down at Jonathan. "This one is even more beautiful than the others."

He had said that about each new arrival. I looked up at him and smiled and felt all those womanly emotions welling up in me.

After Jonathan was born, Abraham mellowed. He never hit the children again and he never again hit me. He had wanted our children to accomplish something in the world rather than be subject to it as he had been. We both wanted that. Even though Abraham had been to college, he always struggled to make a living. The years of the Depression and the responsibility of so many children hadn't made it easier. But Abraham didn't have the soul of a merchant, a trade which could have helped him succeed. He had the soul of an artist, an inventor. He was always tinkering with things. When he worked at the Brooklyn Navy Yard in the '40s, Abraham invented a hole punch, because each time the workers attempted to punch a hole in the metal sheets, the metal crinkled. Abraham's invention fixed that problem. He never got credit for it. He made designs with tiny, ceramic tiles on concrete planters and table tops that he also made. And when he was in his eighties, he even built a loom at our country house and started to weave.

Abraham loved to build. Most of our children, even the girls, had helped Abraham clear the land and build our house over the years. He was always adding a room or cutting a room off. Each year the boys also climbed down into the well Abraham had dug, to clean out the silt and sand. Afterward, it became a tradition to have a playful water fight, because drawing lots of water from the well after it was cleaned, helped it to clear. Abraham always joined in. He liked it when the children helped. He was passing on his trades and the language of his trades. He was passing on the love of art also through his many stories and inventions, although he didn't know it. I was also passing along my love of art without knowing it.

Besides the clothing I made that sometimes seemed to be picked up by fashioned designers to become the new fad, and the dolls I made, I used to carve figurines for the children from double bars of Ivory soap. They were usually the characters I found in the children's books. Sometimes I even colored them. And I had always sung to our children.

Somehow between the two of us, we had given our children something we had never consciously intended to give them. We had given them a love of art, philosophy, and invention. Mariam became a fashion designer and a painter; Helyn a sculptor; Harty a photo colorist; Mitzi, changed her name to Jamie, moved to Chicago and became a singer and model; Amos had a great love for philosophy; Tim for invention, although Tim also opened a clothing store with his wife, Pat; David became a builder; Thea a painter and art director; Adrian an accountant; Jonathan, like Tim, could take apart and put together anything, even when he was a child. At the age of nine he once took apart my radio and fixed it when it stopped working. In fact, he took apart every toy we gave him and put it back together again before he played with it. When Tim was only eight, he had taken apart Abraham's gold pocket watch and also fixed it when it stopped working. At twelve he designed and made a map of the United States for a school project that he outfitted with electricity, so each capital lit up when a probe was touched to its state. Tim had a brilliant imagination.

What neither Abraham nor I could pass on to our children was a sense for business. If they didn't learn how to use their talents in school, they would have to find it out for themselves.

In the early 1950s, the time of the Korean war, while the iceman was still delivering ice to our neighborhood to keep the iceboxes cool, the first military jets began to scream over our heads with a great boom, breaking the sound barrier. That was exciting. It was like two worlds colliding. We'd all run to the window to watch the jets carve smoke-filled gashes in the sky. We didn't know then that those jets signaled the beginning of the end for our small world.

By the mid-fifties the city started forcing us and all of our neighbors out of our homes on West One hundred second Street to build the housing projects. It was a difficult time. Everything was changing, and once again, another place I called home was being torn out from under me. We moved a few doors down at first, then a few blocks away. But each move was temporary because each building was torn down for blocks around to make way for the projects.

In 1957, I finally moved the family to Brooklyn. I had just come in from a long day at work when the phone rang.

"Sano?" a woman's voice said on the other side.

"Yes?" I said.

"Oh, Sano!" she cried. "Is it really you?"

"Yes," I said. "Who is this?"

"It's me, Sano. Arexine. Your sister. Arexine. Do you remember me? Zohra's daughter."

I burst into tears and I could hear her crying on the other side of the line. Twenty-seven years had passed since I held her in my arms. She was five years old when I left Aleppo. Now she was a grown woman with a family of her own.

"How did you find me?" I said when I could control myself.

"I thought you were dead. They said you were dead. Oh, Sano, I'm so happy to hear your voice," she said, and burst out crying again.

It amazed me how anyone could find someone in such a big city, but she had. She said she visited a relative who owned a store on Tenth Avenue in Manhattan and told him about me. She told him she wished she could see me again but she had been told that I had died. She said she had cried and cried.

"She's not dead," her relative said. "She's living somewhere in Brooklyn."

Sonya—who was only two when I left Aleppo—was also in America with her family. I told Arexine how to come to me and invited her, Sonya, and their families for Sunday dinner. When they arrived at the door and I opened it, almost before I could get a look at her, Arexine threw her arms around my neck and held me tight.

"Oh my sister, my sister," she cried and pressed me to herself even more tightly. "My big sister."

Again we both burst into tears as if we had held our whole histories in check for all those years with no one to share it with until then.

41.

MRS.

WHEN ABRAHAM WAS IN his eighties he became ill. He had been living mostly in Spotswood by then because he was afraid to leave his house alone. There had been some vandalism, and once all of the watermelons in his garden had been stolen.

He telephoned me in the city one day to tell me he had fallen outside and couldn't get up. I became frantic. I thought he was still lying outside on the ground. I telephoned our children to see who could drive me to see him. Most of our children were grown and out of the house by then, some with families of their own. It was only after we arrived that I realized Abraham meant he had lain on the ground outside for a long time before he could get himself up and into the house again.

He didn't want to go to the doctor but I insisted. I was sorry I did. They gave him water pills. The effect on him was devastating. He could no longer hold his urine, and in a few days he developed the shakes and became so dizzy and weak he could hardly stand.

"Sano," he said to me, "I don't feel good."

When I asked what he was taking, he showed me the water pills the doctor had given him. They were huge, more for a horse than a man.

"You must stop that medicine immediately," I said.

In a few days his shaking stopped, but his legs became swollen. The doctors gave him another type of water pill, but after taking these medicines, something changed in his body. He was never the same again.

Those of our children who still lived in New York and had cars, often drove out to see him and spend the weekend. Of course, they always took me with them. But when my children couldn't drive me to Spotswood, I went by bus alone, straight from work on Friday evenings to make sure that everything was all right with Abraham. I brought groceries with me and cooked dinner for him when I arrived. On Saturday mornings I did the laundry and changed the sheets on the single bed he slept in by the potbellied stove in his room. I made sure he bathed without falling, and had something clean to wear.

But I was constantly tired from working all week and running back and forth. I tried to get him to stay in the city with me because I worried about him. I'd ask one of our children to go get him. He'd sometimes let them bring him to the city, but after only a few days he wanted to go back to the country again.

He loved it there. That was his home, even though by then almost the whole forest had been cleared, and row upon row of suburban homes were built alongside our land. When he came to the city on one occasion, someone broke his windows, and again Abraham was afraid to leave the house alone. Each time I went to see him he'd ask me to stay, but I couldn't give up my job. Who would support us then? I still had young children living at home. In 1963 our youngest was only thirteen years old. Abraham was eighty-three.

That year I went to the doctor for a persistent cough and trouble with my knees, conditions that developed while visiting with my daughter, Jamie, and her family, who were living in California at the time.

"You seem very nervous," the doctor said. "How old are you?"

"Fifty-three," I said.

"Why are you so nervous?" the doctor said.

I told him about Abraham, that I worried about him. I told him how I traveled back and forth every week to be with him. I was exhausted.

"You can't continue to do this," the doctor said. "Your husband is an old man. He doesn't have too much more time to live. You must forget about him and take care of yourself."

I thanked the doctor for his advice, but of course, I continued as before. Abraham had never learned to drive a car. Neither had I. But at least I could walk to the store or bring things from the city when our children couldn't drive me to see Abraham.

On one of those occasions when the family did drive out, in the summer of 1970, I made a dish Abraham had taught me to make called *argenki-*

tal, with raw chopped meat, bulgur, scallions, tomatoes, and mint. Abraham made a stew with fresh vegetables from the garden. Even when he was in his nineties he still worked in his garden, tilling the soil with only a shovel and his bare hands.

Most of the family came. Amos and Harty were there, and David was there with his wife and small children, as was Tim with his wife and first son. Thea was also there, back from living in Spain and Morocco where she had gone to concentrate on developing her painting, her lifelong dream. Jamie had flown in from Chicago with her two young children. Of course, Adrian and her husband were also there with their first child, and Jonathan was there with a local girl, Norma, who later became his wife. Jonathan had met her when he went to live with Abraham for about six months to care for him. Mariam was living in Mexico at the time, and Helyn was living in Florida where she had married and was raising her family.

We sat around the kitchen table as we had since the mid 1930s when Abraham first began to build our house. But so much had changed since then. Of course there were more children since the house was first built and they were now grown. We didn't use the well any longer. We now had running water and a sewer and even electricity.

With electricity, there was no more need for the kerosene lanterns to light the rooms. But I had liked the days when the kids were young and we had all sat around the shortwave radio in semidarkness listening to *The Shadow*, or the *Lux Playhouse of Stars*. We even had a bathroom now with a tub and toilet. No more warming water for a bath in the big washtub the way we used to—the way we also had in my country when I was a child—or bathing under the rain spout when it rained. And no more going into the woods and digging a hole to relieve ourselves. We even had a stove, so there was no more cooking with wood outside on an open fire. Everything had changed. But the changes had come with a heavy price to our beautiful wilderness.

Abraham sat at the head of the table. It amazed me how smooth his face remained. He had shrunk somewhat over the years, and his once trim six-foot frame had thickened with age, but at ninety, he still had few wrinkles. With the hippie era upon us, Tim let his hair grow a few inches longer. Abraham then let his hair grow longer too, at least where he still had hair. I tried a few times to cut it for him, but he refused.

"I'm a hippie too," he'd say and laugh.

"Oh, Mom," our children would say and also laugh, "at ninety years old he has a right to be a hippie."

As we sat around the kitchen table eating Abraham's stew, Dave said, "Hey, Jamie. Do you remember the time you went outside with me because I was afraid to go out alone at night to pee?"

"No, I don't remember," Jamie said and laughed. "But I hope you're talking about when you were a little boy. I'd hate to think I had to hold your hand to pee when you were a grown man."

Everyone laughed. David laughed too.

"I was around eight years old," David said and turned to the rest of the family. "When we were kids every time I went outside in the dark to pee I saw a king sitting in the garden."

"Why didn't you just use the bathroom, Dad?" his first son "little" Dave said.

"It wasn't like it is now. We were in the middle of the woods then," David said. "We didn't have a bathroom in those days. It was just a country house."

"We didn't have anything but good times," Thea said.

"What do you mean you saw a king sitting in the garden?" Adrian said.

"Yeah! A king. Every time I went out there in the dark. It used to scare the pants off of me"

"That was just the tomatoes," Jonathan said.

"Maybe he was a tomato king," Tim said.

"No, really," David said. "One time Jamie called me a sissy and said she'd go out with me while I peed. When we went outside, there he was. I shouted 'Look! There he is!' Jamie looked like one of those cartoons. She screamed and jumped in the air so high she didn't touch the ground until she was in the house."

"Oh, my God!" Jamie said. "I think I remember."

And everyone laughed again.

"So much for the big-sister act," Harty said. "Remember the creeping well?"

"What was the creeping well?" David's daughter, Lori said.

"When Grampa dug it, it was outside the house about twenty feet away. One day it was just outside the kitchen window. It had moved closer to the house. Then one day it was just inside the kitchen. And later it was where it is now, in the back of the kitchen."

"Mom," Lilli-ann said to Jamie. "How can that happen? How can a well move?"

"Tim," Thea said. "Remember the cranberries? Tim and I used to go out in the swamp with hip boots that would have reached to my neck if my body wasn't in the way. We'd pick pails full of cranberries, remember Tim?"

"Mom," Lilli-ann said. "How can a well move?"

"It wasn't the well that moved," Jamie said. "But it looked like it was the well that was moving. It was the house that was moving."

"Mo-o-m," Lilli-ann said. "How can a house move?"

"I remember when I first found the cranberries in the swamp behind the house," I said. "I waded in and picked some and brought them to show your aunt, Agnes. 'Oh,' she said. 'You mustn't eat those. They're poison.'"

"Mo-o-o-o m," Lilli-ann said. "How can a house move?"

"Because Grampa kept building the house. He kept adding rooms so the house kept getting closer to the well, until the well was inside the house."

David said, "I once saw Pop getting stung by a whole nest of hornets while he was cutting the back of the house off to turn it into a chicken coop. He just shooed the hornets away like they were flies."

"He picks up hot coals with his bare hands too," Thea said. "But I can do that too if I don't have to hold them too long."

"Oh, that's so cool," David's second son Mark said.

"Oh, that's so cool," Thea mimicked and pulled Mark close to give him a hug.

Abraham clucked his tongue on the roof of his mouth.

"You're a hoot," David said to Thea and laughed.

"Oh, Dave," his wife Reggie said. "Remember when we were dating and we'd go to visit Thea in that little room she lived in in Greenwich Village? You were so funny, Thea. She'd say, 'Wait for ten minutes. I just have to make another pair of pants. I don't have a clean pair to wear.' She used to buy a ton of corduroy and sit down and make a new pair of pants right in front of us in ten minutes." Reggie laughed. "Then we'd go to the Gaslight Cafe and listen to folk songs and poetry, and the audience would snap their fingers instead of clapping, remember Dave? The neighbors would complain if they made too much noise so they couldn't clap."

"She was a beatnik," Amos said.

"At least I didn't see kings in the garden," Thea said and laughed.

"You don't believe me but he was really there," David said.

"Mom," Jamie said. "I remember the time you sent me a care package of your Thanksgiving dinner when I first moved to Chicago. When I opened the package, my girlfriend thought the rice in your chestnut stuffing were maggots. She almost fainted."

I had forgotten all about that. "Oh, sugar!" I said. I buried my face in my hands for a moment to laugh with embarrassment. "I packed it in dry ice," I said. "I didn't want you to be left out so far from home. You were so young when you left; only eighteen years old. That was the year Jonathan was born. I wanted all my children with me. I love my children. I remember the refrigerator and then the console TV you sent us from Chicago. They had the biggest red bows I ever saw. That was our first refrigerator and first TV."

"What about me, Sano?" David's wife, Reggie said. "Do you love me too?"

"I love all of you; all my children and all my children's wives and husbands too, and all my grandchildren."

Tim reached for a piece of bread and accidentally dipped his sleeve into his food.

"Look, Pop!" Amos said. "Tim's feeding his clothes."

That was all Abraham needed. He clucked his tongue on the roof of his mouth and made a face that was full of mischief.

"There was once a poor man with ragged clothes who was walking down the road," Abraham began without further introduction. Everyone but the young ones knew what was coming, and Abraham addressed himself mostly to them, stretching out words for dramatic effect.

"The poor man passed a fiiiiine house and heard a man calling, 'Come! Come everyone. Come join the feast!'

"'Ooooh,' the poor man said to himself. 'Gooood. I could use a feast. I'm very hungry.'

"So the poor man went to the table of the rich man's house expecting to join the celebration. But when the poor man tried to take a seat near the head of the table, the host pulled him aside. 'Noooo,' the host said. 'You must sit at the other end of the table. This end is only for honored guests.'"

Abraham shook his head and made a face as if he had a bad taste in his mouth.

"So the poor man sat at the other end of a looooong table with the other poor people. When the food was served, first it went to the head of the table, and little by little, after aaaall the rich guests took what they wanted, the platters were passed down to the other end where the poor man sat. But by the time the platters reached the poor man, everything was gone.

"'I see,' the poor man said to himself. 'Only the rich are honored here. Only those who don't need a feast are the ones who get a feast.' And the poor man went on his way without getting anything to eat.

"One day, again he was walking down the road, and again he heard someone calling, 'Come everyone! Come join the celebration!'

"'Aaaah,' the poor man said to himself. 'This time, even I will eat.' He went to the cupboard where he had stored the eggs of his only chicken, and collected them in an old hat. Then he brought the eggs to a tailor shop and set them on the counter.

"'Tell me,' the poor man said to the tailor. 'If I give you all these eggs, will you lend me a fine suit of clothes for just a few hours?'

"'Yes,' said the tailor rubbing his hands together. 'What a fine bargain I made,' the tailor thought. 'I not only get the eggs, but in a few hours I will also get my suit of clothes back.'

"And so the poor man left the eggs with the tailor, and took the fine suit of clothes home to his little shack. He washed himself and then dressed in his new outfit. He looked very handsome.

"'Oooooh!' said the host when he saw the poor man in his fine clothes. 'Who could this fine gentleman be? I must invite him to my feast. Come!' he said to the poor man. 'Come join us, please!'

"The poor man went to the lower end of the table, but before he could sit the host rushed over and bowed low before him. 'Nooo. Nooo,' said the host. 'A fine gentleman like yourself must sit at the very head of the table. Please. I would be greatly honored.'

"And so the poor man sat at the head of the table where all the finest food was served to him first. Eeeeveryone watched every bite the poor man took. They even watched him chew. They were soooo happy to have such a fine gentleman at their table.

"But with each bite the poor man took, he gave one bite to his fine new clothes. The poor man poured some soup onto his fine vest, and he dipped the edge of his coat into the gravy. The roasted pheasant and quail, he wiped on his lapels.

"'Oooooh!' said the host. 'This man must be very rich indeed. Look how he feeds his fine clothing without worrying. What a great honor it is to have him at my table.' And all the other people at the table looked at the poor man with envy.

"'What is he saying?' someone asked. 'What is he saying? I can't hear him.'

"'Here!' the poor man was saying to his fine suit of clothes. 'Here! You eat too! For the honor is all yours.'"

We all laughed while our grandchildren giggled uncontrollably.

"Wahoo!" Abraham said.

So they continued, reminding each other of the past as they usually did when one of our children was visiting from far away, and Abraham told a few old country jokes and a few more stories; life's last pleasure.

🕊 🕊 🕊

On one of my trips alone to see Abraham, I arrived on the Friday evening bus. That time I walked all the way from Jamestown along Summerhill Road. When I arrived at the house, even before I came through the door, I could hear Abraham singing verses from the Bible like the Arabic chanting of an old mullah calling the people to prayer. He had always loved to sing, maybe as much as he loved to tell stories. And he loved to read his Bible. In Mardin, the town where he was born in southeastern Turkey, there is a monastery where the people still chant in Aramaic, the language of Christ.

I stood listening to him sing from the other room for a while, then went into his bedroom.

"How are you feeling, Pop?" I said. I began calling him Pop when our grandchildren began to grow and call him Grampa.

Abraham looked up from his Bible, clucked his tongue, and shook his head.

"Not a hundred percent," he said.

"Did you eat?" I said.

"A little bit," he said.

His feet and ankles were swollen but he got up and took hold of the cane that was leaning against the side of the bed. Then he followed me into the kitchen, dragging his swollen feet in his worn slippers. "Do you want some tea?" I said

He nodded his head and sat down heavily in a chair. "Maybe," he said.

I filled the teapot with fresh water and put it on the stove to boil, then put away the groceries I brought.

"Sano," Abraham said. "Get the chessboard."

I went into the living room and brought the chessboard and the box of chess pieces back to the kitchen and put them on the table in front of Abraham. I had learned to play years before when Mariam, our oldest daughter, first married and she and her husband lived with us for a short time. Her husband had bought that very same chessboard and chessmen thirty years before. He had sat with Abraham for hours at a time playing game after game. Sometimes I watched, and I learned to play also. Abraham then taught our children to play when some of them were barely old enough to read.

Abraham opened the box and set the pieces on the board in their proper places. Then he stopped and looked at me through the lenses of his glasses; lenses that had grown thicker over the years. His eyes zoomed out at me double their actual size. He clucked his tongue again and shook his head.

"What is it, Pop?" I said.

Abraham slid a pawn up two spaces and I followed with one of mine. Again he clucked his tongue and shook his head, but for a few moments said nothing.

"Why didn't you ever tell me, Sano?" he finally said.

"Tell you what?" I said.

"Did you have sex with the doctor?"

It was a moment before I realized what he was asking. The idea that I had sex with a doctor was so foreign a thought to me that I wasn't sure I had heard him right.

"What are you saying?" I said.

"Did you have sex with the doctor?" he said.

"What are you saying?" I said again, but this time with rising anger in my voice. "How can you ask me that? What doctor? When?"

"The one who examined you when you were pregnant with Jonathan," he said, and again he shook his head and clucked his tongue.

"What doctor that examined me? Jonathan was born twenty years ago," I said. "How can you accuse me of such a thing?" And I burst into tears.

The doctors had been so remote in all the years I had gone to see them. They hadn't even called me by name. "Mrs.," they'd say to address me. Just that. "Mrs."

Only one doctor had spoken to me about something other than the problem at hand. I didn't even remember his name, but he was a kind man. "Mrs.," he had said. "I'm fifty-five years old and only recently I married and had a child. What a mistake I made. All those years that I took care of my mother I never thought of my own life. Now my life is almost done." He shook his head then and pressed the cold stethoscope to my chest to listen with a slight tilt of his head.

That was as close as I had ever come to any of my doctors over the years. I was just one of hundreds of married women who passed through their offices each year. Now the man who I had spent forty-five years of my life with was accusing me of sleeping with one of them. The thought of sleeping with anyone had never crossed my mind in all those years.

"I'm going home," I said, trying to control my tears. "I won't let you accuse me of anything like that."

Abraham clucked his tongue again and gave a short jerk of his head in a typical gesture. "It's all right," he said to calm me. But I got up from the table. I put on my jacket, picked up my purse, and walked out the door.

The street was lit dimly from one streetlamp half a block away, but as I turned down Summerhill Road and headed toward town, the road was dark.

"One ticket for New York City," I said to the ticket salesman at the general store, which was also used as the bus depot.

"That bus just left," he said. "The next one isn't due for a few hours yet. Maybe you can catch one at Jamestown. They leave every half hour from there."

"Excuse me," I said to a man who came in to buy some cigarettes. "Are you going to Jamestown by any chance?"

"I'm passing that way," he said.

"Would you mind dropping me off at the bus station there?" I had never done such a thing in all my life.

"I'm sorry," he said, "but that's not my truck."

"Oh," I said. "I'm sorry to bother you."

I went outside to wait under the streetlamp. The moths and other bugs were already swarming around the light.

"Listen, lady," the man said when he came out of the store. "I guess it won't hurt no one none. Hop in."

On the bus, each time I thought of what Abraham had accused me of, I burst into tears, and when I arrived home I was still so upset I again began to cry.

"What's wrong?" my daughter Harty said.

I covered my face with my hands and tried to control myself. "Your father accused me of having sex with a doctor," I blurted out. "He said I slept with a doctor when I was pregnant with Jonathan." And again I broke down and cried.

Harty picked up the telephone and called Abraham.

"How could you say such a thing to Mom?" she said.

"I know she had sex with the doctor," Abraham said. "She took off all her clothes for him. I heard the nurse tell her to take off all her clothes."

"Oh, Pa!" Harty said. "They tell everyone to take off all their clothes. That doesn't mean she had sex with him. They tell me to take off all my clothes too when I go to the doctor."

Harty said she could hear him clucking his tongue but he didn't say anything for a long time. "Maybe" he said finally.

I realized, perhaps for the first time, that there were still so many American customs Abraham didn't understand. A woman taking off all her clothes to be examined, especially by a male doctor, was one of them. In Turkey in 1905, the year Abraham had left for America, the practice had been taboo. Midwives delivered babies. In small communities, such as the one I had come from, there were no doctors.

All week at work I tried to put the incident out of my mind, but it has always been difficult for me when I'm accused unjustly. I had tried to live my life as I know my mother would have lived hers.

When I returned the following weekend, Abraham was again sitting in his bedroom, this time reading his Bible. When he couldn't find what he was looking for in the English Bible, he'd look in the Arabic Bible and would always find it.

I didn't stop at his bedroom, but walked on into the kitchen, past the room where he had built the giant loom about five years before. When he built it, I had wondered why he would build a loom so late in life.

"Don't you know?" Tim's wife said to me one day. Abraham had confided in Pat while telling her stories. "He built the loom because he loves the sounds of the shuttle and harness. They were the sounds of his childhood; the sounds of his mother who had always sat at her loom weaving."

He had confided many things to Pat over the years—maybe to others also. He loved to tell of his life, and our children's friends and spouses loved to listen. Once I came into a room where Abraham was showing Pat his dentist's instruments from his college days; he kept them in a tool kit in the basement. Pat was a medical student at Columbia University at that time. They were speaking French. I didn't know Abraham could speak French. I guess he had learned it when he went to college years before, or maybe in Syria, where French became the second language.

"He speaks French at least as good as my French teacher," Pat said. "Abraham's a linguist,"

Abraham had grinned mischievously.

Again I brought groceries and set them on the kitchen counter. The chessboard was still sitting on the kitchen table where we had left it, and all the men were still in their places. Even the two pawns Abraham and I had moved forward the week before, sat where we had left them.

I filled the teapot again and set it on the stove and put away the groceries. Abraham came out of his room leaning heavily on his cane. He sat down at the kitchen table as before. Finally I sat at the table too. He clucked his tongue once, then slid the chessboard between us as if a week had not come and gone. He picked up his bishop and slid it diagonally across the board, then leaned back in his chair and looked at me with his owl eyes. He said that when I mentioned Jonathan's birth at the dinner table, all the feelings of betrayal came back to him.

He told me that when he returned to Syria in 1950, he also went to Turkey for the first time since his exile. He was angry because he was sure I had slept with the doctor. It made him think of Warde, the girl he had kidnapped. He said he had never forgotten her even though more than forty-five years had passed since he last saw her, and he was by then seventy years old. He said he went to the house where Warde lived and knocked on the door. A frail old woman with white hair and stooped shoulders answered.

"Are you Warde?" he asked her.

"Yes," she said. "Who are you?"

"I am Abraham," he said. Then he turned and ran away.

I could feel the tears welling up in my eyes again. Abraham shook his head in mock wonder and clucked his tongue before beginning to laugh, and I knew he was laughing at himself. Then he began to clear his throat in short quick spurts the way he always did when he spoke of his mother and sisters; the way he always did when he was trying to hold back his tears.

42

GO WITH GOD

A MONTH BEFORE Abraham's ninety-fourth birthday he developed pneumonia. The family had been to see him, and our daughter Helyn had flown in from Louisiana where she lived with her husband and children by then. We sat at Abraham's bedside in the nursing home listening to him breath.

"Pop. How do you feel?" I said.

"Not a hundred percent," he said.

I poured water into his cup and helped him drink. Helyn told him about her children.

"Sano," Abraham said. "Go out of the room. I want to talk to Helyn alone for a moment."

I left the room and stood in the hall. I opened my pocketbook to take out a handkerchief and saw the letter I had received from the town of Spotswood. It said they were condemning our home and requisitioning our land for a school. I couldn't tell Abraham.

When Abraham first bought the land and built his house—Pop's house we always called it, even though it belonged to all of us— Spotswood, New Jersey was one of those tiny American villages, the kind one rarely sees now except in old books and movies. It had a feed-and-grain store and a lumberyard where they also sold tools and nails, tar paper, and cinder block, all the things one needed to build. Then there was an ice-cream parlor with swivel seats and red plastic booths. There was the doctor's house that looked like two identical houses side by side that was connected by a small corridor in the middle. There was a local saloon/restaurant, and of course there was the church and the old graveyard. All of it sat on the edge of the railroad tracks on one side of the road, and the lake on the other. There was also a small general store on the other end of the village, across the road from old lady Bennett's farm, where the kids sometimes went to get fresh milk. And when she was in her nineties, they'd help her milk her cows at times. There were a few other private village homes on the main road, and then you had left Spotswood. And like us, there were a few farms tucked in the woods, such as the Russian lady's farm where we had also sent the children to buy milk with a little metal milk container to bring it home. Her farm sat on the other side of a golden field of wheat, not too far from our land, but neither could be seen by the other or from any place on the road.

Spotswood stayed that small all through the fifties and into the sixties. We never thought to buy up the land around us. The whole forest seemed to be ours for so many years that when the developers came and began to clear it away and dry up the beautiful streams and cranberry swamp, it came as a surprise. Where once we were surrounded by forest, almost overnight the forest disappeared and we were surrounded by row upon row of look-alike homes, each with a neat patch of lawn and a shrub for atmosphere. They even bulldozed trees on our land. When Abraham protested they said, "Oops. Sorry," but cleared some more.

But even the fact that over the years our beautiful little paradise had become suburbia didn't make Abraham want to stay away. When the new suburban homeowners finally moved in, some set about trying to force Abraham out because his home was so unlike theirs. His was like a tiny farm with chickens and a vineyard, fruit trees, and a garden. He was in his eighties when the families moved in. Most were fine with Abraham, but some children, encouraged by their parents, threw stones at him when he worked in his garden, and continued to throw stones at him even when he was in his nineties.

One family took him to court with the ridiculous claim that his puppy stole their *Sunday Times* each Sunday, then jumped over his low fence to bring it to him. At the age of ninety-three Abraham carried his little dog to court to show the judge the culprit. I went with him. Jonathan and Tim went too. The judge threw the case out, but the mischief went on. Someone even stole all of his chickens. When Abraham bought more, the son of the people who had sued him, warned Abraham the same thing would happen to the new chickens. But no matter what they did, Abraham wouldn't leave.

When Abraham was in his eighties he had said to me, "Sano, I want to live to be a hundred and fifty." But in his nineties he said he had changed his mind. "I want to live forever," he said. And he wanted to live forever in the country on the land that he loved, in the house he had built himself, bit by bit over the years. Abraham loved his land as we had loved our land in Turkey. He had nurtured that land for thirty-eight years, turning the soil for his garden each year with only a shovel, and planting each grain and seed with his own two hands. It was as much a part of him as one of his own children.

I wiped my eyes with my handkerchief and went back into the room where Abraham lay. Helyn stood at the side of the bed. Abraham was breathing heavily. I could feel the muscles in my throat constrict and again my eyes filled with tears.

"You'll have to leave now," the nurse said as she came into the room. "You should go home to get some rest."

I looked at Abraham. His eyes were closed.

"Pop," I said, not knowing if he was sleeping. "I'm leaving now. I'll come back tomorrow." But I couldn't bring myself to go.

Abraham just lay there with his eyes closed. Finally I turned to leave the room.

"Sano," he said. "Go with God."

It was the first time he had ever said that to me in all those years. I burst into tears.

I was uneasy all the way home. Something told me I shouldn't have left. When I walked in the door of the house, the phone rang. Abraham was gone.

When Abraham died, the town made its final move. They gave me a small settlement and set our home on fire. Then they bulldozed away our beautiful fruit trees and vineyard, and leveled the land. The cranberry swamp and the streams had long ago been totally dried, and the once lush cultivation and wilderness became a flat, barren field. That's how it stayed. They never did build the school there. They built it about a quarter mile away. Our land became the very end of the school field, on the other side of which were those first suburban homes.

I was glad Abraham never knew they had finally pushed us off our land. It was as if we had never existed there. It was like history repeating itself.

Book Five

JOURNEY'S END

Like a haphazard tourist
I roamed the earth
Searching for something
I could not name
Until I stood on the hillside
where they once dwelled
And gazed at the majesty
of their skies

43.

ABRAHAM, MY OWN

In Aybasti the next morning, my mother and I were up and dressed bright and early, long before Harry and Ali came to knock on our door. There was no shower in the small hotel. We were lucky there was a toilet on our floor, but even that was primitive. One had to flush it with a pail of water. The only other hotel in Aybasti we were told, was even more primitive than the one we were in, but we were grateful there was a hotel, and we had slept as well as we would have in a luxury suite. As my mother said, "When your eyes are closed all rooms are the same."

I ran down the four dingy flights of stairs and, from a small store, bought the typical Turkish breakfast fixings for my mother and me to eat in our room: bread, olives, feta cheese, and tomatoes. Then I climbed up the four dingy flights again, happy I could still manage it without too much huffing and puffing.

I spread our breakfast out on the small table, using the paper it was wrapped in as a platter, then sliced the bread with the pocketknife I had bought for such occasions, and cut the feta cheese and tomatoes into small cubes to make them easier to pop into our mouths.

Sometime around 9 A.M. I opened the door to Harry's knock.

"Well?" Harry said to my mother from the doorway. "You're finally going to Iondone. Are you excited?"

"I don't know what I feel. I suppose so," she said.

"I'll go arrange for a dolmuç," Ali said, referring to the minibus taxi. "I'll come back to tell you when I find a driver who is willing to take us to Iondone."

"I'll come too," Harry said.

Harry pulled the door to our room closed behind him, and my mother and I looked at each other.

"Well?" I said. "Are you excited? As you said, you've waited a lifetime."

"But what will we find?" my mother said. "Maybe I'm afraid to be excited. I don't want to be disappointed. I keep seeing my mother standing there in the doorway, even though I know it can't be. I used to think my brother might still be alive. That maybe he found his way back home after the turmoil. He's younger than I am, remember. And Uncle Nikolas and his wife stayed behind. Nikolas said he would go and live among the Turks. Who knows? Maybe they went back. But of course he'd be dead by now."

"So many years have passed," I said, trying to silence the growing number of ifs and maybes that were again forming in my mind. I knew it was too much to hope for, but always there was that hope, even for me, that someone of her family would be there. Maybe her brother had returned, or her uncle's children were there with their grandchildren, just like it used to be. Or maybe time had stood still, and they were all there as I had pictured them the night before.

"Do you really think it's possible?" I said. "Do you think your brother might still be alive?"

"I used to think so. But I don't anymore. I looked for him so many times from America. I never found him. But last year I believe he found me. He would have been seventy-seven years old. He came into my mind and my heart so powerfully, and remained there through each day, and through each night for almost a year, as if he were calling out to me, telling me he was there thinking of me, embracing me, reminding me of what we had lost. Then he was gone."

"You've lost so much." I said.

How is it you stayed so generous? is what I wanted to say. How did she continue to do those little things that she did so well? Or rather, how did she continue to have the will to do those things that were above and beyond the call of duty? The warming of the blankets on cold winter nights when we were children before she wrapped us inside; the pies, cakes, and cookies we certainly didn't need, but loved so much. The trinkets she used to make, like the tiny dolls, only an inch and a half long, for which she crocheted minuscule coats, hats, and booties, to pin to our coats. Or the drawstring purses she crocheted for my older sisters that then became the new fashion craze. The beaded American flag pins. The stories and songs.

As a child I remember my mother saying she had made a promise to herself when she was a child, that if she ever had children she would never be mean to them as some were mean to her. She would always be kind. But no one could have blamed a mother of ten for cutting corners. I was the eighth child, yet she still hadn't tired of these rituals. Now her grandchildren and great-grandchildren enjoy the same devotion. God had blessed her hands, which are never still. It's this devotion that keeps her home full of my brothers and sisters and their families almost every Sunday, and keeps us and her grandchildren stopping by to see and help her on other days as well.

"I know what I've lost," my mother said. "But I also know what I've found. I won't say it was easy. Sometimes it was very hard."

"Mom," I said. "Did you know that Pa loved you?"

My mother looked at me as if she was surprised by the question, then bowed her head in contemplation. I knew my father had loved her, but I wondered if she knew.

My father hadn't always been an easy man, but we had loved him just the same. It hadn't occurred to me, except subliminally perhaps, that he was only comfortable communicating in one of three ways: he issued orders, he told stories, and he offered fruit and candy, which usually included Black Jack gum. I don't remember ever seeing Black Jack gum in the candystore, so where he got it was a mystery. And it was a mystery why he chose that gum as one of our treats, but he usually did. And of course, he offered us those wonderful Middle Eastern goodies he brought home on occasion.

My father had never hit me as a child. On more than one occasion when I was six or seven, I woke in the middle of the night because of the same recurring nightmare of some mundane object, like a nut or bolt, or even a blanket, becoming huge and then rolling toward me to crush me. It always frightened me and I'd wake up crying. On one of those occasions my father came and took me from my bed. My mother must have been working nights at the time. Everyone else was still asleep. He sat me down in the dining room near the potbellied stove, just the two of us.

He took out the cocoa and the sugar, and put a tablespoon of each into a little pot. He added a little water and slipped the pot into the top of the stove to cook the cocoa mixture until it almost bubbled over the rim. Then he filled the pot with milk, stirred it until the cocoa was hot, and poured it into a cup. He smacked his lips together noisily and said "yummm," to show me how good the cocoa would taste. Then he told me to drink, and I did. And while I sipped the hot cocoa he sat beside me and stared at the stove. I could smell that earthy scent that was always his coming from his nightshirt. A scent that would one day be mine.

"There was once a faaamous liar named Saha" my father began. "Saha was sooo famous people came from aaaall around just to challenge him to a lie.

"One day a man came from faaar away to challenge Saha. He knocked on the door and Saha's little daughter opened it. 'Who are you?' the little girl asked the man. 'I have come to challenge Saha to a lie,' the man said, 'because *I* am the greatest liar in the world.' 'Oh,' the little girl said. 'My father is not home right now. He is out sewing up a big hole in the sky.' 'How old are you?' the man asked, amazed that the child lied so easily. 'I am five,' the little girl said. 'Oh,' said the man. 'If Saha's daughter is such a liar as this, even at such a young age, then Saha must be the greatest liar after all.' And the man turned around and went on his way."

Then my father brought me back to my bed and tucked me in.

I remembered my sister Helyn once told me about the incident in the hospital on the day my father died. He was lying in bed talking when he turned to my mother and asked her to leave the room. He said he wanted to talk to my sister alone.

"Your mother is still a beautiful woman," my father said. "Maybe she'll find another husband."

"Oh, Pa," my sister said. "Don't be ridiculous."

My mother was sixty-three years old.

"Well?" I said when my mother didn't answer. "Did you know that Pop loved you?"

"When he died I used the money the town of Spotswood gave me for our property to buy my home" my mother said. "Not long after I moved there, I was sitting alone on the back lawn and I had such a strange experience. I looked up at the trees and I thought I saw your father sitting on one of the branches. He was smiling down at me. I shook my head to clear it and then looked again, but he was gone.

"I remember once I overheard him bragging about me to a neighbor. 'My wife has such a beautiful voice,' he said. 'You should hear her sing.' He never told that to me, but when I heard him say it to the neighbor, it made me feel so proud.

"How can I tell you whether I knew he loved me? I lived with your father for over forty-eight years until he died at the age of ninety-four. We raised ten children together, six girls and four boys. We never used the language of love. We talked about love only after our children were grown, and then only about how much we loved them. He was an old-fashioned man. He never kissed me before he left home in all those years. He never kissed me hello. He never took my hand and held it in his. But I knew he loved me in his way. I knew by the way he sometimes called me "my little Sano," or the way he looked at me when everything was fine. I had one man in all my life. That man was Abraham, and that's the way I wanted it to be.

"And I had never planned on having so many children. How I managed is a mystery even to me. Who knows what I could have accomplished without you. But I wouldn't change that for anything in the world. My children are my life. Maybe this was God's plan for me; the cloth He intended me to weave."

44.

JOURNEY'S END

――――――――――――― ❦ ―――――――――――――

A<small>LI KNOCKED ON OUR DOOR</small> to tell us they were ready with transportation, and a few minutes later, Harry, Ali, and the driver of the dolmuç greeted us when my mother and I arrived on the street outside the hotel. Our driver was a tall man with a stocky build and a rather fair complexion for a Turk. Ali introduced us, then we all piled into the dolmuç and started on our long-awaited journey to Iondone.

So close, so close was all I could think as the dolmuç slowly wound its way up the steep, curving, gravel and dirt road toward Iondone. Hazelnut bushes lined the edges of the road, heavy with fruit and a thick layer of dust. Except for Ali and the driver, who conversed in Turkish, we drove in silence. My mother and I stared out the window from the backseat. Harry busied himself with a map. I asked my mother if she recognized anything but she said she did not.

With the road so rough, the driver took extra care to make the hairpin curves required for the ascent. An occasional car going in the opposite direction slowly maneuvered a curve to pass us, and after staring into our windows as they went, rumbled down the mountain, as we rumbled up.

We were on the road for maybe half an hour, and well up the mountain when the dolmuç suddenly came to a stop.

"Why are we stopping?" I said.

"The driver says there's an old man who lives here. He might remember something. He's eighty-seven years old. Even older than you," Ali said, turning to my mother.

On the side of the road was a small house made of wooden planks. It was a simple house and the wood was unpainted, but somehow it had kept its rich natural color. We had seen a few like it on our travels in the area, but most of the houses appeared to be made of mortar.

The driver got out of the dolmuç and Ali followed. My mother and I got out also and waited on the road while the driver went into the house. After only a few moments, our driver reappeared accompanied by a tall, trim man, with only a hint of roundness at the shoulders, and a full salt-and-pepper beard. The man was obviously of advanced age, yet he carried himself in so upright a fashion, barely relying on the cane he carried, that one might have taken him to be much younger than his eighty-seven years. He had one of those faces and figures that were so pleasant and grandfatherly, one would expect to find him engraved in a storybook, in a style of the nineteenth century.

Ali greeted the man cordially in Turkish and questioned him about the past.

"There were three Greek villages," Ali translated when my mother began to recite the description of the villages.

"Rüm," my mother said, referring to the name the Turks called the Greeks.

The man made a tripod with his first three fingers touching at their tips, one to the other, exactly as I had seen my mother do so many times before.

"Look!" Ali said to my mother. "He does the same thing with his fingers as you do with yours."

"Her family were blacksmiths," Ali said to the man. "Do you remember them? They were the only blacksmiths in the area."

"Yes," the man said. "We used to spread manure on their fields, and they made our tools in return. I was fifteen when they took them away. I remember."

"He actually remembers my mother's family?" I said, stunned to be so close to a living, breathing part of something that had for so long been only a fairy tale.

"Yes," Ali said. "He remembers."

"I asked him to come with us to show us," our driver said through Ali, "but he refused. He said some Greeks came some time ago and were very angry. He said he doesn't want any trouble."

"How do you say papa in Turkish?" I asked Ali.

"*Baba,*" he said.

I slipped my arm under and around the old man's arm. "Come with us, *Baba*," I said in Turkish.

The old man hesitated, obviously bewildered by my gesture. He looked at Ali, and Ali nodded, but he was still hesitant.

"Come, *Baba*," I said again.

"All right," he said after a moment more.

Ali helped the man into the front seat of the dolmuç and climbed in after. My mother and I climbed into the back again beside Harry. Then the driver put the dolmuç into gear and again resumed our slow drive up the dry, pitted, dirt road toward Iondone.

We slowly scaled another hill and rounded yet another corner. The sky was clear and blue and one green hillside rolled into another.

"There!" the old man said and pointed.

The dolmuç pulled to an abrupt stop, and we each followed the line of his finger to look where he pointed, but all I saw was a small wooden shack on the side of the road, and the same green rolling hills.

"It was there," he said.

"What was there?" I said.

"That was the town called Iondone," the old man said, still pointing to the empty hills.

"Where?" my mother said. "Where?" And I could hear an anguish rising in her voice. It was a sound I had not heard before, except when one of us had been badly injured as children, and of course, when my eldest brother, Amos, had died of an aneurysm at the age of forty-six.

"There," the man said again.

"But there's nothing there! How can that be? There's nothing there! There were over two hundred and fifty homes in Iondone. Where? Where?" my mother said, as if demanding he produce the village he pointed to.

The old man looked down at his lap nervously and said something to the driver in a low voice.

"He said, maybe the woman who lives in that house knows something," our driver said through Ali.

We got out of the dolmuç and the driver went to the shack. A few minutes later he came out accompanied by a woman of about forty-five years of age. She looked from one to the other, then recited some facts to Ali without expression.

"She says she knows your house," Ali said. "She says she lived in your house."

My mother also made a tripod of her three fingers, and pointed to one of her fingers to indicate which of the three villages her home was in.

"Yes," Ali said. "She says that's the village where she lived. She says she can show you if you like, but it's a muddy trip down the cow path to the other hillside."

I could see there was a spark of hope rekindling in my mother's eyes. *Maybe her house was still there,* I said to myself, feeling that same spark of hope rekindle in me.

The woman indicated the way with a gesture toward the cow path, and Ali, the driver, the woman, my mother, and I started toward it. Harry's game leg made it difficult for him to make the trek, so he and the old man stayed behind.

Once on the muddy path our feet sunk into the gooey earth and slurped out again with each step. Our driver broke a branch from a small tree and gave it to my mother to use as a walking stick, but he walked close to her, obviously ready to catch her if she were to fall.

The trip down the hill through the mud and up the other side was long, and my mother's angina made the trip slow. Periodically we stopped to let her heart rest, and finally we made our way up the far hillside, about three quarters of a mile from the main road. We climbed to the top and walked toward a flat area where the hill began to descend again on the other side. Curiously, a little calf was tied to an old tree near a pile of stones. The stones were obviously the only remains of an old foundation to a home.

The little calf stared at us and my mother and I stared at it. There seemed no logical reason for it to be there. No houses were near. In fact, the only house in the whole area was the little shack that belonged to the woman on the main road.

"This was your house," the woman said, ignoring the calf.

The pile of stones she pointed to formed a small rectangle the size of a one-car garage, but the sides of the rectangle had been knocked down so that the stones filled in the space where the animals would have once lived under the house.

"No," my mother said. "That can't be." And I could again hear the anguish in her voice. "Our house was bigger."

"Yes," the woman said. "Your house was there."

The woman pointed to a place just a few feet away where a bed of tiny wildflowers grew in a perfect rectangle the size of a large house.

"We tore it down and built this one with the wood and stones," the woman continued through Ali. "Then we tore this one down and used the wood for the fire."

"There was an oven," my mother said, as if proving to the woman that she was mistaken.

The woman pointed to an empty place near where the house once stood.

"And our blacksmith shop?"

The woman pointed to another spot not far away. A small strip of dirt road, like a foot path, began and ended a few feet away.

"And the mill?" my mother asked.

"Down at the bottom of this ravine," Ali translated. "But it's no longer there."

"But why did they destroy all the houses?" my mother said. "I thought at least the houses would be here. Why didn't they live in them instead of destroying them?"

"She said they were looking for gold. They tore the houses apart because they heard people hid their gold," Ali said.

My mother smiled wistfully and her eyes filled with tears. "The only things we buried were our pots and pans."

She pointed to a spot near where the house once stood and the woman's head jerked to look at the spot, as if my mother had finally pointed out the treasure for which she had searched so long.

"We buried them there," my mother said. "We thought we were coming back."

"If you had come a few months later," Ali translated, "even these stones would be gone."

"The pear trees?" my mother said. "Where are the pear trees?"

The woman shrugged.

"She said they bought the houses from the Greeks before they left. She says the land belongs to her."

My mother ignored the last. She knew it wasn't true.

"Can this really be the place?" my mother said.

We surveyed the mountains. Except for the pile of stones the woman claimed came from my mother's home, not even a stone, or a log, or a road, could be seen anywhere. There was no sign that the three Greek villages had ever existed, or that thousands of people ever quietly lived their lives there for perhaps thousands of years.

Was that it? All there was? Wildflowers growing in a perfect rectangle the size of my mother's home, and a little calf inexplicably tied to an old tree nearby? I knelt down in the wildflowers and looked out over the beautiful grassy landscape. The clouds billowed up from the edge of the mountains in great white tufts. I could feel the tears welling up in my eyes for something lost. Or maybe for something found. I had a family at last, just long enough to know they were gone.

As the tears rolled down my cheeks, I collected wildflowers from the spot and tucked them between the pages of my little book. I scooped up a handful of soil and wrapped it in a cloth. Then my mother and I, and the people who had brought us there, walked back down the hillside and up the other, to the road in Iondone.

Harry was sitting on a stone near the dolmuç. The old man was already gone.

"Have some potatoes before you go," the woman said. "I boiled them before you came."

She went into her little shack and came out with a bowl full of boiled potatoes, a small bowl of salt, and a pitcher of fresh water. My mother, Ali, and I sat on the grass. The driver kneeled beside me to wash his hands and struggled with the pitcher of water.

"Give it to me," I said motioning toward the pitcher. "I'll pour it for you."

The driver looked at Ali, and Ali told him what I said. The driver protested shyly, but I jerked my head in a Middle Eastern gesture that said it was all right; that no more protests were needed. He handed me the pitcher then, put his hands beneath it, and rubbed them together as I poured the water over them the way I had done for my own father as a child; as my mother had done for hers. Then we ate some potatoes sprinkled with salt, climbed back into the dolmuç, and slowly drove back down the dusty road to Aybasti.

In Aybasti, Ali and the driver of the dolmuç stood with us in the street waiting for another dolmuç to take us to Fatsa, a town on the Black Sea; the town my grandfather and great-grandfather used to go to for supplies. Harry was coming with us. I had asked my mother if she wanted to stay on for a few days, but she shook her head, no. We had traveled so far and my mother had waited so long to get there, yet we both felt an inexplicable need to escape that place. It wasn't like me to leave so quickly. I don't think it's like my mother either. To this day neither I nor my mother understand why we left so soon.

"The driver wants to reduce the price he said he would charge you to take you to Iondone," Ali said.

"He doesn't have to," I said.

"I know," Ali said. " And he knows too. But he wants to."

I looked at the driver and he looked back at me with a somber face and a slight, wistful smile. I paid him what Ali told me to pay, and he waited there with Ali to say good-bye until our dolmuç came. When it arrived, Harry, my mother, and I squeezed into the overcrowded van. The passengers made room for my mother and me to sit beside a woman and her child. Harry sat beside a man.

Through the open window we thanked Ali and the driver and waved our good-byes as the dolmuç pulled away and headed down the road.

45.

A DIAMOND IN THE ASH

In Fatsa, the motel we checked into rested amid the pines that lined the shore of the Black Sea. It was late afternoon when we arrived. My mother and I brought our bags to our room. Harry went to his. Then I left my mother and went to sit in the shade of the pines. She came to find me weeping for a life and family I had never known.

"What's the matter, sweetheart?" my mother said.

"Mom," I said. "I never felt the stories you told about your family were real. I mean, I knew they were, but I could never feel the people you talked about. They sounded like stories of beautiful people who lived long ago but that was all. They were your people but never mine, until I stood on your land and looked out at those beautiful mountains and that glorious sky."

My mother sat beside me on the bench and took my hand in both of hers. "As we drove up the mountain in the dolmuç," she said, "I couldn't help wondering if they would be there. My heart was racing. Even though I knew it could never be, it took all my strength to convince myself that I wouldn't find them waiting because I had never seen my home without my mother inside. In my mind, as the dolmuç slowly climbed the mountain, I could picture the cows roaming in the pasture; I could picture the garden and the pear trees. When I was a child, Mother used to send us out early in the morning before anyone else when the pears were ripe, to collect the ones that had fallen to the ground. Other families did the same, because the trees belonged to the whole village. Sometimes I'd climb up into those pear trees just like a little monkey.

"When we arrived and I saw those empty hills my heart sank. Maybe it even stopped beating. I couldn't believe that was our land. The land around Iondone looked right, but the land the woman said was ours looked so steep. I thought it was flatter on top of the hill. It was flat for a long distance where the garden used to be. And I thought at least they would have kept the homes. I thought they would have lived in them. To think, thousands of years of history and one's life can be summed up in a pile of stones. But when I saw that little calf tied to that old tree, my heart jumped. 'Wait for me,' I told Mata the day I left. It was as if my little Mata had waited for me for all these years as I had asked. I wanted to go to her and put my arms around her neck. I wanted to press her furry face to mine as I had with Mata when I was a child, but I was afraid to touch her. I was afraid she would vanish beneath my hand; would vanish like everything else had vanished.

"It was only recently that I wondered what would have been if my father had refused to leave our land and had hidden us among the Turks as my uncle had done. But I don't know the fate of my uncle, so I'll never know what our fate might have been.

"Sometimes, when I sit alone, I see through closed eyes the sun streaming through the clouds and splashing through the orchards of my youth. I see my mother laying the wash on a grassy hillside. And when I lift my voice in song, I hear my father's voice in mine as I sing the songs that he sang sitting by the fire. I think of those simple things one thinks will always last; those throw-away things; those things like breathing that connect the big events, because they're the real things. They're the wings of the butterfly, the tooth of the shark, the roots of the mighty oak. They're the threads from which the fabric is woven. Even though my legs have slowed now, and my back is slightly bent, and my eyes no longer see the bright colors of a sunrise without strain; even in my darkest hours, I need only watch a flower tilt its lovely face to drink the rain, or hear my children laughing, to know that life is good. Breath is God's gift. Life is our reward. The rest is up to us."

My mother had been speaking as if she had drifted away to some inner world that had kept her strong all these many years. Her last sentence stuck in my mind. "The rest is up to us?" Did I believe that? I suppose a part of me did, but there was that other nagging part that couldn't help asking, what about when you have to contend with others? When your life is in their hands? When they control your fate? Is that really up to us?

When I stood on my mother's land, for the first time in my life I could actually see her as a child running down the hillside with Mata running by her side; her long black hair; her dress billowing behind her. I could see the others running too, Cristodula and Yanni, and little Nastasía. I saw my grandmother as my mother had described her, spreading out the wash on a beautiful grassy knoll while Mathea and Maria lay in their crib. My grandfather was also there stacking wood for the long winter, and my great-grandfather, with his slightly stooped shoulders and graying mustache was sitting by the fire. Even his wife sat crocheting beside him. For the first time in my life they were as alive for me as if they stood before me.

Was that what I had searched for all my life? My heritage? Who and what I am? Was that what my wanderlust had been about from such an early age? No guidebooks could hold that key. I felt changed in some inexplicable way. I had history. I had a people. I had love that went beyond the present. That went beyond my own lifetime and my own small life. A love that was somehow ancient. That was connected to the beginning of time.

I looked at my mother sitting beside me and I understood what it was that was up to us. What we make of it. Not what we make of what we can't control. But what we make of what we can control.

And I realized why I had become my mother's protector as a child; what it was I had always tried to protect in her. It was her innocence. Her generosity. Her unconditional love that allowed her to perform as our mother, no matter what stones we or others threw in her path. There was nothing not to love about my mother when I was a child. You could sink into her ample bosom and all your sorrows would melt away.

But the innocence I had presumed to protect in my mother was not innocence at all, I realized now, but rather a profound worldliness; a profound wisdom. My mother's unconditional love and generosity were not based on not knowing the world, but knowing all too well the capriciousness of fate and the tentative hold we have on those we love.

"Maybe they're home at last," my mother said. "Maybe they're in the wind . . . in the grass . . . in the stones that once were their shelter, and the wildflowers that guard their claim to the earth."

My mother looked out through the shade of the pines to the Black Sea. It sparkled like diamonds.

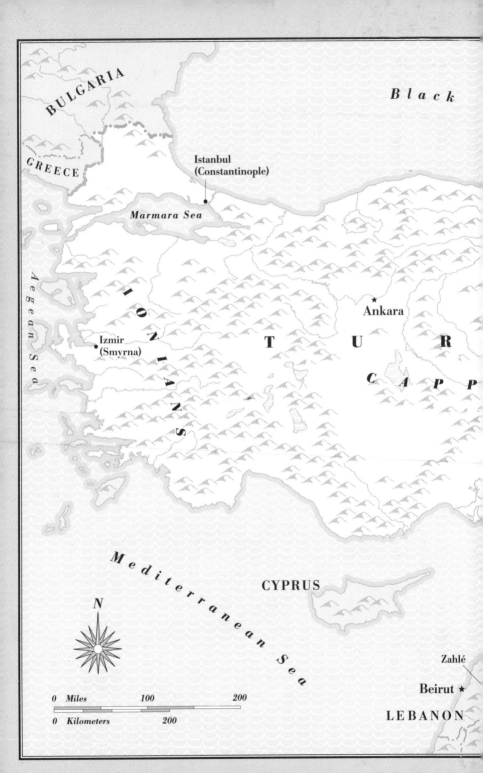